The Cable/Broadband Communications Book

Volume 2, 1980–1981

Edited by Mary Louise Hollowell

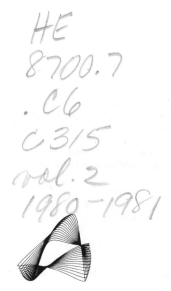

Knowledge Industry Publications, Inc.
White Plains, New York

The Video Bookshelf

The Cable/Broadband Communications Book
Volume 2, 1980–1981

Grateful acknowledgment is made for permission to print the following: "Computers and the Cable: An Overview," © 1980 by Gary H. Arlen; "Non-Pay Programming: Explosive Growth via Satellite," © 1979 by John P. Taylor; "Direct Broadcast Satellites: The U.S. Position," by Wilson P. Dizard, slightly edited version of a paper originally appearing in the April 1980 issue of *Journal of Communications*, © 1980 by the Annenburg School of Communications, University of Pennsylvania.

ISBN 0-914236-79-2

Contents

Acknowledgments

Grateful acknowledgment is made to all of the contributing authors to this volume, and to the numerous persons in the field (too many to mention individually) who took the time to confer with me on subjects that should be covered in this volume and on the most suitable individuals to cover the topics I chose. For helping with one or more of the following tasks—proofreading the manuscript, helping with the glossary, answering my many questions regarding the content of my Introduction-Overview—a special thanks to these individuals: Gary Arlen, Lynne Bradley, James A. Brown, Jr., Jacqueline Eagle, Paul Fox, Corliss Harris, William H. Johnson, Howard Liberman, Robert Powers, Jean Rice, George Shapiro, and Christopher Weaver. And most of all, thanks to Dominick Anfuso, my invaluable assistant on the entire project.

Introduction—Overview

By 1980, many of the "blue sky" promises of cable TV a decade ago had become reality or were on the horizon. Sparking the incredible growth of the last few years was commencement of satellite delivery of pay programming to cable TV systems by Home Box Office (HBO), in 1975. As we enter the 1980s, the communications satellite is an integral part of the domesic communications system in the United States, and cable television has come of age as a major delivery system to the home.

The Cable/Broadband Communications Book attempts to provide comprehensive, authoritative coverage of developments in the field. The CBCB is a reference tool oriented to the professional looking for in-depth treatment of a particular subject or subjects. I hope that this volume will be of value also to the layman, who may wish to read it straight through (my recommendation is for the novice to read at least Chapter 1 and Chapter 2 before dipping into other chapters that might have special interest for you). I have divided the book into sections as follows: Ownership and Regulatory Framework, Local Needs and Services, The Cable/Satellite Connection, and The Cable/Computer Connection.

This volume of the CBCB is being published in fall 1980 and the cut-off date for material covered in its 13 chapters was, for the most part, April 1980. As we go to press in October 1980, I am updating here some of the book's contents with information about developments which seem to me to be the most significant and interesting since the cut-off date. After reading any particular chapter, you may wish to update it further by checking this introduction again to review what in it may relate to that chapter (the information here in many cases overlaps the topics of several chapters).

In cable television ownership, structure, and regulation, there have been a number of recent developments. For example, the proposed merger of the Cox and General Electric cable interests, mentioned in Chapter 1 of this book, was reviewed and approved by the FCC with a finding that their merger would neither create any undue concentration of control in the cable industry nor have other anti-competitive consequences. Even though neither Cox nor G.E. is a pay cable programmer or packager, the Commission went out of its way to express its concern about this type of vertical integration and the possibility that the merged company might develop in this direction. Although the merger was approved by the FCC, the parties fell into disagreement and the merger finally did not occur. In Canada, a merger of two major firms (Canadian Cablesystems, Ltd. and Premier Communications Ltd.) was also approved, with the merger applicants, who will serve about one million subscribers, promising regulatory authorities that they would install two-way videotex terminals in approximately ten thousand homes in Vancouver if they were permitted to merge.

Further developments relating to vertical integration (in cable ownership-program supplier relationships) were also evident. They came in the area of pay TV. Chuck Dolan's "Rainbow" service, described in Chapter 8, became the basis for a new pay cable venture: Dolan's Cablevision Systems and three other multiple system operators (MSOs)—Cox Cable, Daniels & Associates, and Comcast—joined together to create a satellite-distributed program service called the Rainbow Network. And, creating much excitment and controversy was the announcement by Getty Oil Co. and four major motion picture companies—MCA, Twentieth Century-Fox, Columbia, and Paramount—of their new joint venture, Premiere pay TV service. The Justice Department promptly challenged this organization under the antitrust laws.

Under Premiere's plan, the motion picture companies involved would deny their new films to competing suppliers until nine months after the films had been made available to Premiere. Premiere officials say this is the only way for an outside company to get into the pay television business and provide any viable competition. Some others outside the firm agree that an outfit with the finances and clout like that of Premiere is the only kind that could offer any real competition to Home Box Office, the largest pay television company. Spokesmen from HBO have expressed opposition to Premiere, as have other pay TV and cable industry people, including executives of the National Cable Television Association (NCTA). Premiere executives point out that the largest pay cable companies are themselves connected to large cable MSOs with significant resources and control. They also express surprise at the quickness of the Justice Department action against the companies involved in Premiere, since Justice has been investigating HBO for quite some time with no action yet. Burt Harris, chairman and chief executive of Premiere, is quoted in *Broadcasting* (August 11, 1980) as saying, "If they tackle us, they should tackle all vertical arrangements." (For details on ownership of pay cable companies, see Chapter 8.)

Some other developments in the area of ownership discussed in Chapter 1 of this book are as follows: (1) In the cable-télephone crossownership area, FCC Commissioner Joseph Fogarty wrote an article in the August 4, 1980 *Telephony* magazine, expressing doubts as to the continued validity of the rules which prevent telephone companies from owning cable TV systems in their local exchange areas. At an FCC Commission meeting in October 1980, the Commission instructed its staff to draft a *Notice of Proposed Rule Making* amending the rules to give telephone companies greater flexibility to install cable TV systems in rural areas and a *Notice of Inquiry* to explore the continued validity of the telephone crossownership rules even in urban areas. (2)Executives of both ABC and CBS have given speeches suggesting that their companies might again be interested in cable ownership if the network-cable TV crossownership rules were lifted. FCC Chairman Charles Ferris is reported as having indicated that he was not averse to the Commission rethinking this rule as well to determine if its rationale continued to be valid. (3)On the question of local ownership, much unfavorable publicity has been directed in newspaper editorials and elsewhere to the so-called "rent-a-citizen" problem in cable TV franchise proceedings, in which a major cable company takes on local partners solely for the favorable political contacts these partners have with local officials.

Another regulatory issued covered in this volume and subject of recent developments is that of signal carriage and exclusivity. On July 22, 1980, the FCC voted to eliminate most of its cable television distant signal carriage and syndicated exclusivity rules, thus terminating the Economic and Exclusivity Inquiries discussed in some detail in Chapter 2. But appeals from the action have been filed by broadcast interests, and motions for stay pending judicial review have been filed with both the FCC and the court. Appeals to Congress in terms of an amended copyright law are also promised; in fact, some members of the House and Senate have expressed their displeasure with the FCC ruling and their intention to consider (in early 1981) revision of the Copyright Act to deal with the problems they see flowing from the FCC action.

Thus while the cable industry came close to having alleviated its problems with distant signals, still another hurdle has been placed in the way. But on another front, recent action in the Senate has generated a new hope for the industry—regarding local government control and access requirements. Legislation introduced in June 1980, S. 2827, to amend the Communications Act of 1934, contained provisions that would change the nature of local regulation of cable TV. Essentially, local governments would not be allowed to regulate rates for basic subscriber service, nor to require any program origination. The local government would be prohibited from controlling content in any way, which means that cities and states could not have a dedicated government access channel and could not require a cable system to carry access programs at no cost or to provide free or low-cost studio time to the public for access programming. Furthermore, the bill would make these provisions retroactive. S.2827 came at a time when relations between the cable industry and its "public interest" opponents—cities, consumer groups, and the like—seemed to be fairly good. But consideration of this bill could again create the kind of open hostility that was prevalent in the early 1970s. The National Cable Television Association responded favorably to the cable provisions of the bill. The National League of

Cities, the American Association of State Colleges and Universities, the National Federation of Local Cable Programmers, and the Office of Communications, United Church of Christ came in strong opposition to it.

Local government opponents to the cable provisions of the bill saw it as taking all rights away from cities and making current franchsing a futile activity: cable operators could make any number of promises on the basis of which franchises would be granted, and then passage of the bill as written could wipe out all the agreements being made now. Neither the local governments nor the public interest groups have any confidence that cable operators would voluntarily provide the access that is now being provided because of franchise agreements (and of course local government access would be wiped out in any case). S.2827 was originally scheduled for markup without a hearing, but public outcry about the cable provisions apparently helped to delay that action. No further action is expected this session; it is expected that the bill will be reintroduced early in the next session and hearings scheduled at that time. (For more understanding of the issues involved here, see Chapters 2 and 6. Also, you may wish to consult Chapter 3 to see how the states are currently involved in cable regulation.)

The unauthorized receipt of television signals is another issue of concern. There is a question of whether intercepting signals not intended for the individual is a violation of either the Communications Act or the Copyright Act, or both. But at least one judge (in Los Angeles) has ruled in an over-the-air subscription TV (STV) case, that it was acceptable for individuals to use decoders that were not authorized by the STV service, because "broadcasting remains broadcasting." Other cases are being brought, though, and the FCC has now issued a Public Notice supporting court enforcement of criminal and civic penalties for the unauthorized manufacture, sale, distribution, and use of illegal decoders.

The issue is of at least some importance to cable operators, not just from individuals tapping in to the cable system, but also from persons setting up their own earth stations to receive signals being delivered to the cable system via satellite. The signals cable operators receive via satellite are not now scrambled, and large, "backyard antennas" designed for the purpose can easily pick them up. There has been a recent upsurge in the sale and building of such antennas. On the positive side, technical complexities and costs of these, make it seem unlikely that a real mass market will develop. Also, better scrambling devices are being developed and before long signals that are being transmitted to cable systems via satellite will be scrambled. This should be of some help.

Because an increasing (albeit still small) number of homes are directly picking up satellite signals that were intended for cable systems and other means of delivery to the home, one might think that this has something to do with Direct Broadcast Satellite (DBS), but it doesn't.

The communications satellite has been a welcome addition to the "media mix" in the United States thus far because it has served as an adjunct to other media. But DBS is another matter, for theoretically it could provide strong competition to the other video media. Those satellite signals now being picked up directly by individuals with their backyard antennas were not *intended* for direct reception; such signals are part of the "fixed-satellite service." The signals of DBS, or "broadcast-satellite service," *are* intended for direct reception, and the technology for that service would be higher-powered satellites than those currently used for fixed-satellite service, thus allowing for lower-powered (and lower-cost) earth stations for individual reception.

DBS is the subject of political debate on the international front; that debate and the U.S. position are explained in Chapter 4 of this book. Even as the international political questions remain at issue, however, DBS is making developments in some foreign countries, with support of the governments. In the United States, though, DBS would be a commercial venture and would have to prove economically viable. Presently many experts believe that DBS is not practicable in the United States for the near future, despite some claims to the contrary. Not only must the technology advance enough to bring down the costs of individual receivers, but also problems related to piracy of signals, handling of payments for programming, and development of a federal regulatory scheme for the service need to be solved.

The FCC is studying the issue of DBS, and staff reports have been prepared and presented to the Commission. On October 2, 1980, the FCC issued a *Notice of Inquiry* asking for comments on the Staff Report on Policies for Regulation of Direct Broadcast Satellites. That report recommends that the FCC enact no specific technical standards or content regulation. It also states that for regulatory purposes DBS simply does not fit well into any of the current "boxes," such as common carrier or broadcasting, for example. The report recommends that rather than attempt to *make* it fit into one of these categories, the FCC set up a new category for DBS. As of the middle of October 1980, no applications for DBS service had been filed with the FCC, though apparently Comsat was still intending to file (its earlier plans for a joint venture with Sears Roebuck & Co. fell through). At the October 2 Commission meeting, FCC Office of Plans and Policy staff indications were that the soonest any DBS services could begin after authorization would be 1983.

In the meantime, other new means of delivering programming could be underway which have some significance in the cable/broadband arena. In September 1980, the FCC issued a *Notice of Proposed Rule*

Making for new VHF drop-ins, thus allowing for new, strong over-the-air broadcast signals. Of even more significance for the domestic communications network, perhaps, is the other *Notice of Proposed Rule Making* issued at the same time: for "low-power television stations" which the FCC would license in a manner similar to television translator stations, but which would be permitted to originate programming. Low-power, or "mini-TV" stations would have a limited reach that could provide specialized programming to parts of a community. Costs for building and operating such a station would be very low in comparison with the costs of building a conventional TV station. Only one station per community would be allowed per licensee, but there would be no restrictions on the number of markets for a licensee.

One of the purposes behind the proposal for low-power TV stations was to provide an ownership and programming opening for minorities and nonprofit groups. One of the larger proposals filed thus far is that of a minority-owned firm, Community Television Network (CTN), which has filed applications for stations in 15 cities across the country, to be linked by satellite. Founded by three former FCC broadcast attorneys, CTN would be the first minority-owned national broadcast television network (see Chapter 9 for information on BET, black-owned cable TV network).

Most of the applications at this time, however, seem to be from established commercial firms with some involvement in broadcasting or cable TV, a situation of concern to some "public interest" activists. They fear that many interested and capable minority and/or nonprofit groups will be left out because they may not have the resources to put together a plan and file for a license so quickly as the firms that are filing now.

The proposed low-power TV stations represent new competition in the broadcasting and cable industries—opening the way not only for more local programming but also for whole new specialized networks, such as the one proposed by Community Television Network, which could compete for the advertising dollar much like a special-interest magazine might (they can also provide pay TV programming). Another progressive use of communications technology is that demonstrated by the recent proposal to establish an advertiser-supported "country television" network through the use of television translator stations linked by satellite. Sears Roebuck & Co., through its Allstate Insurance Co. subsidiary, is financing the newly formed Neighborhood TV Co., which has filed for 98 applications with the FCC for UHF translator stations in cities across the nation. Neighborhood TV Co. intends to transmit the signal of KUSK-TV, Prescott, Arizona, which is scheduled to go on the air in 1981 with programming of rodeos, country music, comedy, cowboy dramas, and related fare.

Chapter 9 of this book includes discussion of independent television stations that have become "superstations" through being carried to cable systems via satellite. If the Neighborhood TV Co. filings are approved, KUSK-TV could become a superstation of sorts too, with translators instead of cable being used as the relay to the home receiver. If Sears' innovative proposal is approved, it seems likely that others will soon follow.

Translator and low-power television stations are especially important in areas that could not easily be served by cable, but in wired areas they could also expand the viewer options and thus offer an alternative to subscribing to cable TV. Because of this and other new competition, certainly cable operators will have to show a lot of initiative if they are to continue in the growth trend now underway.

Bringing in more entertainment and news programming via satellite, described in Chapters 8 and 9, is of course important to cable's development. But so are demonstrating more initiative and willingness to become involved in the public service applications the technology is so capable of providing. Chapter 5 of this book presents a discussion of the ascertainment of community needs. Such study could be very helpful to the cable company recognizing that it can be more than strictly a conveyor of news and entertainment. There are markets in the government and community services area that can be developed by the enterprising cable operator, through proper planning and some give and take. A reading of Chapters 6, 7, and 9 can give you a long list of the opportunities for development, as well as some models to consider and questions to ask.

One of the most publicized new offerings of the cable TV industry is that of two-way interactive programming. Small-scale experiments were conducted by some systems years ago, but it has been only in the last year or two that the cable industry has begun to show practical applications. The cable system in Reading, Pennsylvania, even without sophisticated technology now available has been providing two-way services for years. Reading's experience has been written about and talked about for a long time, but little effort had been made to emulate that experience. Then came Warner Amex's QUBE system in Columbus, Ohio, with sophisticated equipment, multiple offerings, and all the media hype necessary to make two-way cable (and thus cable TV per se) seem a desirable commodity all over the country. The QUBE system and its publicity have helped to usher in another phase of the communications revolution. (Both QUBE and Reading as well as the Japanese experience with two-way interactive programming are described in Chapter 12.)

Again, cable TV is not the only industry capable of offering two-way services to television viewers. Chapters 11, 12, and 13 all deal in some way with two-way services, whether delivered by cable or by other technologies or by combinations. Since those papers were written, a number of developments have occurred in the home information utility-videotex area (in this book, *videotex* is used as the generic term for the delivery of computer-generated data into the home usually using the television set as a display device). Some of the developments are as follows:

The Electronics Industries Association (EIA) subcommittee studying teletext, reported in Chapter 13, has not yet come to agreement for recommending standards to the FCC, but in summer 1980, CBS filed with the FCC a proposal that the Antiope format developed in France be adopted as the United States technical standard for teletext. The FCC will be examining the CBS proposal and other forthcoming ones, but no final action is expected for some time (perhaps years), and likely the technical standard adopted will be some kind of hybrid of the various ones submitted.

Cox Cable has confirmed its plans for an information and service retrieval test and major new entities are entering the field too. For example, Readers Digest recently acquired majority ownership of "The Source," and many other publishers have begun to establish divisions to become Information Providers (IPs). AT&T has stepped up its activities in videotex, too, as have many newspaper organizations. Some other new players include Texas Instruments, N.A. Philips, and GTE.

The trend in videotex for at least the short term is towards transactional services, such as banking at home and shopping at home. It may take a bit longer to gain wide public acceptance of a televised information service for sale; the public is used to a large amount of textual information being provided free of charge on the television screen and being available in newspapers and magazines as well (though of course not with the timeliness, user flexibility, and comprehensive supporting data that a videotex service could provide).

Several new experiments have been announced and/or begun in the past few months, and new studies have started as well. For instance, the National Science Foundation has awarded a contract to the Institute for the Future, for a 20-month study of the technological and social effects of videotex in the United States over the next 20 years. And the National Cable Television Association has set up an engineering subcommittee to conduct tests to help develop cross-compatibility between the various transmission systems in cable television with regard to videotex services.

A Madison Avenue rite of passage marking cable TV's coming of age is the formation in fall 1980 of the Cable Television Advertising Bureau (CTAB). Another mark of recognition of the advances in cable/broadband is the increase in trade publications as well as the stepped up coverage of the field in jouranlistic and business magazines. In the trade publication field, for example, *CableVision*, formerly a bi-weekly, has begun weekly publication; Gary Arlen, author of Chapter 11 of this book, has initiated a newsletter called *International Videotex Teletext News*; Paul Kagan has added to his string of special-interest cable-related newsletters with two more in 1980, *Cable TV Security* and *Cable TV Advertising*; and Fairchild Publications has initiated a weekly newspaper, *Multichannel News*. (Numerous other publications in the field are among the resources cited at the end of each chapter of this book. Also included in the resource lists are individuals and organizations you may wish to consult for further exploration of a particular subject.)

Two technologies not discussed in depth in this volume are videodiscs and fiber optics. A comprehensive discussion of each of these was presented in Volume 1 (1977-1978). To briefly update: Some companies have videodiscs on the market now, and additional ones (with incompatible formats) will be arriving in the stores in 1981. Because of the superior quality of both audio and video on videodisc, it eventually will not only prove a viable competitor to videotape and videocassette, but also may offer some competition to other media—such as cable TV, MDS, and broadcast television—which provide similar programming. Fiber optics technology is now in use in a limited way in the telephone and cable TV industries, but its potential for very high capacity for carrying information is not realized in practice at this time. It could have a larger role in what we now call "cable television systems" as the fiber connections problems are solved, because it would be cheaper and more easily maintained, and would occupy less space than does coaxial cable, with a much higher channel capacity.

The cable/broadband communications field is a complicated one, and the changes are constant, relentless, and sometimes explosive. I hope that the chapters in this book provide you with a better understanding of the developments, and the issues, in the field. And that this introduction-overview helps to bring focus to the subject with all its diverse elements.

—Mary Louise Hollowell

The information presented here was gathered from (a)my experience as a writer and publisher in the field, (b)contributors to this volume and other communications experts who fed me information and were on call to verify certain statements I was writing, and (c)recent issues of the following periodicals: Broadcasting, The Home Video Report, Multichannel News, *and* VideoNews.

William H. Johnson

1. Structure and Ownership Of the Cable TV Industry

Industry ownership patterns result from happenstance, the force of individual genius and personality, the interplay of economic forces, and federal and state governmental policies. The resulting structures are commonly thought to strongly influence performance. In the telecommunications field, many who are currently involved in regulation regard regulation of industry as a superior means of furthering industry conduct "in the public interest" to regulation directly controlling conduct. When feasible, this school of thought suggests, prescriptive codes of conduct and processes of review should be replaced with structural controls—hopefully positioning private incentives so as to draw out the desired conduct without any need for continuing detailed oversight.

This concern with structure has a long history in telecommunications and in other areas of regulation. Because much of what has occurred in other areas in the past has relevance to current issues of cable television ownership, it may be helpful to list an unscientific sample of some past decisions affecting ownership structures. In the early part of this century railroads were prohibited from carrying coal and other

William H. Johnson is Chief of the Policy Review and Development Division of the Cable Television Bureau, Federal Communications Commission. The views expressed herein are those of the author and do not necessarily reflect the views of the Federal Communications Commission.

commodities in which the carrier had an interest. Much later, airplane manufacturers were forced out of the airline transportation business. In the telecommunications field, AT&T was forced out of the telegraph business when in 1913 it sold its interest in the Western Union Company. (In the mid-1960s debate was ongoing as to whether there should be a complete record communications/voice communications separation, with the Bell System forced out of the teletypewriter exchange communications business.) In 1926, the Bell System left the field of broadcasting, over which it had considerable control through its ownership of patents, broadcasting stations, interconnection facilities, and an equipment manufacturing affiliate, when it sold its stations and associated network to NBC. Later the FCC forced NBC to sell one of its two networks, creating in the process the ABC radio network. In 1941, the FCC adopted policies prohibiting any one entity from owning more than three television stations (raised to five in 1944 and then to five VHF and two UHF in 1954).

In 1948, after injunctive remedies attacking specific behavior in the market were for the most part shown to be fruitless, the producers, distributors, and exhibitors of motion pictures (RKO, Paramount, Twentieth Century-Fox, Warner Brothers, and Loew's) were ordered to divorce their production from their exhibition (theatre ownership) operations. In 1956, a suit which had been brought to divorce Western Electric from the Bell System ended in a consent decree prohibiting AT&T for the most part from engaging in any business other than the furnishing of common carrier communications services.

In 1966, litigation instituted by the Justice Department resulted in the International Telephone & Telegraph Company (ITT) deciding not to take over ABC, even though this merger had been approved by the FCC. FCC rules adopted in 1970 preclude ABC, CBS, and NBC from engaging in the television program syndication business. In 1975, FCC rules were adopted prospectively prohibiting daily newspapers and radio and television stations in the same area being commonly owned.

It has also been suggested from time-to-time that the three television networks be required to sell those television stations that they now own and that the Bell System sell its manufacturing affiliate, Western Electric, or that the AT&T long lines operations be separated in ownership from the 23 associated Bell System companies that operate local telephone exchanges. These suggestions have not yet been adopted by the FCC, the courts, or the Congress.

Each of the actions or proposals listed above finds a potential counterpart in the cable television area. In each there is a tension between the real or perceived conflict of interest involved and the economic efficiencies or other forces that created the structure in the first place. The most visible of these conflicts involves the control of cable systems by local broadcasters.

Broadcast Station and Network Ownership

According to some accounts, the first cable television system was constructed in Astoria, Oregon, in 1949. It was built by the owner of a local radio station. From this start, broadcast involvement grew until in 1972, in excess of 37 percent of all cable television systems were reportedly owned by broadcasters.

This picture is in some respects deceptive, however. While the primary concern, at least of the FCC, has been with television broadcasters owning cable systems in their local service area, the 37 percent figure included both radio stations and commonly owned television stations not serving the same geographic area.

As a result of governmental pressures, local TV ownership of cable systems has been greatly reduced in recent years. While the FCC has been concerned, probably from its very creation, with the question of media diversity, cable was not thought of until the late 1960s as a media capable of editorial opinions but rather as a passive "community antenna." When this attitude changed, rules were adopted forbidding the creation of new cross-ownership interests between cable systems and local television broadcasting stations.

Those who had acquired both a cable system and a television broadcast station in the same area before 1970 were required to sell one of the two. These rules were justified as fostering economic competition and as creating additional diversity of ownership and viewpoints among the media. Although the divestiture requirement was never fully implemented, as a result of changing policies and court appeals, and is a matter still pending before the FCC, such interests have been decreasing rather steadily in recent years. This no doubt out of a realization that the risk of involuntary divestiture will continue to exist regardless of what is actually required by present policy. If all of the sales transactions already publicly announced are completed, only about one and a half percent of cable subscribers will be on systems that are cross-owned with local television stations.

Fee rules also forbid the three major national television networks (ABC, CBS, and NBC) to own cable systems. Of the three networks, CBS was the only one with major investments in the cable business, owning what is now Viacom International which took over both CBS's syndication business and its cable operations.

Newspaper Ownership

In a relatively small number of communities cable systems are commonly owned with a local newspaper. Many years ago newspapers hedged their bets on the future by participating heavily in the ownership of radio and television stations. To some extent these same owners became cable television owners as well and for the same reasons.

Beyond this, however, all of the predictions in the late 1960s about the use of cable systems to distribute whole newspapers in facsimile edition directly to the homes of subscribers were of real concern to newspaper owners. During that period the American Newspaper Publishers Association was regularly reporting to its members concerning developments in the field of cable television, and in comments filed with the FCC the ANPA quoted the director of its advanced research program at MIT as stating:

> Electronic delivery of news to selected clientele is a forerunner of home delivery of the news by electronic means. During the next ten years there will be a vast expansion of broadband/cable facilities on a one-to-many basis; that is, from one central transmitting source, such as cable-tv station, to many homes.

"Electronic delivery of news and information to the home is now in the offing," said the ANPA in 1971, "and is the subject of current newspaper technological research."

However, with the apparent failure of the cable facsimile newspaper idea to make any more progress in the 1970s than the radio newspaper facsimile idea of the 1930s, as well perhaps as the result of heightened sensitivities of public officials to media concentration issues, it has become relatively infrequent in recent years to hear of newspapers bidding for cable franchises in their home towns, although there are some signs that the interest of newspaper companies is reviving.

As a consequence the FCC issued an interim opinion in the proceeding in which it had proposed to prohibit newspaper-cable ownership in the same area. In this decision the Commission declined to adopt the proposed rule but promised a continuing review to determine if abuses were developing. The Commission said:

> Our review of the most recently filed cable ownership reports suggests that newspaper cable ownership in the same market area represents only a very minor portion of the industry and that there is no definable pattern of growing newspaper involvement similar, for example, to that in the early stage of radio and television broadcasting.
>
> *   *   *   *
>
> If rules are to be adopted, it would be preferable they be adopted at an early date so that equities, later difficult to displace, do not develop but they should not be adopted so early that they cure a hypothetical rather than a real problem. For now, we believe, this dictates a policy of watchful waiting. . . .

It should not be assumed from this absence of any strong trend toward local newspaper ownership, however, that some of the great newspaper chains and publishing companies are not heavily involved.

In terms of subscribers, Time, Inc., publisher of *Time, Life, People, Money, Sports Illustrated,* and *Fortune,* is now the second largest cable system owner. Times Mirror Co., publisher of the *Los Angeles Times* and a chain of newspapers across the country, is the sixth largest owner. Among the other cable operators that have corporate relatives in the newspaper world are Cox Cable Communications, the fifth largest cable system* operator (Cox Newspapers), NewChannels, the seventeenth largest system operator (Newhouse newspapers), Telecable, the nineteenth largest (Landmark Communications), and Colony Communications, thirty-first (Providence *Journal*). In spring 1980 it was announced that the *New York Times* is proposing to purchase a 42,000 subscriber cable system in the Camden-Burlington, New Jersey, area.

Newspaper-cable cross-ownership is also a matter of concern to local and state regulatory authorities. Massachusetts, for example, excludes from cable ownership "newspaper media and their affiliates in their major circulation areas." Rhode Island, in the franchising process, has considered newspaper ownership to represent a demerit in terms of comparative qualifications among applicants. In Connecticut, the Times Mirror Co., in early 1980, was ordered to sell either its Hartford newspaper or its Hartford cable television system by the Connecticut Division of Public Utility Control.

Telephone Company Ownership

The cable television business bears more than a superficial resemblance to that of telephone companies—wires strung on utility poles delivering communications services to residential and business subscribers.

During the early years of cable television, when it would have been natural for the telephone industry to become heavily involved, pent up demands for telephone service following World War II and the Korean War apparently occupied the telephone industry full time. There was also some feeling at the time, perhaps, that cable television was a phenomenon destined to have a short life, ending when the FCC lifted its freeze on the licensing of new television facilities. In any case, the telephone industry did not take advantage of some very considerable advantages in the early years, including existing sources of capital, installation crews, local office and repair facilities, control over and familiarity with local utility poles, and often operating rights and easements broad enough to allow for the provision of cable television service without the need for additional municipal approvals.

---

*The ranking of multiple system operators according to size in this paper is based on *1979 Television Digest* data.

In 1956, the Bell System companies became subject to an antitrust consent decree which has been generally interpreted as precluding direct provision of cable services to subscribers so long as such services were not legally defined as common carriage. (It is interesting to speculate on whether the cable business would have been defined as common carriage had the Bell System companies become involved. The industry is subject to public utility regulation in several states and, although ultimately unsuccessful, plausable arguments favoring common carrier regulation were set forth in several court proceedings. In any case it is possible that the consent decree may not be as restrictive in this area as its popular interpretation usually suggests. In other areas the decree increasingly has become the subject of some revised interpretation.)

Notwithstanding the constraints of the consent decree, the Bell System in the late 1960s probably had almost as much money invested in the cable television business as any other company. This was accomplished by constructing cable distribution plant and leasing it to an independent retail cable operator pursuant to a common carrier tariff.

The second, third, and fourth largest telephone operating companies, General, United, and Continental, became directly involved in cable television during this period through separate corporate subsidiaries. After a relatively short period, however, the FCC adopted rules prohibiting telephone companies from engaging in the retail cable television business in the same areas where they were providing telephone service. This rule was articulated as necessary to prevent telephone companies eliminating competition in the provision of broadband communication services.

More recently the FCC has been giving consideration to exempting systems in rural areas from this ban because of a feeling that telephone companies may be able to provide cable service in some areas where that would not be economically feasible for an independent operator. Suggestions have also been made that the entire prohibition be eliminated. This too will no doubt be explored by the Commission as it continues the reevaluation of its cable television rules.

Given present technology and existing plant investments, even if both telephone and cable services were provided by the same entity, there would still be two wires entering each residence and little if any electronic integration of the twisted pair wire telephone and coaxial cable video services. Technical developments hold open the prospect of both services (and many more) being transmitted over a single coaxial cable or fiber optic system. This potential for greater efficiency associated with a one wire system has caused considerable apprehension in the cable television industry and has been the focus of some attention in connection with efforts to rewrite the Communications Act of 1934. Roughly speaking, what seems to be involved in this debate, beyond the obvious self-interests of the parties, is: (1) a real concern that telephone companies and particularly the Bell System not become in any way involved with control over the content of television programming; (2) a desire not to decide for or against any particular technology but to leave this choice to competition in the market; and (3) a concern that such competition be "full and fair," with special concern reserved for assuring that monopoly revenues from telephone services are not to be used to subsidize telephone-owned cable television type services in a predatory manner.

In the spring of 1979, telephone and cable television industry representatives reached a tentative agreement on the outlines of a legislative detente. Cable systems would distribute video entertainment programming, telephone companies would provide telephone service, and both would compete in the provision of data and those other telecommunications services whose growth is predicted to be of considerable magnitude in the years ahead.

Ownership by Program Suppliers and Distributors

The principal recommendation of the 1974 Report to the President of the Cabinet Committee on Cable Communications was as follows:

> Control of cable distribution facilities should be separated from control of programming and other services provided over the channels on those distribution facilities.

As the Report said:

> By separating the distribution function in cable, which is a natural monopoly, from the programming functions, which can be highly competitive, the dangers of intrusion and influence in programming can be avoided while the wide variety of competitors vying for the public's attention can be expected to produce a diversity of programming.

Perhaps as a bow to "political realities" the Report, in a footnote, conceded to the cable operator one or two channels for his own use. Moreover, the policy was not to be implemented until 50 percent of households nationwide were cable subscribers.

In 1972, the FCC had considered this idea and found it not necessarily wrong but rather premature at that stage of the industry's development. Other reports and studies, both private and governmental, state and federal, have also toyed with the idea of forcing a total or partial separation of ownership between cable programming and system ownership.

These proposals are very much the intellectual children of the "commodities clause" which prohibited railroads from carrying products in which they had an interest and the motion picture company consent decrees which separated the major film producers from theater ownership. The conception is basically that system operators distributing their own programming will have an incentive to refuse access to programming provided by others or to extract unwarranted concessions for such distribution since it will be regarded as competitive with the system's own programming.

A particularly interesting aspect of these proposals is the suggestion that they would reduce government regulation. This argument assumes that cable systems will be distributing 30, 40, or 50 channels of programming and that complete and undiluted operator control over all these channels is either violative of the antitrust laws (under the case law suggesting that a vertically integrated company controlling a "bottleneck" facility must make it available to competitors) or otherwise so inconsistent with democratic principals as to require some regulation. The options then given are: (1) content regulations such as the broadcast fairness and equal time rules; (2) common carrier regulation, involving channel leasing and the regulation of rates therefor; or (3) separations, under which the operator's only source of nonsubscriber revenues would be from channel leasing so that his private incentives would be to expand channel usage and system capacity. Given this oversimplified version of the options, it can be seen that the first two would involve continued detailed regulation. The last might not although even that is not at all clear.

In these areas as in others involving horizontal or vertical integration, the claim is sometimes made that cross-ownership is necessary to strengthen cable television in its program origination functions. In 1972 the Commission embraced this rationale in connection with a proposal by the Hughes Aircraft Company to own a private space satellite system for distributing programming to its own and other cable systems. The Commission said:

> It may take an entrepreneur with the aggressiveness, imagination and resources of Hughes to pioneer CATV network operations. If Hughes' ownership of communications satellite facilities would further its objective of making available to the CATV viewing public a wide diversity of special interest programs, and [it] is willing to undertake that investment, we fail to see why it should be deterred from doing so.

Today, almost all cable operators distribute some nonbroadcast programming over which they have legal, if not always practical, editorial control. The programming involved ranges from the most primitive time and weather channels to highly sophisticated local originations with two-way subscriber feedback. Much of the programming is pay television and other nonbroadcast programming received via space satellites. In addition, a number of the larger multiple system operators are very deeply involved in program production, ownership, or distribution.

Teleprompter, the largest cable system operator, is a 50 percent owner, along with Viacom International, the seventh largest operator, of Showtime, a satellite distributed pay cable program service. Viacom is itself a major syndicator of television programming, having taken over the program syndication business of CBS when it was forced out by FCC rule. Confirming the obvious, that vertically integrated companies favor their own affiliates, Teleprompter switched many of its own cable systems from the Home Box Office pay television service to Showtime when it acquired its ownership interest in Showtime.

American TV and Communications, the second largest cable operator, is now owned by Time, Inc., which is also owner of Home Box Office, the largest distributor of pay cable television programming. In November of 1978 the FCC approved the merger of Time and ATC. In doing so the Commission considered whether the merger ought to be disapproved because of the possibility that competitive market foreclosure would result from the tendency of ATC cable systems to rely primarily or exclusively on Home Box Office pay programming. Although some concern was expressed, the ease of entry into the business and its substantial growth potential were weighed against the potential for anticompetitive conduct. It is worth noting that the Commission relied on the leased access channel rules as a means of assuring continued access to independent program suppliers. These rules have since been found by the Supreme Court to exceed the Commission's jurisdiction and are no longer in force.

Warner Amex, the third largest multiple system operator is affiliated with both the Warner Brothers motion picture and television program production companies and with affiliates that supply pay television programming (Star Channel) and children's television programming (Nickelodeon) for cable use.

Because Warner Amex has a corporate relationship to one of the companies subject to the consent decree that separated motion picture production from exhibition, it has been suggested that its present involvement in pay cable television might be a type of exhibition prohibited by the decree. This suggestion, made by the National Association of Theatre Owners, has not met with a favorable response from either the FCC or the Department of Justice.

The tenth largest multiple system owner, UA-Columbia Cablevision, is also involved in distributing programming to cable systems by satellite. It distributes both sports events from Madison Square Garden and a children's program called Calliope.

In light of the concerns expressed that cable system operators with programming affiliates would tend to reduce competitive program offerings to obtain the most revenues for their own programming, recent experiments suggesting that more offerings, particularly in the pay television area, tend to increase the total revenues received rather than simply divide what is available are of particular importance in terms of developing trends.

Multiple Ownership

The telephone industry is dominated by the Bell System, television broadcasting by the three national networks, and the motion picture industry by its seven major producers. The cable television industry is more like the newspaper field. It is not dominated by any single firm but it does have a number of large multiple system owners comparable to the Tribune, Newhouse, Scripps, Gannett, Knight, Hearst, and Times Mirror chains in the newspaper world.

Teleprompter, the largest of the multiple system operators serves about 8.4 percent of all subscribers, the five largest (Teleprompter, American TV and Communications, Community Tele-Communications, Warner Amex, and Cox Cable) serve 28 percent, and the 50 largest, 77 percent.

What pattern might be considered optimal depends in part on values associated with national media ownership diversity and the extent to which cable systems may be considered to have a media "voice." It also depends on economic issues relating to franchise competition, economies of scale, incentives to engage in research and development, and relationships with other industries with which cable competes, serves, or obtains equipment or programming. As with so much in the cable television area, ambiguities as to the essential nature of cable television confuse the issue. Is it interstate or intrastate, competitive or monopoly, communications carrier or software supplier, show-biz or high technology, ma and pa or big business, technological achievement or program marketing scheme?

Industry structures, including multiple ownership, are subject to review in theory by the FCC through its radio licensing and rule making powers, by the Department of Justice and the Federal Trade Commission through their enforcement of the antitrust laws, and by state and local governments principally through the franchising process. Because no radio station license may be assigned or transferred without FCC approval and because all major cable system operators make extensive use of microwave radio in connective with their operations, all mergers among the large multiple system operators require FCC approval.

Under FCC rules, a single entity may own no more than seven television stations. As cable's potential for program origination became recognized, multiple ownership rules were proposed as well for cable television. The Commission's rule making proposal issued in 1968 said:

> It is contemplated that such rules would limit the total number of subscribers on a nationwide basis, based on the number of subscribers, the size of the communities, and the regional concentration.

One of the specific alternatives proposed for consideration was a two million subscriber limit on the operations of any single entity. As of

April 1980, this proposal was still pending, having never been specifically accepted or rejected. As indicated above, however, ownership structures are reviewed in the radio station licensing process.

Given the state of the cable television industry at the time the two million subscriber limit was proposed, that maximum was not a significant barrier to a considerable amount of merger or acquisition activity. Some of this activity was, in fact, a direct consequence of FCC rules forcing local television broadcasters and telephone companies out of the cable television business.

In 1970, the FCC, with the apparent approval of the Department of Justice, consented to the merger of the largest cable company (H & B American) and the third largest (Teleprompter). In applying for approval of the merger the companies stated that the greater financial strength of the two companies combined would facilitate the creation and distribution of television programming of a type which is "generally not featured on broadcast television stations. For example, concerts, live theatre performance, women's and children's programs, sports, and the like. ...." Explicit reliance was placed on this promise when the merger was approved.

There followed a period in which a considerable number of mergers took place, until in 1972 the merger of Cox Cable, then the fifth largest operator, and ATC, then the fourth largest operator, was proposed. As the FCC was on the verge of acting on the request for its consent to the merger, the Department of Justice filed suit against the two companies under the antitrust laws. As a consequence, the merger was called off by the participants, establishing what appeared to be a sort of *de facto* multiple ownership rule.

As a consequence, the FCC rule making proceeding was never finalized and for a period of time the merger trend tapered off. More recently the trend has experienced some resurgence. For example, in 1978 the FCC approved the merger of ATC (second largest) and Time, Inc. (twenty-third largest). Also approved was the merger of Communications Properties (eighth largest) and Times Mirror (twenty-sixth largest). Cox (fifth largest) and General Electric (fifteenth largest) in October of 1978 announced their plans to merge.

Notwithstanding those mergers that have already taken place, concentration within the fifty largest multiple system owners is about the same in 1979 as it was in 1972. (Using one technical measure of concentration, the Gini Coefficient was .53 in 1972 and .51 in 1979. The Gini coefficient in an industry of equal size firms would be zero and approaching one in an industry with a single dominant firm.)

In 1972, the four largest multiple system operators had 28 percent of the subscribers and the top 8, 41 percent. In 1979, even if the subscribers of General Electric are attributed to Cox to account for the proposed merger, the Time owned Manhattan Cable and ATC subscribers are combined, and the subscribers of Athena (which is owned in part by TCI) are attributed to TCI, the top four companies have 25 percent of all subscribers and the eight largest, 39 percent.

Although these are traditional measures of industry concentration, they may not be of much relevance to the cable industry where firms generally do not compete with each other except in the highly artificial competition for franchises. These measures, however, do give some indication of trends in the industry.

Equipment Suppliers

One of the most prominent features of the domestic telephone industry is the integration within the Bell Telephone system of research and development (Bell Laboratories), equipment manufacturing (Western Electric), local distribution facilities (23 associated Bell telephone companies), and intercity facilities (AT&T long lines).

In the early days of the cable television industry, significant vertical integration between equipment suppliers and system operators also looked like a real possibility. Among the very first cable systems were those built with equipment supplied by the Jerrold Electronics Corporation. By 1954, 80 percent of all systems were built with Jerrold equipment. Jerrold sold only complete systems not system parts. Every system came with a continuing service contract for which Jerrold received $500 a subscriber and $.25 per subscriber per month. In some instances, when Jerrold failed to sell its equipment it threatened to or actually installed a competing system of its own. Jerrold was also a system owner, purchasing some systems which were then supplied only with Jerrold equipment.

Antitrust suits by the Department of Justice and private parties, however, terminated all further Jerrold cable system purchases between 1959 and 1962. The service contract and complete system sales requirements were also terminated. Although this did not end Jerrold's system ownership (which increased after 1962), it did assure that the Bell system type of vertical integration would not develop in the cable industry. In 1971, Jerrold, then the sixth largest system operator, sold its systems to Sammons Communications. Jerrold is now part of the General Instrument Corporation.

Other companies also have combined cable system ownership with electronics equipment manufacturing (Hughes Aircraft, General Telephone & Electronics, General Electric, Vikoa, etc.), but none has dominated either the equipment supply or system ownership markets.

There exists a number of functions, beyond the distribution of television programming, that cable systems are technically capable of performing and which they might economically perform if only a certain critical mass were reached in which each service contributed to but would not individually support the required capital investment. These are principally the interactive services such as meter reading, power control, facsimile retrieval services, per program pay television, and computer assisted learning.

An internal IBM study of some years ago concluded that many of these services were indeed feasible but that what was missing and needed in order to bring them into being was a sophisticated entity skilled in marketing, computers, and transmission systems, to undertake the entrepreneural task of developing, packaging, and marketing these services. The study did not, however, volunteer IBM for the task.

It is possible that the absence in the cable business of companies that combine system ownership with equipment manufacturing and associated research and development has contributed to the difficulties encountered in developing these services. As the 1980s begin, however, new interest and effort are being placed on these services, many of which are described in detail in other chapters of this book.

Television Receiver Repair and Sales

A common provision in cable television franchises prohibits the system operator from servicing or selling television sets. For example, a model franchise of the California League of Cities prohibits the system operator from, directly or indirectly, engaging in the business of selling at retail, leasing, renting, repairing, or servicing television sets or radios. A survey undertaken in New York several years ago found such prohibitions in 15 of 18 franchises surveyed. Such restrictions, carried over from one franchise to the next, are perhaps symptomatic of the manner and mileau in which cable ownership policy has developed.

In the earliest phase of the industry's history, cable systems were frequently created as adjuncts to appliance stores. Where television reception was poor, receiver sales were likely to be slow and the showroom model's performance not likely to impress potential buyers. The solution in some cases was the creation of a community antenna system. Later, companies in the television repair and sales business became concerned that operators of cable systems would squeeze them out of the repair and sales business as a result of the system operators entree into the homes of subscribers. It is undoubtedly true that the system operator would have a significant advantage in the sales and repair field because a major percentage of complaints relating to cable service upon investigation relate to the subscriber's television receiver.

These local restrictions on receiver sales and repair are a kind of structural regulation intended to preclude one type of vertical integration. Not being a glamorous issue, little has been written on the economics and merits of such restrictions. It would appear, however, that there would be considerable cost saving involved in having a cable television service person complete the repair job whether the problem was the system or the receiver. On the other hand, it is likely that consumers would suspect that the cable operator was shifting the blame for cable faults to set faults in order to increase revenues. In any case, system operators do not appear very much interested in moving into television set repair and sales. Such regulations, however, in 1980 caught General Electric in their net. In Connecticut there is such a restriction which the Division of Public Utility Control has ruled would preclude General Electric assuming ownership of systems there in connection with the pending Cox-General Electric merger.

If in the future, the television set becomes the focus of a more elaborate home communications system and telephone companies are permitted to return to the cable business, a real conflict will be presented between the traditional approaches to the sale and repair of terminal devices taken by the two industries and their regulators.

Miscellaneous Ownership Issues

There are a number of other issues of ownership which are also of considerable importance but which have not received much regulatory attention and which will be mentioned only briefly.

Microwave Common Carriers

Much television programming is delivered to cable television communities over the facilities of microwave radio common carriers. These carriers came into existence many years ago, even before policies were developed encouraging competition in interstate microwave communications, because cable operators needed a service of lower quality and less expense than that which the established telephone carriers were offering. FCC rules permit such a carrier to have an ownership interest in no more than 50 percent of its customers—that is cable systems receiving programming. The question has also been raised as to whether such carriers should be permitted any ownership interest in the programming transmitted. This question remains unresolved at the present time.

Many cable system owners are also the licensees of common carrier microwave systems, including Teleprompter, ATC, Times Mirror, Community Tele-Communications, Service Electric, NewChannels, etc. Warner Amex is the owner of a resale common carrier making use of satellite channels to distribute broadcast signals to cable systems.

In theory, cross-ownerships between carriers and customers could result in incentives to discriminate in both rates and routes in favor of affiliates. There is, however, both competition among carriers and the possibility of private microwave construction which provides system operators with some possible alternatives in the event discrimination occurs. (Such discrimination would also violate common carrier law.)

Multipoint Distribution Service Common Carriers

Multipoint distribution service (MDS) stations are omni-directional common carrier radio stations that operate much like UHF television stations except that the former sell communications time pursuant to tariff and can be received only with the aid of some additional equipment. These stations primarily serve as a means of delivering pay television programming to hotels and apartment buildings but some also provide such services to individual homes. They are thus directly competitive with both cable television systems and broadcast subscription television stations. They are also used in some instances as a means of delivering pay television programming from a central location to the headends of cable systems.

No rules prohibit cable operators from operating MDS stations and a number of operators do have MDS licenses.

Alien Ownership

The Communications Act contains provisions that limit the ability of aliens to hold radio licenses in the United States. These restrictions were included mostly because of concerns by the U.S. Navy that foreign countries would obtain technical information of military value from station ownership and could use stations for military purposes during time of war. The possibility that stations might be used for the dissemination of propaganda may also provide a rationale for restrictions of this type.

Although cable television is not included within these restrictions, the FCC once proposed that they be extended to cable apparently at least in part out of a concern that foreign oil money might be invested in large sums in the cable business. However, FCC investigation found little outside ownership and that mostly Canadian. The proposed rules were accordingly not adopted although the Commission did promise to continue to monitor the situation.

With the Canadian cable industry now reaching nearly 50 percent of Canada's population and with pay cable not yet permitted in that country, Canadian cable operators have been turning increasingly in recent years to the U.S. market, obtaining franchises in cities such as Syracuse, New York; Fresno, California; and Fort Lauderdale, Florida with promises of highly sophisticated operations. In response, the FCC has again been requested to adopt alien ownership restrictions, and has again declined to do so.

Municipal or Federal Government Ownership

A frequently considered option in the franchising process is government ownership. In the final decision, most cities do not select this option, but there are a number of city owned systems in operation, including those in Opp, Alabama; Frankfort, Kentucky; and San Bruno, California. The federal government also operates a number of systems on military bases in places such as Ft. Sill, Oklahoma; Ft. Leonard Wood, Missouri; and F. Rucker, Alabama. (Several dozen subscriber-owned systems are also in operation.)

Such ownership is, of course, anathema to the cable television industry, which has argued that governmental ownership sacrifices certain First Amendment values and opens possibilities of political abuse. While these are real concerns, structural devices seem to have been used with considerable success to blunt such criticisms with respect to other governmentally owned or controlled media, particularly in the field of public broadcasting.

Local Ownership

In its search for criteria to distinguish among competing broadcast station applicants, the FCC has sometimes awarded a plus to owners that will actually live in the community served, particularly if these owners are "integrated" into management.

Local ownership is also pushed as an advantage in cable television franchise contests. In so-called "80-20" deals, major multiple system owners (MSO) become partners with local individuals who the MSO's assume have political influence or other appeals to those awarding the franchise. Although such ownership interests may be of some assistance in assuring that cable operations are responsive to local needs, they also have considerable potential for abuse if the local owners are not real contributors of either money or expertise but merely window dressing in the franchise competition.

Conglomerate Ownership

In 1969, several years after the abortive ITT-ABC merger, the FCC commenced a proceeding looking into various questions relating to the ownership of broadcast stations by licensees with substantial non-broadcast business interests.

In commencing this proceeding the Commission said:

> It will look for evidence that such holdings by conglomerates or by any person or entity with other large-scale business interests contribute to technical innovation, stability, greater programming efforts, either locally or on a syndicated basis, or the formation of additional networks. It will also look for possible hazards to the fair and free presentation of material by the stations owned by conglomerates or any person or entity with other large-scale business interests, reciprocity arrangements in advertising,

lack of licensee responsibility due to inadequate supervision by top officials, siphoning of broadcast profits for other operations or acquisitions, increased leverage either in the broadcast or nonbroadcast fields, and the possible impediments to technological developments.

In 1975, in a less than one page opinion, the Commission terminated the proceeding and concluded that further action was not needed.

Many of the issues raised in this broadcast proceeding could also be raised with respect to cable television owning companies. Many cable system owners are diversified corporations, although most are basically involved in communications related fields. Some are more classic versions of conglomerates with businesses having no apparent relationship whatsoever under one corporate roof. Cox Broadcasting, for example, is involved not only in radio, television, and cable television, but in running automobile auctions; Cablecom-General is owned by the General Tire & Rubber Co.; Rollins is associated with the Orkin Exterminating Company; and in late 1979, American Express acquired a half interest in Warner Cable.

Theatre Ownership

A number of the multiple cable system operators also have interests in motion picture theatres. UA-Columbia Cablevision, for example, is partially owned in common with United Artists Theatre Circuit. Wometco Communications, Plains TV Corp., Midwest Video, and others are also affiliated with theatre owners.

For many years organizations of theatre owners successfully lobbied against the introduction of any type of pay television system, either wire or broadcast, in the United States. They were prominently featured amongst the opponents of pay television before the FCC and were prime movers in the California referendum (later found unconstitutional) in which pay television was outlawed in that state.

These violent contests between the cable and theatre businesses in public forums do not appear, however, to have had any visible impact on the competitive vigor of those companies that have a foot in each camp.

Conclusion

In describing a 1936 amendment to one of the antitrust laws, the Senate Report indicated an intention that the law apply to anticompetitive conduct in its incipience—"to catch the weed in the seed will keep it from coming to flower."

Back in the same era Justice Cardozo observed that "often a liberal antidote of experience supplies a sovereign cure for a paralyzing abstraction built upon a theory."

In considering public policy relating to industry structure there is a very considerable tension between the desire to attack problems in their incipiency and the need for actual experience to give meaning to sterile theory. This is certainly true in the cable television field where theoretical grounds for concern are abundant. The real challenge in considering new policies or revisiting old ones is to gather and interpret the available evidence from both the cable television and related fields that is being made available by actual experience.

Resources

Historical Precedents

1. Railroad Commodities Clause: 49 U.S.C.A. 1(8); *Deleware, Lt. W.R.* v. *U.S.*, 231 U.S. 363 (1913).
2. Aircraft construction - airline ownership separation: Civil Aeronautics Act, Section 408(a).
3. Early decisions on telephone industry: *Investigation of the telephone industry in the United States* (House Doc. 340, 76th Congress, 1st Session, 1939).
4. Motion picture production/exhibition divestiture: Paramount Consent decree, CCH 1948-1949 Trade Cases, 62,377, *U.S.* v. *Paramount Pictures*, 334 U.S. 131 (1948).
5. American Broadcasting Company - Paramount Merger Case: *Paramount Television Productions, Inc.*, 17 FCC 2d 264 (1953).
6. American Broadcasting Company - International Telephone & Telegraph merger proceeding: *ABC-ITT Merger*, 7 FCC 2d 245 (1966) affirmed on reconsideration 9 FCC 546 (1967).
7. Bell System Antitrust Consent Decree: *U.S.* v. *Western Electric Co.*, 1956 Trade Case 71,134 (D.N.J.).
8. Conglomerate Proceeding: *Notice of Inquiry in Docket 18449*, 16 FCC 2d 436 (1969); *Memorandum Opinion and Order in Docket 18449*, FCC 75-711, ___ FCC 2d ___(1975).
9. Television networks excluded from the syndication business: *Report and Order in Docket 12782*, 23 FCC 2d 382 (1970).
10. Newspaper- Television station cross-ownership: *Second Report and Order in Docket 18110*, 50 FCC 2d 1046 (1975).

General Cable Television References Including Discussions of Ownership

1. Sloan Commission on Cable Communications, *On the Cable, The Television of Abundance* (1971).
2. Federal Communications Commission, *Cable Television Report and Order*, 36 FCC 2d 143 (1972).
3. Cabinet Committee on Cable Communications, *Cable Report to the President* (January 14, 1974).
4. Staff of the House Subcommittee on Communications, *Cable Television: Promise versus Regulatory Performance* (1976).
5. Kalba Bowen Associates, *Separating Content from Conduit?* (1977).

Specific Cable Television Ownership Decisions

1. Jerrold Electronics Antitrust Cases: *U.S.* v. *Jerrold Electronics Corp.*, 187 F. Supp. 545 (E.D. Pa. 1960); *Jerrold Electronics* v. *Wescoast Broadcasting*, 341 F. 2d 653 (9th Cir. 1965).
2. Microwave common carrier ownership of CATV systems or programming: *First Report and Order and Further Notice of Proposed Rule Making in Docket 15586*, 1 FCC 2d 897 (1965); *Notice of Proposed Rule Making in Docket 20490*, 55 FCC 2d 36 (1975).
3. CATV—Telephone cross-ownership: *First Report and Order in Docket 18509*, 21 FCC 2d 307 (1970); *General Telephone Co. of the S.W.* v. *FCC*, 449 F. 2d 851 (5th Cir. 1971); *Clarification and Notice of Proposed Rule Making in CC Docket 78-219*, 69 FCC 2d 1097 (1978); *Report and Order in CC Docket 78-219*, FCC 79-775, ___ FCC 2d ___ (December 11, 1979).
4. TV-CATV cross-ownership rule: *Second Report and Order in Docket 18397*, 23 FCC 816 (1970); *Second Report and Order in Docket 20423*, 55 FCC 2d 540 (1975).
5. CBS—Viacom divestiture: *Iacopi* v. *FCC*, 451 F 2d 1142 (1971); *Network Television Broadcasting*, 35 FCC 2d 411 (1972).
6. Newspaper, radio, and multiple ownership: *Notice of Proposed Rule Making and of Inquiry in Docket 18891*, 23 FCC 2d 833 (1970).
7. Newspaper—CATV cross-ownership: *First Report and Order in Docket 18891*, 52 FCC 2d 170 (1975).
8. Foreign ownership: *Report and Order in Docket 20621*, 59 FCC 2d 723 (1976).
9. H & B—TPT merger: *Teleprompter Transmission of Kansas, Inc.*, 25 FCC 2d 469 (1970).
10. Warner—Cypress merger: *Warner Communications Inc.*, 37 FCC 2d 260 (1973).
11. Athena—Tele-Communications, Inc. merger: *Athena Communications Corp.*, 47 FCC 2d 535 (1974).
12. Time, Inc.—ATC merger: *American TV & Communications Corporation*, 70 FCC 2d 2175 (1978).

Industry Structure Generally

1. Caves, Richard, *American Industry: Structure, Conduct, Performance*, Prentice-Hall, Inc., 1977.
2. McGee, John S., *In Defense of Industrial Concentraion*, Praeger Publishers, 1971.
3. Borchardt, Kurt, *Structure and Performance of the U.S. Communications Industry*, Harvard College, 1970.
4. Needham, Douglas, *The Economics of Industrial Structure, Conduct and Performance*, Holt, Rinehart, and Winston, 1978.
5. Conant, Michael, *Antitrust in the Motion Picture Industry*, Arno Press, 1960.
6. Bureau of Competition, Federal Trade Commission, *Proceedings of the Symposium on Media Concentration*, December 14 and 15, 1978.

George H. Shapiro

2. Up The Hill and Down: Perspectives on Federal Regulation

From the inception of FCC regulation of cable television in 1965 until early 1975, the nature and scope of the FCC's rules governing the operation of cable television grew steadily in both scope and complexity. By the end of this period, no broadcast signals could be added by cable systems without obtaining prior approval from the FCC; there were severe restrictions on the programming cable systems could offer for an extra per channel or per program charge (pay programming); all new local franchises and most franchise amendments had to be submitted to the FCC for review and certification as consistent with federal franchise standards adopted by the FCC; and cable system compliance with elaborate channel capacity and access requirements was reviewed whenever the FCC approved the addition of new broadcast signals or passed on the validity of new franchises or amendments.

George H. Shapiro is a member of the law firm of Arent, Fox, Kintner, Plotkin & Kahn, Washington, D.C. Detailed descriptions of the history and operation of the FCC's rules applicable to cable television are set forth in Mr. Shapiro's papers in Cable Handbook 1975–1976 *and* The Cable/Broadband Communications Book *(Vol. 1) 1977–1978. This paper does not repeat most of that discussion but instead sets forth the author's perspective on that history and regulatory developments (up to April 1, 1980) since 1977.*

By early 1975, however, a process of retrenchment had begun. Thereafter, this process was substantially furthered by three developments: (1) passage of copyright legislation by the Congress which resolved some of the regulatory problems with which the FCC sought to deal in its rules; (2) Court decisions invalidating several of the theoretical underpinnings of the FCC's regulatory structure; and (3) a fresh look by the FCC itself at those regulatory underpinnings. Unfortunately, the result to date has not been a consistent and defensible scheme of regulation (or deregulation) or even a clear view of the nature of the cable medium, where it is going, and how, if at all, it should be regulated. Instead, the FCC has created an administrative quagmire by stripping its Cable Television Bureau of most of its personnel prior to the time that it has decided how much of its regulatory scheme to dismantle or what direction future federal regulation should take. Several of the developments which have led to the present disarray in the FCC's regulatory program for cable television will be discussed below, as well as some of the issues which the FCC and/or the Congress need to consider and resolve if cable systems of the 1980s are to develop to their full potential.

Signal Carriage and Exclusivity

The early stages in the FCC's regulatory retrenchment of its cable regulatory program were described at pp. 10-13 of the 1977-1978 volume of the *Cable/Broadband Communications Book*. As noted therein, the March 1977 decision of the United States Court of Appeals for the District of Columbia in *Home Box Office, Inc.* v. *FCC* played a crucial role in fostering this development. That decision struck down the FCC's pay cable rules, which had restricted the types of pay programming cable systems could offer their subscribers. The pay cable rules had been adopted at a time when a basic premise of FCC regulation of cable systems was that cable systems supplemented the service provided by television stations and that cable systems should not be permitted to engage in activities which might affect the programming offered by television stations or the revenues they earn from providing that programming. The Court concluded, however, that the Commission had "in no way justified its position that cable television must be a supplement to, rather than an equal of, broadcast television." Moreover, in ruling on a First Amendment challenge to the pay cable rules, the Court stressed the fact that rules impinging on speech can be valid only if they serve an important or substantial governmental interest, which must be demonstrated in the rule making context by "a record that convincingly shows a problem to exist and that relates the oroffered solution in the statutory mandate of the agency." The Court held that the pay cable rules failed to meet this test, and in remanding the case to the FCC, the Court reminded the FCC that "prior restraints on speech are heavily disfavored and can be sustained only where the proponent of the restraint can convincingly demonstrate a need."

The Court's conclusion that cable could not be regulated as a mere supplement to broadcasting and the requirement of a convincing showing of need to support restrictive rules were not lost on the FCC. In June 1977, shortly after the *Home Box Office* decision, the FCC initiated a *Notice of Inquiry in Docket No. 21284* to inquire into the economic relationship between broadcasting and cable television (the Economic Inquiry), designed to test the validity of the following "intuitive model" upon which its prior cable television regulatory model had been based:

(a) the increase in viewing options available from cable television services will diffuse rather than expand the audience and reduce the average audience for local stations;

(b) a reduction in average audience translates into reduced revenues;

(c) reduced revenues will, without coincident reductions in costs, reduce profits;

(d) station licensees will cut costs rather than accepting reduced profits;

(e) the reduction in costs will translate into a reduction of service to the public.

In May 1979, the FCC released a detailed *Report* in the Economic Inquiry. Based upon econometric analysis and case studies, the FCC concluded that the effect on local station audiences from elimination of the signal carriage rules appeared to be small. The predicted audience loss, in all but extreme cases, was estimated to be less than ten percent for the foreseeable future, with that loss likely to be offset in a short time by increases in population and the level of economic activity. The FCC found only a "weak relationship" between broadcasters' revenues and the amount of local public service programming they broadcast. Based upon the conclusions in the *Report*, the FCC issued a *Notice of Proposed Rule Making* proposing the elimination of its rules restricting the signals cable systems carry.

In late 1976, prior to the *Home Box Office* decision, the FCC had adopted *Notice of Inquiry in Docket No. 20988* on a related matter, questioning whether its syndicated exclusivity rules should be retained, modified or abandoned (the Exclusivity Inquiry). The FCC initially stated that "a long drawn out proceeding delaying any decision is not contemplated" and that its "goal would be to terminate that proceeding and adopt any appropriate amendments by January 1, 1978." Nevertheless, apparently because of the relationship of the issues in the Exclusivity Inquiry to the issues in the Economic Inquiry, a decision was delayed and the FCC's *Report* in the Exclusivity Inquiry was not issued until May 1979, simultaneously with its *Report* in the Economic Inquiry. The *Report* in the Exclusivity Inquiry concluded that the near–term effect on broadcast stations of eliminating the syndicated exclusivity rules would in the short-term result in loss of no more than one percent of the local station's current audiences and that the long-term effect could theoretically approach nine percent for some stations. The FCC concluded that this amount of impact would not significantly harm any broadcaster because increases in population and advertising demand will give broadcasters improved financial conditions in the long-term. The FCC also found that the syndicated exclusivity rules were not necessary to protect the interests of program producers in order to insure the continued production of television programming and that any effect on program supply from elimination of the syndicated exclusivity rules would be felt as a reduction in the *rate* of increase, rather than an actual reduction in the *supply* of programming. Thus, the FCC also proposed elimination of the syndicated exclusivity rules.

Despite its conclusions in its *Reports* in the Economic Inquiry and the Exclusivity Inquiry, the FCC has thus far failed to eliminate or modify its signal carriage and syndicated exclusivity rules, primarily because of a dispute over the extent to which copyright owners and broadcasters may or should retain program rights in television programs carried by cable systems.

The dispute over program rights now focuses on the 1976 Copyright Law and a Petition filed in 1979 by the National Telecommunications and Information Administration (NTIA) of the United States Department of Commerce. The 1976 Copyright Law provided for a system of compulsory licensing of cable television transmission of broadcast signals based upon a statutorily prescribed fee scheduled. The Copyright Law also established a Copyright Royalty Tribunal, which reviews and can make changes in the compulsry license fees at five-year intervals and in the event of changes in the FCC's signal carriage and exclusivity rules. NTIA believed that elimination of the distant signal and syndicated exclusivity rules would exempt the development of cable systems from the restraints imposed by the commercial marketplace, and in its Petition, filed shortly by before the Economic Inquiry and Exclusivity Inquiry *Reports* were issued, NTIA urged that the FCC not eliminate its signal carriage rules unless cable systems generally are required to obtain the consent of the originating television stations for the retransmission of their programs. NTIA's retransmission consent proposal would thus require cable systems to negotiate with, and presumably pay, broadcast stations and copyright owners for program rights, thereby in the view of NTIA, retaining the distribution of television programming to cable systems in the competitive marketplace.

At the time the FCC adopted the Economic Inquiry and Exclusivity Inquiry *Reports,* the staff of the Cable Television Bureau and the FCC General Counsel urged the FCC to reject the NTIA Petition, primarily because they believed that the Congress had rejected retransmission consent at the time it adopted the compulsory licensing provisions of the Copyright Law. However, a majority of the Commissioners would not vote to issue the Economic Inquiry and Exclusivity Inquiry *Reports*, and the related proposals to eliminate the distant signal and syndicated exclusivity rules, unless the question of retransmission consent or some other form of protection for program rights was left open. Thus, while at one point the FCC's *Notice of Proposed Rule Making* to eliminate distant signal and syndicated exclusivity rules states that the FCC believes that it should deny the retransmission consent proposal, at another point comment on the following matter is requested:

> It may also be necessary to take actions that will facilitate the development of market institutions that will protect and adequately reward holders of program rights. Retransmission consent, full copyright liability, and pre-transmission notification are among the ways to address this issue. The Commission's preference would be to give markets the opportunity to work and to impose regulatory judgments on how transmissions shall take place only on demonstration that a private market will not work. Nevertheless, on *a priori* grounds it might be the case that further Commission policy should be developed in this area. Therefore the Commission invites further comment on how the markets in program rights may develop, and what actions, if any, the Commission can legally take that would serve that end.

The fact that a majority of the Commissioners voted, contrary to the recommendations of the FCC staff, to include retransmission consent in the FCC rule making proposal demonstrates that the FCC itself is not yet convinced by the Economic Inquiry and Exclusivity *Reports* that the distant signal and syndicated exclusivity rules should be rescinded.

The controversy over program rights thus threatens to further delay action on the FCC's proposals to eliminate the signal carriage and syndicated exclusivity rules, and could have a substantial effect on the outcome. A recent court decision, however, may facilitate resolution of the program rights issue. In November 1979, the United States Court of Appeals for the District of Columbia Circuit, in *Geller* v. *FCC*, recognizing that the FCC's 1972 rules were in part adopted in order to facilitate the passage of copyright legislation, ordered the FCC to conduct proceedings to determine whether, in light of passage of the 1976 Copyright Law, there is any basis for the continued existence of the rules. The Court's decision seems to indicate that the protection provided in the current rules for broadcasters and program producers by the distant signal and syndicated exclusivity rules may have been superseded by the Copyright Law, and if the FCC concludes otherwise, the *Home Box Office* decision would seem to require that the FCC base any such conclusion on a strong evidentiary record. But the evidence to date, as shown in the *Reports* in the Economic and Exclusivity Inquiry, is that FCC regulation of program rights would be unjustified.

The administration of the existing rules regulating signal carriage has, since the *Home Box Office* decision, also caused considerable problems. While the FCC has been unable to come to any final decisions in the proceeding dealing with the distant signal and syndicated exclusivity rules, the econometric analysis used in the Economic Inquiry and Exclusivity Inquiry *Reports* and the proceedings leading to the issuance of those *Reports* has resulted in a new standard for acting on waivers of those rules which in most instances thus far considered by the FCC has led to grant of the requested waivers. Utilizing the formula set forth in the *Notice of Proposed Rule Making* initiating the Economic Inquiry and relying on the reasoning of the *Home Box Office* case, cable systems in 1978 began seeking waivers of the distant signal rules by attempting to show that adding signals would not adversely affect local broadcast stations. In reconsidering a decision waiving its distant signal rules for a cable system in Arlington, Virginia (the ARTEC case), the FCC in November 1978 adopted the new waiver standard by (1) eliminating a former requirement that cable systems show some kind of unique circumstances to support grant of a waiver, and (2) specifying that cable systems could establish a prima facie case in support of a waiver if they could establish that waiver of the rules would have only a minimal economic impact on local broadcast stations. Then the burden shifts to the local broadcasters to establish the need for the continued protection afforded by the current rules, and if they are unable to meet that burden, the cable system's waiver is granted.

After the ARTEC decision (the validity of which is currently being challenged in the courts), numerous cable systems filed requests for similar waivers of the rules. But the FCC found itself in a dilemma. In October 1978, the FCC had eliminated its requirement that cable systems obtain certificates of compliance, and shortly thereafter it began a major reduction in the staff of the Cable Television Bureau. In the meantime, numerous waiver requests in accordance with the ARTEC procedures were filed, and very few were acted upon. In July 1979, a group of cable operators sought an order from the United States Court of Appeals for the District of Columbia Circuit to compel FCC action on their waiver requests. The FCC's response was as follows:

> The Cable Television Bureau staff has informed Commission Counsel that by the end of July, there were over 275 petitions for special relief pending before the Bureau, including 130 petitions requiring application of the *ARTEC II* waiver procedures. The Bureau has only five staff attorneys, in addition to supervisory personnel, to handle special relief requests, as well as other legal matters within the Bureau. This large number of relief requests, exacerbated by the scarcity of personnel available to review those requests, has necessarily limited the number of *ARTEC II* related petitions processed. ...

The situation has only become worse since that time.

Thus, notwithstanding the FCC's initial constructive reaction to the *Home Box Office* decision and the FCC's own findings regarding the lack of adverse impact that would be expected from elimination of its signal carriage and syndicated exclusivity rules, the outcome of the proceeding proposing elimination of those rules remains uncertain, and in the meantime, numerous requests for waiver of those rules remain untouched because of the absence of staff to review them to determine whether they comply with current waiver standards.

Access and Channel Capacity

Court decisions have also invalidated the FCC's efforts to make cable channels available to all comers merely for the asking. The FCC's 1972 rules set forth elaborate access and channel capacity requirements applicable to cable systems in the 100 largest television markets. These rules imposed on all cable systems commencing operation in those markets after March 31, 1972, the following requirements: (1) a minimum channel capacity of at least 20 channels; (2) a minimum of 4 channels set aside for first-come, nondiscriminatory access by members of the public without program content control by the cable operator; and (3) a requirement that cable systems increase the number of access channels when minimum usage criteria for existing access channels are met. Cable systems already in operation on March 31, 1972, were given until March 31, 1977, to come into compliance with these requirements, but in the meantime they were permitted to add new distant signals only if they added an access channel for each new distant signal they added. Notwithstanding the abundance of channels the FCC thus sought to make available to the public, in all but a limited number of instances the access channels remained idle (in part for reasons discussed in Chapter 6 of this book) but could not be used to provide most other services. In addition many cable operators were unwilling to add signals utilizing their existing channel capacity because, in order to do so, they would also have had to add access channels, which in many instances would have required the installation of converters in the homes of all subscribers and in some instances complete rewiring of the cable system and/or the replacement of all existing amplifiers in the system. Such investments made little sense to cable operators when the additional channel capacity to provide access channels would be largely idle or under-utilized. Similar considerations also made the 1977 rebuild requirements for existing top 100 market systems seem totally divorced from reality, particularly in view of the economic recession in 1974-75 and the tight money situation then prevailing. Thus, in February 1975, the FCC began a rule making proceeding proposing to suspend the 1977 rebuild requirement until the FCC could reevaluate its access and channel capacity requirements.

Shortly thereafter, in June 1975, the FCC commenced a further rule making proceeding to modify its access and channel capacity requirements. New rules, which for the most part considerably scaled down those requirements, were adopted in 1976. While the FCC retained its minimum channel capacity rule, no cable system was required to install converters solely in order to provide access so long as a single channel was available for that use. The applicability of the access and channel capacity rules was expanded from the top 100 markets to systems in all markets, but systems with less than 3,500 subscribers were exempted. Existing systems with no unused activated channel capacity were permitted to provide access to the extent possible on their currently utilized channels (such as on a channel blacked out to provide network nonduplication). Converter installation requirements were significantly reduced. The compliance date for the modified channel capacity requirements was postponed until 1986, by which time the FCC believed that natural economic forces would result in most cable systems increasing their channel capacities.

The 1976 access rules were challenged in court by Midwest Video Corporation, a company operating exclusively in smaller television markets, to whom the access rules had not previously been applicable. In a sweeping decision issued in February 1978, the United States Court of Appeals for the Eighth Circuit, in *Midwest Video Corporation* v. *FCC*, set aside the access and channel capacity rules as exceeding the FCC's jurisdiction. Furthermore, the Court, while explicitly declining to rest its decision on First and Fifth Amendment grounds, left no doubt that it thought that the rules also violated those provisions. Thereafter, in April 1979 the Supreme Court in *FCC* v. *Midwest Video Corporation,* affirmed the Eighth Circuit's decision on jurisdictional grounds. Moreover, while declining to reach the constitutional issues discussed by the Eighth Circuit, the Court in a footnote acknowledged that the First Amendment challenge to the access rules was "not frivolous."

The Supreme Court decision has significant implications for future efforts to regulate cable television, at both the federal and state levels. The Court concluded that the access rules imposed common carrier obligations on cable systems because they required cable operators to make their facilities available to all comers on a first-come, nondiscriminatory basis and because they divorced the cable operator from content control on the access channels. In an earlier decision, the Court had determined that the FCC's authority over cable television derived from the broadcast provisions of the Communications Act, where common carrier regulation was prohibited and where the policy of the Communications Act was to preserve editorial control of programming in the broadcast licensee. The Court stated:

... Congress has restricted the Commission's ability to advance objectives associated with public access at the expense of the journalistic freedom of persons engaged in broadcasting.

That limitation is not one having peculiar applicability to television broadcasting. Its force is not diminished by the variant technology involved in cable transmissions. Cable operators now share with broadcasters a significant amount of editorial discretion regarding what their programming will include.

The Supreme Court has, in a case involving newspapers, also recognized that the First Amendment protects the editorial function, and accordingly, the *Midwest Video* decision, aside from making it clear that the FCC cannot, under existing statutes, require access on a common carrier basis, also raises questions about whether the First Amendment will invalidate state and municipal access requirements in cable television franchises.

While it is possible, even after the *Midwest Video* decision, that the FCC could attempt to develop a record that would support the adoption of channel capacity and studio requirements which were eliminated along with the access rules, it is unlikely, absent a change in the Communications Act, that the FCC will again seek to impose common-carrier type access requirements. Public interest groups have filed a petition urging that the FCC impose an obligation on cable systems to originate programming under their control, similar to the mandatory origination rule which the Supreme Court had previously upheld as imposing obligations on cable systems analogous to those imposed on broadcasters. It is questionable, however, whether the FCC will adopt this proposal in light of its earlier determination that effective local programming cannot be mandated by law, its current efforts to withdraw from much of its regulation of cable systems, and the fact that a substantial portion of the cable industry now voluntarily engages in program origination which provides programming opportunities for local individuals and groups.

Federal Regulation of State and Local Franchises and Federal Preemption

As a result of its interpretation of court decisions and its own deregulatory efforts in other areas, the FCC is also withdrawing or has withdrawn from virtually all aspects of state and local franchise regulation and may be moving to eliminate its preemption of state and local regulatory efforts in other areas. The FCC first embarked on its regulation of state and local franchising in 1972 in its *Cable Television Report and Order*. Initially the FCC rule on franchise standards required the following: (1) that local franchising authorities consider the legal, character, financial, technical, and other qualifications of franchise applicants and the adequancy and feasibility of their construction arrangements; (2) that franchises be issued in public proceedings affording due process; and (3) that franchises contain provisions requiring early implementation and completion of construction, a fifteen-year limit on their duration, subscriber rate regulation for traditional cable services, investigation and resolution of subscriber complaints about service, automatic incorporation into franchises of changes in the FCC's franchise requirements, and a limitation of franchise fees to three percent (or five percent if the franchise fee is used for a local cable television regulatory program) of gross revenues from the provision of traditional cable television services.

In 1974, in its *Clarification of Rules and Notice of Proposed Rule Making in Docket Nos. 20018-20024*, the FCC sought comment on expanding its franchise standards to include the following: (1) more specific rules on the type of public proceeding required for the selection of a franchise; (2) specific guidelines and requirements on the information to be considered prior to selection of the franchisee; (3) line extension and density provisions; (4) changes in the duration of franchises and a review of the franchise by franchising authorities at five-year intervals; (5) provisions relating to the expiration or cancellation of franchises and the continuance of service thereafter; (6) provisions on the assignment or transfer of control of franchises; and (7) specific provisions on what local government official will be directly responsible for receiving and acting on subscriber complaints.

In late 1974, the FCC adopted rules concerning the line extension and density provisions in franchises and the identification of local officials responsible for subscriber complaints. In early 1975, however, the regulatory momentum had begun to change, and the proceeding on modification of the franchise duration and the adoption of a five-year review procedure was terminated without the adoption of rules. Then in December 1976, the FCC initiated a rule making proceeding in Docket No. 21002, proposing simplification of its certificate of compliance procedure (which as noted above was subsequently eliminated) and proposing elimination of its franchise standards. In its *Report and Order* in that proceeding, released in September 1977, the FCC eliminated all of the franchise standards except for the franchise fee limitation, and it modified that limitation to permit the revenue from pay cable, leased channel and other non-traditional cable services to be included within the revenue base on which franchise fees are levied. Petitions for reconsideration of this action were filed by a number of parties, and those petitions were denied in April 1979. In that denial, however, the FCC questioned whether, in light of the fact that all of its cable rules were being reevaluated, there was any reason to retain the franchise fee limit in any form, and thus proposed complete elimination of the franchise fee limit.

This action came less than two weeks after the Supreme Court decision in the *Midwest Video* case, invalidating the access rules. The FCC indicated that one reason why it was proposing elimination of the franchise fee limit was that the access rules had required cable systems to provide access channels at less than profit-maximizing rates and that, with the invalidation of the access rules, there may be no need to insure that cable revenues are not drained away by high local fees.

State and municipal regulation of cable television has also been affected, not only by the FCC's franchise standards, but also by the preemptive force of other FCC rules and policies. The current areas of FCC preemption are as follows:

1. The FCC has preempted state and municipal efforts to regulate the terms and conditions of broadcast signal carriage.

2. The FCC has preempted state and municipal franchise provisions prohibiting cable systems from originating programming.

3. The FCC has preempted state and municipal franchise provisions prohibiting or regulating the provision of pay cable services, including the regulation of the rates charged for pay cable services. An effort by the State of New York to regulate pay cable rates was invalidated by the United States Court of Appeals in *Brookhaven Cable TV, Inc.* v. *Kelly,* which thus upheld the FCC's authority in this area.

4. The FCC has preempted state and municipal governments from adopting cable television technical standards unless a waiver of the preemption policy is obtained from the FCC.

5. The FCC preempted state and municipal governments from adopting channel capacity and access requirements more burdensome than those provided for in the FCC's rules unless the FCC concluded that any such requirements were reasonable and necessary for a planned local program for use of the channels and facilities involved.

Two of these areas of preemption have been either eliminated or questioned by recent FCC and court decisions. While there has been no specific decision on the matter, it is likely, in light of the invalidation of the access rules in the *Midwest Video* case, that there is presently no longer any federal preemption of state and municipal access requirements (if such requirements can survive constitutional challenge after the *Midwest Video* case). Moreover, in its further rule making proceeding on franchise fees, the FCC raised questions about whether, if the franchise fee limitation is removed, there is any further basis to prohibit state and municipal rate regulation of pay cable services. It is not likely that that question will be resolved in the current phase of the franchise fee proceeding, but it could be considered in further proceedings. If it is, the question of whether to retain the FCC's preemptive policies in other areas could also be considered.

Conclusion

Thus, at this late stage in the development of cable television, virtually every major premise in the FCC's regulation of cable television to date has either been invalidated by the courts, has been withdrawn by the FCC itself, or is currently under intensive review and subject to withdrawal or substantial revision in currently pending proceedings at the FCC. A number of factors have had a role in influencing both the courts and the FCC to reach the decisions and take the actions discussed above. Some of the more important factors are the following: [1]

1. The nature of the cable television industry has changed and continues to change substantially in relatively short periods of time, and these changes have regulatory implications. For example, it is questionable whether 10 years ago it would have been possible to convince the Supreme Court of the importance of editorial function to the operation of cable television systems—the principal basis on which the Court invalidated the access rules. It was the advent of satellite communications, which now offers cable systems a wide variety of fare from which to select—e.g., pay cable services, religious programs, sports channels, children's programs, foreign language programs, Congressional debates, distant major television stations—which made it possible to see the cable operator as an editor selecting from a wide variety of program fare to develop an attractive service package to market to his subscribers. Other satellite-delivered services loom on the horizon—an all news channel, programming directed to the elderly—and other services will undoubtedly be developed in the future, such as teletext and information retrieval. Already two courts have analogized cable systems to newspapers, and if the editorial function of cable operators continues to increase, First Amendment considerations could well become paramount in determining the future role of not only federal, but also state and local regulation of at least the video services provided by cable television systems. On the other hand, various types of non-video services are also developing and could constitute a significant part of the service provided by cable systems in the future—for example, burglar alarm and detection services, automatic meter reading and utility load management, point-to-point data transmission, check cashing and verification, automated fund transfers, and the ordering of consumer items on two-way responsive cable systems. Many of these new and emerging services—both video and non-video—are described in detail in other chapters of this book. Some of these types of services may invite common carrier, consumer protection, and other types of regulation, and cable systems may be regulated one way for some of the services they provide and other ways for other services.

2. The nature and extent of any type of future regulation of cable television will be significantly determined by the extent of the competitive alternatives available. The FCC has recognized the extent to which competition is an effective regulator in a number of areas, most recently in the common carrier area. Most present cable services are subject to considerable competition from a number of alternative services, and competition is likely to increase in the future. For example, the FCC's efforts to make UHF television competitive with VHF television finally seem to have succeeded, and the number of television stations has expanded in recent years. The FCC has under consideration a proposal for further expansion of television services, particularly in small and rural communities, in a pending inquiry on low power television services. Pay cable services are duplicated in many communities by MDS services. Broadcast pay television stations have begun commercial operation in several communities, and applications are currently pending before the FCC for many more. Videotape recorders are giving consumers additional choices, and a significant development of the videocassette and videodisc market is expected over the next few years. Television stations are experimenting with providing teletext and other information services. The Communications Satellite Corporation has announced plans for direct satellite-to-home services and other similar proposals will surely follow. Specialized common carriers are proliferating and offering a wide variety of services and will have the capability to offer even more services. The need for regulation of these services diminishes as competitive services continue to develop.

3. Technology will also affect the nature of any future regulation. Fiber optics and laser technology are also developing, and those and other technologies will have an impact on the number and types of services cable systems can provide and the types of competitive alternatives that will develop. For example, if telephone companies develop fiber optics plants with abundant channel capacities, parties may offer services competitive to those of cable systems on telephone company plants, or cable operators could conceivably lease telephone company or other common carrier fibers to provide their services, perhaps in competition with others providing similar services on the same fiber.

These and other considerations indicate that the deregulatory trend currently evident at the FCC is likely to continue, but it is important that the FCC recognize that a significant role for federal regulation remains. At least for the foreseeable future, cable television will continue to be a form of interstate communication by wire, which is within the FCC's regulatory ambit, and it will continue to be a means for distributing national programming, primarily by satellite. Proposals to eliminate franchise fee limitations, or reduce the extent of federal preemption in such areas to pay cable rate regulation, may subject cable television to discriminatory and hobbling forms of taxation through the franchise fee mechanism, impede its ability to compete with the other developing forms of communication, and subject cable operators to a bewildering array of conflicting state and local regulations. As described in detail in Chapter 3 of this book, the interstate service provided by common carriers is already exempt from most forms of state regulation, and such media directly competitive with cable television as broadcast pay television and MDS already operate in an environment where state or municipal rate regulation is prohibited. Additionally, in the past, cable systems have been subjected to anticompetitive practices on the part of telephone companies through their control of the poles to which cable operators attached their cable, and there is likely to be a continuing need to insure that at least those parties regulated by the FCC do not engage in similar or other anticompetitive practices that adversely affect the competitive environment in which national telecommunications systems are developing. As the FCC proceeds on its deregulatory course, and as Congress debates a wide variety of proposals for revising the Communications Act, they should keep these and similar considerations in mind and not permit deregulation to become the abandonment of any federal role in insuring that cable television, as a national medium of communications, is able to offer its services in the marketplace on fair and equal terms with other communications media.

Resources Mentioned

1. *Home Box Office* v. *FCC,* 567 F.2d 9, *cert. denied* 434 U.S. 829 (1977).
2. *Notice of Inquiry in Docket No. 21284* (Economic Inquiry), 65 FCC 2d 9 (1977).
3. *Notice of Inquiry in Docket No. 20988* (Exclusivity Inquiry), 61 FCC 2d 746 (1976).
4. *Report in Docket No. 21284* (Economic Inquiry), 71 FCC 2d 632 (1979).
5. *Report in Docket No. 20988* (Exclusivity Inquiry), 71 FCC 2d 951 (1979).
6. *Notice of Proposed Rule Making in Docket Nos. 20988 and 21284* (Economic and Exclusivity Inquiries), 71 FCC 2d 1004 (1979).
7. *Geller* v. *FCC,* ___ F.2d ___, 46 RR2d 721 (1979).
8. *Report and Order in Docket No. 20508* (Modifications in Channel Capacity and Access Channel Rules), 59 FCC 2d 294 (1976).
9. *Midwest Video Corporation* v. *FCC,* 571 F.2d 1025 (1978), *aff'd sub nom. FCC* v. *Midwest Video Corporation,* 440 U.S. 689 (1979).
10. *Cable Television Report and Order,* 36 FCC 2d 143 (1972).
11. *Clarification of Rules and Notice of Proposed Rule Making in Docket Nos. 20018-10024,* 46 FCC 2d 175 (1974).
12. *Report and Order in Docket No. 21002* (Modification of Franchise Standards and Certificate of Compliance Procedures), 66 FCC 2d 380 (1977).

Note: References to FCC 2d are to the Federal Communications Commission Reports, published by the Government Printing Office. References to RR and RR2d are to Pike and Fischer Radio Regulation. One or both of these publications are available at many law libraries throughout the country and at the Federal Communications Commission library, located on the sixth floor at 1919 M Street, N.W., Washington, D.C. Docket volumes, containing comments filed by interested parties and documents issued by the Commission, are available to the public at the Commission's Public Reference Room on the second floor at 1919 M Street, N.W.

Sharon A. Briley

3. State Involvement in Cable TV and Other Communications Services: A Current Review

Traditionally, state involvement in communications matters has been limited to regulating intrastate telephone and telegraph services, to the extent permitted by the Communications Act of 1934. The act firmly implanted the concept of federal-state cooperation and, by amendment in 1971, authorized for this purpose the use of joint boards, consisting of federal and state members.

As new technologies have developed, the potential for new state roles has increased. For example, the evolution of cable television has provided an unprecedented opportunity for states to deal with regulatory issues concerning video communications services. Every state government has been involved to some degree with the subject of cable television, which now serves some citizens in every state. The character of such involvement ranges from total absence of policy to complex regulation. Laws and regulations in the states cover a wide variety of areas of cable television service—from standards for drilling holes in buildings

Sharon A. Briley is the Cable TV Specialist and Policy Analyst for the Policy Review and Development Division, Cable Television Bureau, Federal Communications Commission. She is the creator and author of the FCC publication on cable TV state regulation and of annual legislative reports since 1973. The views expressed herein are those of the author and do not necessarily reflect the views of the Federal Communications Commission.

served by the cable company to requirements that subscribers receive their program guides in advance of the program transmission. Most typically, state laws and regulations are concerned with franchising, rates, pole attachments, theft of service, taxation and fees, programming, and the provision of good service.

In addition to cable television, states have become increasingly interested in the effects of other developing technologies, such as multipoint distribution service (MDS). State utility commissions in Alaska and Rhode Island, for example, have considered regulating MDS. Also in the common carrier field, terminal equipment has attracted state interest; the New York Public Service Commission recently adopted regulations concerning customer wiring. Also, a two-way data case involving a telephone company challenge to a cable company's offering of a home security service is a current topic of interest on the New Jersey Board of Public Utilities, which is well aware that its jurisdiction to regulate intrastate services is not preempted. The older, unregulated technology of master antenna television (MATV) has given state agencies in Connecticut, Delaware, and New York some concerns which may result in regulatory decisions.

Some states which have had considerable experience in cable television regulation at either a state or municipal level have "deregulated" or are considering deregulatory measures, particularly in the areas of rates and franchising. These states include California, Massachusetts, Minnesota, New Jersey, and New York.

As public awareness of new communications services increases, citizens and governments face many choices in dealing with the issues confronting them: What services should be made available and how can they be provided most efficiently? Who should own and control the services? What regulations should be imposed, if any, and by whom? Within these broad questions may be hundreds of others requiring answers. This paper will discuss some states's efforts at answering these and other questions in its overview of state involvement in electronic communications, primarily cable television.

Federal-State Relations

Debate involving the relationship between the federal and state governments has been an integral part of American government since its inception. The Constitution, in Amendment X, provides the following guidance: "The powers not delegated to the United States by the Constitution, nor prohibited by it to the States, are reserved to the States respectively, or to the people." Edward S. Corwin's treatise on the Constitution documents his conclusion that the Tenth Amendment does not "shield the States nor their political subdivisions from the impact of any authority granted to the Federal Government." The words of the court in *Case* v. *Bowles* in 1946 are equally relevant today: "There is no general doctrine implied in the Federal Constitution that the two governments, national and state, are each to exercise its powers so as not to interfere with the free and full exercise of the other." Thus, while the potential for conflict in federal and state government actions is inherent in the nature of American government, the general welfare of the nation is probably improved as a result of the freedom of both levels of government to act.

Federal, State and Local Jurisdiction

The "government" of communications services involves decision making by Congress, the Federal Communications Commission (FCC), and the courts. The parameters of state involvement in communications matters are defined ultimately by Congress in the Communications Act of 1934, which established a dual regulatory plan under which the FCC regulates interstate services, facilities, and rates, and the states regulate intrastate and exchange services and rates. The FCC has concurrent jurisdiction with the states to the extent that facilities are commonly used for intrastate and interstate communications. However, the courts have upheld the federal Commission's jurisdiction to preempt conflicting state regulation in cases where there is a need for uniformity or when state regulations may undercut federal policies. A recent example is the North Carolina Utilities Commission's 1973 proposal to prohibit telephone companies in the state from providing intrastate service through customer-provided terminal equipment, to which the FCC responded in Docket No. 19528 that a uniform national policy on interconnection is essential because the same facilities and terminal devices are used for both intrastate and interstate service. The U.S. Supreme Court upheld the FCC's authority to preempt state regulations in such cases.

Jurisdiction at any level of government may be granted by legislation or it may be asserted in the absence of legislative mandate. At the federal level, no law originally granted express authority to the FCC to regulate any aspect of cable television. After having declined to assert jurisdiction in 1958, the FCC adopted rules in 1965 relating to the licensing of common carrier microwave stations serving cable TV systems. In 1966 the Commission proposed to assert jurisdiction over non-microwave cable TV systems, in its *Notice of Inquiry and Notice of Proposed Rule Making in Docket No. 15971*, stating that it would welcome congressional guidance as to policy and clarification of authority, "which would lay the troublesome jurisdictional question at [sic] rest." In asserting jurisdiction in its *Second Report and Order* in that proceeding, the Commission stated that it would ask Congress "to consider the appropriate relationship of Federal to State-local jurisdiction in the CATV field, with particular reference to initial franchising, rate regulation and extension of service." The U.S. Supreme Court, in *U.S.* v. *Southwestern Cable Co.*, upheld the Commission's action on the basis that the FCC had authority to regulate services "ancillary" to broadcasting. In 1970, the Commission began a separate proceeding, Docket No. 18892, concerning "Federal-State or Local Relationships," which was concluded in the *Cable Television Report and Order in 1972*, the foundation of the present rules. Since then, with no congressional action forthcoming, several significant court cases have both supported and struck down parts of the Commission's cable television regulations. Chapter 2 of this book contains a discussion of these cases—supporting jurisdiction to preempt pay cable rates and to require originations of programing, and opposing FCC regulation of the content of pay cable channels, the regulation of two-way nonvideo services (i.e., leased channels), and the imposition of access and channel capacity requirements.

The authority of all states regulating cable television on a comprehensive basis, termed "regulating states" in this paper, is supported by state statute. The U.S. Supreme Court, in the 1968 case of *TV Pix, Inc.* v. *Taylor*, upheld the constitutionality of a state statute granting the Nevada Public Service Commission jurisdiction to regulate cable television. In the absence of congressional preemption, the Court said, states have the right and power to regulate cable television. The Court also noted the local character of cable television, which results in little need for national uniformity which would preclude state action. However, even with apparent comprehensive regulatory authority in areas not federally preempted, jurisdictional questions arise as a result of statutory limitations. For example, in Connecticut the Division of Public Utilities Control (DPUC), in which the state statute vested the first state authority to regulate cable television, has asked the state attorney general for an opinion on the scope of its authority. State regulators are seeking to determine the Division's authority to require companies to adhere to franchise application promises and to require companies to grant public access time. Also in Connecticut, the statutory reference to cable's use of public streets or highways limits the state's ability to regulate MATV systems on private property. The state agency, which has recently developed new policies on extension of service, is particularly concerned about an MATV system providing one package of service at a single rate to a large condominium in a nonfranchised locality. According to an agency spokesperson, the other homes in the franchise area will probably not obtain cable service, because the remaining portion is unattractive to cable entrepreneurs. The state attorney general has said informally that the state does not have jurisdiction over MATV systems.

In New York, also, statutory language excluding from the definition of cable television any system which serves fewer than 50 subscribers and excluding any MATV system, limits the state's jurisdiction on

MATV matters. The state issued two clarifications of policy on the definition of MATV, affirming its narrowness. A system is not an MATV if it carries programming from any source other than local broadcast signals.

A similar case of limitations within the state statutes is found in Delaware, where an incorporated municipality set rates lower in the municipality than the state set them for the same cable company operating in the unincorporated parts of the franchise area, which the state has sole jurisdiction to regulate. To attempt to alleviate the resulting limitation on the state's authority, a state senator sponsored legislation in 1979 to give the Public Service Commission authority to regulate rates uniformly throughout the state. Introduced in late March, five amendments were attached to the bill by the end of June, including one granting to incorporated municipalities the power to elect to retain their rate-making authority, but to establish "just and reasonable rates by applying rate-making standards consistent with those utilized by the [state] Commission."

Jurisdictional doubts are expressed even more frequently at the local level, generally municipalities or counties, where the first regulations on cable television were applied under the powers of local governments to control the use of streets and grant rights of way. In Pennsylvania, the long-debated issue of franchising authority of certain municipalities is indicative of statutory vagueness. The state Supreme Court, in *Borough of Scottsdale* v. *National Cable Television Corporation* (decided December 27, 1977), upheld the right of municipalities, including boroughs, to grant "franchises" and to regulate rates and rate increases, over a dissent which asserted that municipalities possess only powers that are expressly granted to them. The Borough Code, said the majority, authorizes boroughs, a type of municipality, to regulate the streets and public ways. This authorization permits the borough "to grant cable television franchises and to impose conditions upon the installation, use and maintenance of cable television wires placed beneath municipal streets." Rate regulation was interpreted not to be regulation of the use of the streets. This case did not address the unresolved question of franchising authority for second class townships, which the county court, in its 1977 ruling in *Lower Nazareth Township* v. *Service Electric Cable TV, Inc.*, held to be absent from the Second Class Township Code. The Pennsylvania State Association of Township Supervisors has interpreted the general powers of second class townships to permit the adoption of any laws or regulations which are not inconsistent with the laws and Constitution of the Commonwealth and has cited the statutory authority of second class townships to grant permits containing restrictions and regulations relating to the installation and maintenance of utilities as applicable to cable television systems. Although various decisions have been reached, the debate continues on these franchising issues.

Federal Preemptions

Equally important in determining the bounds of local jurisdiction is federal preemption of regulation, a topic which this author addressed in the 1977-1978 volume of the *Cable/Broadband Communications Book*. The areas of preemption, preventing state or local governments from adopting laws or regulations on these subjects, include signal carriage, pay cable, and technical standards. In the areas of access and pay cable, the degree of federal preemption has changed since comprehensive regulations were adopted by the FCC in 1972. The other major areas of federal regulation affecting cable television include cross-ownership, copyright, equal employment opportunity, political cablecasting, fairness and equal time, sponsorship, obscenity, and cable television relay (CARS microwave) services.

Historically, there have been few cases of friction between the federal and state governments over cable television regulation, the predominant source of friction having been pay cable. In the case of *Brookhaven Cable TV, Inc.* v. *New York State Commission on Cable Television*, the state, supported by the National Association of Regulatory Utility Commissioners (NARUC), challenged the FCC's authority to regulate or preempt regulation of pay cable rates. The U.S. Court of Appeals for the Second Circuit, in its 1978 decision upholding the FCC's authority, held that the state's 1976 ruling on the subject had to yield to FCC preemption, on both constitutional and statutory grounds.

In addition to New York, the Connecticut DPUC and the Connecticut legislature have evidenced concern about pay cable. A bill to prohibit extra charges for pay cable service has been introduced, though unsuccessfully, several times. A law was passed in early 1980 regarding premium services, requiring companies to furnish subscribers, by the first day of each month, a written listing of programs for the month and to refund or credit subscribers if they are billed for unreceived services. One issue of concern to the Connecticut DPUC is whether the state may adopt rules concerning placement of commercial broadcast channels in premium packages in light of the FCC's preemption. The question surfaced as a result of a cable system's removal of an educational station from its basic service to allow subscribers to receive a movie channel service in its place without need of a converter. Converters were then required in order to view the educational channel. The state currently has no jurisdiction to deal with the complaints which arose in this instance, which were resolved by the company offering converters free of charge to those subscribers who wished to view the educational channel.

State regulators in Connecticut have been limited also by the simultaneous jurisdiction to regulate basic subscriber rates and lack thereof to regulate pay cable rates. In a rate case decision in October 1978, the state allowed a cable company to increase rates for basic service by one dollar on the basis of the company's claim of total revenue needed. Subsequently, the company lowered the premium service rates by one dollar, an action benefiting only those subscribers receiving pay cable service. State regulators may prefer not having to segregate the revenues if the company does not, but resolution of the state's dilemma might conflict with the intent of the present federal preemption of pay service regulation, which is intended to allow the marketplace to regulate rates. State governments, however, are no more isolated from the marketplace regulation philosophy than is the federal government, and recent state rate decisions provide evidence of similar attitudes at both levels. The Massachusetts *Notice of Inquiry* on competition standards (issued in December 1979), for example, makes reference to the pay cable preemption, stating that "this Commission [MCC] as a matter of policy, if not jurisdictional decree, has determined that such services should not be price regulated by the government at this time." The California bill, discussed later in this paper, also reflects a similar attitude in its rate deregulation formula.

Two of pay cable's competitors, MDS and MATV services, also escape state regulation to the extent that they relate to the FCC's preemptive powers. In its September 1978 declaratory ruling in *Orth-O-Vision*, the FCC held that the New York Commission on Cable Television's regulations that MATV systems carrying programs transmitted by MDS stations must comply with cable television franchising requirements were invalid. The FCC said that these state regulations were intended to eliminate or curtail MDS as a competitor of pay cable offered by cable systems. The FCC did not address the issues "relating to the state's jurisdiction to regulate MATV systems generally," but only the "state's authority to regulate MDS stations indirectly. . . ." The Commission offered the following rationale.

> We hold that the state's action in this area is an impermissible interference with interstate communications that is properly within the jurisdiction of the Commission [FCC]. Merely because the state disclaims any intent to regulate MDS does not ameliorate the practical effect of its action, which is direct interference with an integral, federally-regulated portion of the interstate communications network.

Prior to its decision in *Brookhaven*, the U.S. Court of Appeals for the Second Circuit in the same year upheld, in *New York State Commission on Cable Television* v. *FCC*, an FCC decision limiting the combined state and local franchise fee in New York to a total not exceeding the federal limit. The FCC had set the limit for the state at four percent.

Although the FCC also preempts the area of technical standards for cable systems, some state regulatory agencies have their own technical regulations, having obtained a waiver from the FCC, or have references to the FCC regulations. The Office of Cable Television in New Jersey obtained a waiver from the FCC to impose its own more stringent technical standards. Massachusetts regulations require that local licensing authorities adopt minimum technical standards conforming with FCC regulations.

To summarize, states generally may adopt laws in any area not preempted at the federal level, provided that they do not contradict any federal policies or regulations. For further discussion of pertinent cases involving state challenges to federal preemptions and federal contests of state actions, please refer to Chapter 2 of this book.

The Mutual Influence of Federal and State Actions

As some of the prior discussion demonstrates, actions of the federal government frequently influence state activities, both official and unofficial. The state of Delaware, for example, initially became involved in cable television as a result of an industry bill enacted to create a means for cable companies to comply with the FCC's franchising regulations. Municipalities in Delaware had authority to franchise; counties did not have authority. This justification for state regulation has since been removed at the federal level. As many as 500 operating systems, however, were unfranchised at the time the FCC's standards were mandatory.

Some state and local governments have preferred previous federal regulations. A current example is Rhode Island's preference for using, as a model for state regulation purposes, the FCC's rules as they were in 1974. Former administrator Archie Smith's franchising Order, adopted in 1974, contained the franchise standards and access provisions based on the FCC rules.

Deregulation at the federal level will not necessarily prompt state actions to fill the void. Assuming that federal preemptions are not imposed, for example, on signal carriage or franchise fees, the purpose of federal deregulatory actions would most likely be defeated if state or local governments were to impose similar regulations in their place. Similarly, if the federal preemption of pay cable rate regulation were removed, state or local governments might regulate the rates, thus controlling the otherwise free market in which buyers and sellers of pay cable services now operate.

On the other hand, in the area of access programming, states are more free to regulate without federal constraints. Note, however, that the communications field is particularly susceptible to First Amendment limitations, to which states are no less subject than is the federal government. Chapters 2 and 6 of this book provide discussions of the U.S. Supreme Court's 1979 decision in *Midwest Video Corp.* v. *FCC,* which struck down the FCC's access and channel capacity requirements on jurisdictional grounds. State interest in access has grown as a result of the

FCC's regulatory support from 1972 to 1979 and has increased further among state and local governments in the absence of federal support. Some state regulatory activities concerning access are described later in this paper and in greater detail in Chapter 6 of this book.

In turn, states often influence federal government actions, primarily through participation in rule making proceedings and court cases. In areas of mutual concern related to common carrier communications, the Federal-State Communications Joint Board Act of 1971 amended the Communications Act of 1934 to provide for a joint board consisting of three FCC commissioners and four state commissioners nominated by the National Association of Regulatory Utility Commissioners to recommend a decision. On cable television matters, NARUC, a quasi-governmental, nonprofit organization founded in 1889, often represents the viewpoints of state utility commissions. NARUC has acted on behalf of the state commissions by giving testimony before Congress on the state role in cable television regulation, developing model acts and legislation, and supporting the states as parties to cases on federal-state jurisdiction issues. NARUC was instrumental in developing the congressional legislation, adopted in 1978, concerning pole attachments. Perhaps the most significant case relative to cable television to which NARUC was a party was *NARUC* v. *FCC* in which the U.S. Court of Appeals for the D.C. Circuit upheld NARUC's challenge to the FCC's preemption of point-to-point nonvideo channels on the grounds that it violated the Communications Act because it was regulation of intrastate communications for hire via cable.

States have participated individually in many rule makings concerning cable television regulation, the New York State Commission on Cable Television (NYCC) being the most active in both FCC rule makings and court cases. The NYCC filed comments in the FCC proceedings on pay cable (Docket No. 19554), line extension (Docket No. 20020), financial reporting forms (Docket No. 20247), duplicative regulation (Docket No. 20272), the 1977 rebuild requirement (Docket No. 20363), rate regulation (Docket No. 20681), and deletion of franchise standards (Docket No. 21002). (The NYCC also holds the record for conducting its own rule makings.) State cable commissions in both Minnesota and New York filed supporting comments in the definition proceeding (Docket No. 20561), leading to a reduction in the regulatory burden on small cable systems. Minnesota and New York have taken similar state actions. The two state commissions also filed in the proceeding on local complaint procedures (Docket No. 20024). The Massachusetts Cable Commission (MCC), which has a smaller staff than the New York and Minnesota commissions, has not participated in rule makings but did file, in 1977, in support of a cable company seeking a waiver, subsequently granted, of the distant signal carriage rules. The New Jersey Office of Cable Television (OCT) of the Board of Public Utilities represented the state in requesting a waiver, partially granted in 1978, to allow cable systems in New Jersey to carry signals of TV stations licensed to the state and certain other state-oriented programming from stations located outside of the state. More recently, the Office filed comments in opposition to the petition, subsequently denied, to restrict foreign ownership of cable systems in the United States.

Proposed Congressional Legislation

The proposed Telecommunications Act of 1979 (H.R. 6121), as introduced, would change the present regulatory responsibilities of the states in two major respects. First, state and federal actions regulating terminal equipment would be prohibited. In effect, the new statute would remove the present possibility of states making regulatory decisions regarding terminal equipment. The other major change is related to the bill's concept of intraexchange and interexchange. States presently set rates and boundaries for intraexchange (local) service; the bill clearly allows this authority to remain with the states. It also clearly grants jurisdiction to the FCC to regulate interexchange services and facilities as well as intraexchange services based in the provision of interexchange service. The FCC would have authority, however, to delegate powers to the states to set access charges. Any powers not specifically granted to the federal government in the bill would be within state jurisdiction.

To implement these provisions, Section 231 of the bill establishes a 45-month Transitional Joint Board, consisting to two state and three federal commissioners appointed by the chairman of the FCC, with responsibilities as follows: (1) to insure orderly transition from separation and settlements to a system of access charges; (2) to insure equitable treatment to customers of basic telecommunications service and of competing carriers; (3) to insure equitable treatment in matters involving terminal equipment already in use; and (4) to develop methods for recovery of investment in plant currently allocated to interexchange service. Decisions of the Joint Board could be appealed only to the U.S. Court of Appeals for the D.C. Circuit. The Board would be responsible for reporting annually to Congress. Following the life of the transitional board, the permanent Federal-State Joint Board which currently exists would continue to implement and establish jurisdictional separation procedures.

Proposed legislation S. 611 and S. 622 in the U.S. Senate would allocate jurisdiction to the federal and state governments in the same basic manner as the House bill. The primary difference between them, and even between the two Senate bills, is in the functioning of the Transitional Joint Board.

State Activities and Interests

Since 1974, no additional states have chosen comprehensive plans for cable television regulation. Therefore, the summary below remains unchanged. Eleven states regulate cable television on a comprehensive basis through an agency of the state: Alaska, Connecticut, Delaware, Hawaii, Massachusetts, Minnesota, Nevada, New Jersey, New York, Rhode Island, and Vermont. Only five of these states—Connecticut, Rhode Island, Vermont, Hawaii, and Alaska (in chronological order of enactment of their enabling statutes)—have preempted local franchising and all of these, with the exception of Hawaii, regulate through state utility commissions. Delaware, Nevada, and New Jersey are the only states regulating through state utility commissions that allow local franchising as well. In Delaware, however, municipalities grant franchises, and the state commission is limited to granting them only in unincorporated areas outside of municipalities. Massachusetts, Minnesota, and New York are the only states where independent commissions have been established solely for the purpose of regulating cable television.

Although state regulation of cable television in seven states is the responsibility of public utility commissions, cable is usually not clearly defined or regulated as a public utility. In all of these states except Alaska, cable television is defined separately from other regulated services. In Alaska, although the enabling statute does not refer to cable television *per se,* cable TV is implied in the term "telecommunications services," describing transmissions via cable. All of these states have recognized in some way the unique differences between cable television and traditional public utilities.

The debate on cable television's definition continues. In Connecticut, the first state to regulate cable, the question of whether or not it is a public utility has been an issue since the first debate about how to regulate it. Some states have defined it in negative terms—in New York and Illinois, the court and utility commission, respectively, have defined it not to be a telephone service. Even more frequently the question of whether cable television is, or will become, a common carrier is raised. A recent letter from the attorney general in Colorado to a city attorney in the Denver area suggested that considering cable television to be a natural monopoly might be violating antitrust laws.

Although there are a limited number of regulating states, involvement in cable television and developing communications technologies pervades state law in many other states. Table 3-1 indicates the general subject matter of state laws affecting cable television adopted through 1979.

Table 3-1: State Laws on Cable Television

Year Adopted[1]

Subject	1979	1978	1977	1976	1975	1974	1973	Pre-197
1. Complaints			TN					
2. Construction or Equipment	CT/2² (17)³		CT		MA	CT		
3. Definition				CT(18) NY(18)			NC	SD(7)
4. Earth Stations Location	CT(2)							
5. Educational Uses				WI				
6. Forfeitures				SC(7, 12)		NY(18)		VT
7. Franchising or Right-of-Way (a)Municipality	NE(15)				IA	ME NH KS	IL	IN '71 NE '69 NC '71 SD '72
(b)County			MD(15)	LA	IL IN	NE NC		
(c)Municipalities and Counties			TN(12, 15, 17)	SC(6, 12)		AZ MN		MI '72 NV NJ '72 NY('73) UT '53 VA '72
(d)Other (Townships, Boroughs, etc.)	OH							
8. Landlord-Tenant Relationships			MA	CT	CT MA			
9. Liability	NY				CT		MS	
10. Occupational Licensing (a)Exemption	NM			IN				

[1]Effective date noted in parenthesis if other than year of adoption
²Number following / indicates number of bills on same subject
³Number(s) in parentheses indicates other subjects listed that same bill addresses
⁴(A) indicates amendment to existing law
⁵The laws in this category encompass many of the other subjects listed; summaries of these laws may be found in *Cable Television State Regulation—A Survey of Franchising and Other State Law Regula tions*, which the FCC publishes periodically

Table 3-1: State Laws on Cable Television

Year Adopted[1]

Subject	1979	1978	1977	1976	1975	1974	1973	Pre-1973
11. Ownership	MT NC			ME			MS	
12. Pole Attachment	OR WA	CT(18) MA NY	CA('78) TN(7)	SC(7)				
13. Programming or Channel Use	CA							
14. Property Damage or Removal	NY(9)		NM TN(7)		CT	CT		
15. Rates	CA('80) CT(18) MA(18) NE		MA(20) MD TN(7)					
16. Safety			CT	VT(17, 18)		CT		
17. Service (a)Abandonment						ME		
(b)Disconnections				VT(17c, 18)				
(c)Extensions	CT(2)	MN(18)		MN(17d, 18) VT(17b, 18)				
(d)Interconnection				MN(17c, 18)				
(e)Theft	FL(A)[4] IL MO(A) VA	FL(A) NC OK VA	GA HA MN MO MT NJ NM OH SC TN	AK AZ CT FL KS	CA NY	DE(18) MT	IN ME NC NH WA	AR MD '69 VA VT '72
18. State regulation[5] (Comprehensive) (a)Independent New Commission							MN	MA '71 NY '73

Table 3-1: State Laws on Cable Television

Year Adopted[1]

Subject	1979	1978	1977	1976	1975	1974	1973	Pre-1973
(b)Existing Utility Commission						DE(17)		AK '70 CT '63 NJ '72 NV '67 RI '69 VT '70
(c)Other Agency								HA '70
(d)Amendments	CT(15) MA(15)	CT(12) MN(17)	NV	CT(3) NY(3) VT(16, 17)	CT MA	NY/5		
19. Study Committees		PA		HA LA MI	MA	MA/2 MI SC	IA	
20. Taxation or Fees (a)Tax Imposition					IL WI	CT	FL IL	AL MS
(b)Exemption	NY		FL	SD	WA	CT LA		
(c)Assessment		AZ(A)			AK	MT		AZ
(d)State or Franchise Fee			MA(15)	SC(7)	NY	CT		

The level of state regulatory activity and interest in cable television and other developing broadband communications services has increased in the past few years. It reflects a growing general public awareness of these services, as well as concentrated efforts of legislators, the industry, and other interest groups. Although interest continues to be shown in comprehensive state regulation, as indicated in the table, proposed and enacted legislation since 1974 has concentrated more on specific areas.

The 1977-1978 study of state regulation conducted by a Harvard group under a National Science Foundation Grant, observes, on the basis of research conducted by this author, that the trend could indicate several things: (1) the industry, municipalities, or legislators may be attempting to "fine tune" previously comprehensive regulation so that it is more congruent with their interests; (2) the industry may be gaining political strength, since existing piecemeal regulation generally benefits the industry; and, (3) the regulatory mood of the times is to regulate only where problems exist. Unfortunately, an evaluation of the comparative effectiveness of specific (as opposed to comprehensive) regulation, defined in terms of satisfying legislative objectives, remains inconclusive, perhaps even impossible.

Some of the state agencies in regulating states have faced legislation which threatens their very existence, or at least their present place within the state organization. In 1979 in both New York and Minnesota, bills were introduced, respectively, to transfer the present independent commission's powers to the PSC and to abolish the state commission entirely. In 1978, a legislator in Minnesota proposed to transfer the state commission's authority to the state Department of Commerce. By contrast, in that same year a legislator in New Jersey proposed making the Office of Cable Television an independent agency rather than an entity subordinate to the PUC.

Several other states have some involvement with cable television on a state level. In Virginia, the Public Telecommunications Council does not regulate cable television, but is required to keep franchises on hand and to review them from an educational interest perspective. Several other state agencies, such as highway and tax departments, are involved in certain aspects of cable television company activities. In 1979, state agencies in California and North Carolina became involved with cable television on a nonregulatory basis. The most notable effort, resulting in a nontraditional approach to regulation, was in North Carolina, where a year-long Task Force on Public Telecommunications proposed not to regulate but to establish a state-level resource center for telecommunications services. Legislative action then created the Agency for Public Telecommunications, which could prove to be a model in public telecommunications planning. The agency, both a nonprofit corporation and a state agency, began operating in October 1979. It is providing telecommunications information resources, technical assistance, and production services for state programs and agencies, as well as developing public radio.

Other recent study efforts have been undertaken or are continuing in various forms in Georgia, Nebraska, Pennsylvania, and Virginia. In Georgia and Nebraska specific legislators have taken interest in cable TV issues. In the latter, the governor has authorized a legislative study commission, which includes on its list the problem, perhaps not unique to the state, of chipmunks eating into cables. In Pennsylvania, more than one legislative study has been conducted. The most recent, by the Local Government Commission, proposes a semiregulatory role by a Bureau of Cable Television established within the state's Department of Community Affairs. The report, released in November 1979, also recommends legislation granting franchising powers to all local governments, including second class townships. Noting that the PUC is currently over-burdened with regulatory functions, the report proposes that the new Bureau would provide technical expertise and assistance, adjudicate pole attachment and rate disputes at the request of cable companies, establish guidelines for construction and maintenance standards for the protection of public safety, maintain various records, require a uniform system of accounts, set reporting standards, and compile an annual report about cable television in the state. It also suggests that the legislature adopt a theft-of-service law and permit municipal ownership where private industry opts not to operate.

Increased activity in the states, however, does not correlate with increased regulation. In fact, much recent activity reflects a deregulatory mode similar to the trend at the federal level. In Alaska, California, Massachusetts, Minnesota, and New York, state legislatures have adopted or proposed some degree of deregulation.

A discussion of state activities in various subject areas may be more useful for comparison purposes than a state-by-state summary, although innumerable variances in state laws, budgets, commission staffs, industry and consumer problems, political administrations, interest group pressures, regulatory purposes, and other factors make comparative analyses virtually impossible. For purposes of this review, state activities in the following areas are included: franchising, programming, pole attachment, ownership, rates, quality and provision of service (including extension and interconnection of services), and taxation. Brief histories and descriptions of state cable regulations through 1977 may be found in the 1977-1978 volume of the *Cable/Broadband Communications Book.*

Franchising

In exchange for the award of a cable television franchise, local governments have traditionally levied a cost, usually in the form of a franchise fee. As cable television has become more popular, companies desiring to construct in the same community began to compete by offering higher franchise fees and/or additional services. This situation led local municipal authorities to a more active and involved role in franchising.

Most state statutes authorize local governments to grant franchises. Each year franchising authority and procedures have been major legislative topics. Recent efforts have resulted in the passage of several new television companies to provide service. In Nebraska in 1979, the township trustees, to grant townships authority to contract with cable television companies to provide serv ice. In Nebraska in 1979, the legislature adopted a bill to allow municipalities to grant franchises without going through elections and without containing procedures for public hearings on rate increases.

Franchising problems have sometimes inspired, and continue to prompt, interest in cable television on the state level. State regulation itself was instituted particularly in response to franchising problems in Massachusetts and New Jersey. More recently, in Virginia, the action of the Richmond City Council in reawarding a franchise to one company after granting it previously to another encouraged the establishment of a governor's commission on cable television. A case pending as of April 1980 in the U.S. Court of Appeals for the Tenth Circuit, *Community Communications Co.* v. *City of Boulder*, involves the issue of whether a city is impeding competition, and thereby possibly violating antitrust laws, in placing a moratorium on a previously authorized cable system's extension of service within its permitted area.

As noted earlier in this chapter, only five of the regulating states have preempted local franchising—Alaska, Connecticut, Hawaii, Rhode Island, and Vermont. The state agencies responsible for granting certificates to cable companies generally have jurisdiction to prescribe terms and conditions of company operation. For example, the DPUC in Connecticut has the authority to specify in its certificate of public convenience and necessity, at the time of issuance or any time thereafter, any terms and conditions it determines to be required for the public interest. The division has the power to suspend or revoke a certificate for due cause, including failure to exercise the certificate within two years of issuance or for failure to provide adequate service. However, the certificate need no longer be limited to a 15-year duration; by Public Act 79–533, the legislature revised the statute to require perpetual franchises, revokable or transferable only if the certificate holder "fails to provide adequate service." Pending legislation in 1980 proposes that the decision as to whether the franchise term is fixed or unlimited should be returned to the DPUC.

As of October 1979, Rhode Island's Division of Public Utilities and Carriers (RIDPUC) has been freed from the deadlock resulting from the case of *Rollins, Inc.* v. *Archie Smith* which had been pending in the state Supreme Court since 1974. The Division is now reexamining, and finding outdated, the franchising plan which Archie Smith, former Administrator, had issued in 1974. The major focus of attention at present is upon administrative and complaint procedures, construction timetables, and community access. The RIDPUC is also reevaluating its statutory jurisdiction. A proposed bill, S. 2593, would amend Chapter 39-19 of the statutes to include a 15-year franchise term, a maximum renewal term of 10 years, criteria for franchise renewals, and provisions for the applicants to pay for investigation and hearing expenses.

The three independent state commissions—in Massachusetts, Minnesota, and New York—have set mandatory franchising standards for local governments. Each of them have recently made revisions of a deregulatory nature.

New licensing procedures in Massachusetts, established in the MCC's *Report and Order in Docket No. R-3*, which became effective November 21, 1979, streamlined regulations in the following ways: (1) issuing authorities, as franchising authorities are termed in Massachusetts, have the discretion, rather than the obligation, to appoint cable advisory committees (CACs); (2) only one round of advertising for applications, rather than two separate opportunities, in one trade journal and the local newspaper is required; and (3) no hearing is required on a CAC report; instead, comments on possible license specifications and requirements may be made during the final hearings to assess applicant qualifications. Also in 1979, the state legislature transformed the agency structurally from one of seven part-time to one full-time commissioner, since obtaining sufficient quorums was sometimes difficult.

In April 1980 the state legislature in Minnesota approved recent revisions which the Minnesota Cable Communications Board (MCCB) made to ease, speed, and clarify all of its rules. In this process, the Board consolidated franchise standards dealing with similar issues. An industry proposal to reduce regulations on systems with fewer than 1,000 subscribers was not adopted; as the MCCB favored, regulations were revised uniformly for all systems.

In New York, the legislature enacted Chapter 713 of the Laws of 1979, which relaxed franchising procedures for smaller cable systems. Subsequently, in Docket No. 90167, the NYCC revised its franchising procedures accordingly.

Ownership

Both at the state and local levels, as well as the federal level, ownership is a subject of rising interest. (For further discussion of structure and ownership of the cable TV industry see Chapter 1.) Some state laws specifically authorize certain types of ownership. For example, a law adopted in Maine in 1976 permitted municipalities to operate telecommunications systems; a 1973 Massachusetts statute authorized municipal lighting plants to operate and maintain community antenna television systems; and, a law adopted in Montana in 1979 authorized rural telephone cooperatives to establish, maintain, and operate cable television and broadband systems and facilities for the benefit of their telephone customers. More statutes and proposals recently are focusing on problems of telecommunications service in rural areas. A new law, Chapter 586 in North Carolina, also adopted in 1979, addresses the provision of broadband services to rural areas of the state by means of telephone membership corporations. Technically, the law includes broadband services in the meaning of the terms "telephone service" and "telephone business."

Some municipalities have shown interest in maintaining the owner-ship powers which they currently hold. In Pennsylvania, for example, a 1979 bill proposed to preclude any prohibition of ownership by twenty-some municipalities which own or operate nonprofit corporations provid-ing cable television service. The bill also proposed that authority be given to boroughs to own and operate cable services. A number of munic-ipal ownership-related proposals are being introduced in 1980 legislative sessions.

Evidence is abundant that state interest in issues of concentration of ownership is increasing. On February 20, 1980, the Connecticut DPUC, on the basis of a state regulation adopted in 1977, decided that General Electric cannot both sell or repair television sets and own a cable system. The decision is significant in light of the proposed General Electric-Cox Broadcasting merger, pending FCC authorization, which would result in GE ownership of the Manchester, Connecticut, cable system. The poten-tial for conflicting state and federal agency decisions is apparent. An even more significant state ownership decision was the Connecticut DPUC's decision in Docket No. 791003, March 7, 1980, to prevent the Times Mirror Company from holding the franchises for a number of ca-ble system communities in the Hartford area while simultaneously own-ing the daily newspaper, *The Hartford Courant.* Among its findings of fact, the DPUC's decision stated: "Common ownership of a newspaper and a CATV system in the same market area has the potential of having a negative impact upon the development of the cable franchise." The state gave Times Mirror the choice of terminating its ownership of the newspaper or of its two cable companies.

Unlike Connecticut's, the Massachusetts statutes contain a specific prohibition of newspaper-cable cross-ownership in a "major circulation area." An advisory opinion clarifying the MCC's regulation is forthcom-ing.

Pole Attachment

In response to their congressionally-mandated option granted February 21, 1978, by the Communications Act Amendments of 1978, P.L. No. 95-234, 18 states and Puerto Rico have certified to the FCC that they have jurisdiction to regulate the rates, terms, and conditions of agreements between cable television and utility companies for attach-ments of cable television company transmission lines to utility-owned poles. The rate of certification logically has decreased, however, since mid-1979. Between then and October 1979 only four states—Indiana, Nebraska, Oregon, and Washington—had certified jurisdiction to the FCC. Although legislation granting jurisdiction to the utility commis-sions was proposed in 15 states in 1979, only 2 bills were adopted—those in Oregon and Washington. Between November 1979 and April 1980, no additional states had certified jurisdiction.

Several reasons for the cautious state legislative action are possible. For one, the inherent delays in the legislative procedure itself cause some bills to fail. For another, more substantive, reason, the states have no prior experience in this complex area of regulation. The statutory authority of all of the utility commissions with comprehensive jurisdiction to regulate cable television, except the Rhode Island PUC, already included authority to regulate pole attachments at the time the congressional law was passed. However, between that time and February 28, 1980, when it adopted the reconsideration of its *Memorandum Opinion and Second Report and Order in CC Docket No. 78-144*, the FCC had been developing regulations to implement the federal obligations pursuant to the law. These regulations and the cases which will follow may assist states in dealing with some of the difficult issues which will arise in state cases as well.

Probably the issues which have provoked the most controversy have been the amount of usable space on each pole and the amount of space occupied by cable. In California, the PUC in September 1979 issued a decision in a long-standing case setting a rate per pole at $12, considerably higher than the FCC's formula would produce, primarily due to the state commission's interpretation of usable space. States are entirely free, however, to adopt and interpret their own law and devise their own formula. The only requirement is that they consider the interest of subscribers to both utility and cable services.

The state of New Jersey's proposed regulations are more similar to the FCC's interpretation. As of spring 1980 the state Board of Public Utilities was reviewing the hearing examiner's Report and Recommendations to the Board of Public Utilities Commissioners in Docket No. 769-C-6206 proposing uniform operational and rate structures throughout the state. The Board's Office of Cable Television in 1976 established a Joint Utility-Cable Commission, now permanent, to discuss pole attachment problems. General opinion at the state level is that the committee, unique to New Jersey, has been an effective means of resolving problems in this area.

Even states which have certified their regulatory jurisdiction to the FCC sometimes have been challenged. Notably, the Teleprompter Corporation sued the Florida Public Service Commission concerning the state agency's pole rate jurisdiction. The state Supreme Court, having heard oral arguments, was expected to decide the case by mid-1980. The Public Service Commission staff has suggested that legislative authority be pursued.

Pole attachment debates will continue into the 1980s, resulting in further regulatory and legislative decisions.

Programming and Channel Use

Programming, tangential to the provision of service and quality of that service, is attracting greater attention among states. Some of it arises from consumer complaints about types of programs available, as often received about conventional broadcasting. Signal carriage being preempted, some states are proposing or taking actions concerning non-broadcast, or originated programming, particularly access.

Since the *Midwest Video* v. *FCC* decision was upheld in the U.S. Supreme Court in April 1979, several states have shown interest in access regulation. Prior to that decision, any government adopting rules in excess of the FCC maximum standards would have needed to obtain a waiver of the federal standards. Also prior to that decision, the only state regulations which contained any reference to access were in Minnesota.

Many supporters of public access now believe that states could safeguard the concept in the absence of federal government mandate. Some efforts, therefore, are being pursued to promote state involvement in access regulation. In New York, the state commission in January 1980 released a *Notice of Inquiry and Proposed Rule Making in Docket No. 90174*, proposing rules on channels and facilities for locally originated educational and public service programming. The PUC in Rhode Island is supporting the formation of a special legislative commission, with broad representation from state government, industry, and community organizations, to promote community programming. The proposed legislation, introduced early in 1980, instructs the commission to study the feasibility of imposing a gross receipts tax on cable companies operating in the state to provide funding.

Some state regulators are requiring operators to follow through on initial commitments to community programming. In its rate case on *Coastal Cable TV* in December 1978, the Connecticut Public Utilities Control Authority, as it was named at the time, directed the company to review its original 1972 proposal, which anticipated providing local closed circuit public service programming during the second year of operation, and to "present a detailed plan including timetable showing how those commitments will be met, or to document with supporting cost data and other reasons why the company is unable to meet its local origination commitments."

Further discussion of community and access programming is contained in Chapter 6 of this book.

Service

Several states are involved in activities concerned with the quality and availability of service. Efforts to provide cable service in rural areas, link communities with common interests, or provide a larger base for programming have led to the development of a number of state policies, each with somewhat different emphasis, determined by individual state differences. Both types of state commissions—utilities and independents—have shown interest in this policy area. Commissions in New Jersey, Connecticut, and Vermont as well as in New York and Minnesota have both statutory authority and adopted policies. They pursue similar objectives through interconnection policies in Minnesota, New Jersey, and New York, and line extension provisions in New York and Vermont.

Although state support is useful, evidence is abundant that state regulation alone cannot cause interconnection or extension of service. In most cases, in fact, the initiative does not come from the state but from cable companies or program suppliers who, for their own purposes, link together two or more systems or decide that it is economically feasible to extend service.

The state regulatory agencies in New York and Minnesota have received legislative mandates to consider regional factors in reviewing franchises. Thus, both agencies include interconnection in their official statewide development plans. In January 1980, the NYCC began a rule making proceeding on cable television line extension practices. In promoting interconnections, the NYCC has concentrated on structural techniques, such as the use of cable systems by school districts and physical interconnection of systems in certain regions. The MCCB, on the other hand, has emphasized program development. It has developed more projects than any other state to promote interconnection, primarily through means of supplying information and technical assistance. The state agency has participated in demonstrations of shared programming, through both live interconnection and "bicycling" of videotapes. The stated objective of the MCCB is essentially to act as a catalyst for establishing a program and service network, which would gradually become independent of the state agency. Structural methods are now authorized due to a 1979 statutory revision allowing the MCCB to regulate line extensions outside of metropolitan areas.

Regulations in Connecticut have attempted to fulfill the objective of statewide cable service by districting and interconnection policies. The PUCA approved, in December 1978, in Docket No. 760207, a new statewide extension policy setting criteria for extension of service to new areas, in the following order of priority:

1. complete construction in the primary franchise area, defined as containing 80 residential dwelling units (RDUs) per mile;
2. extend service to all contiguous areas if there are at least 70 RDUs or 35 prospective subscribers per mile, at a rate of at least 25 percent of street miles per year;
3. extend service to all non-contiguous areas; and

4. extend service to any area where prospective subscribers have agreed to contribution-in-aid of construction, if there are at least 15 prospective subscribers per mile.

One question of interpretation which has arisen is whether the rules prohibit any construction in less dense areas where extension could be a drain on rate payers in areas where density is at minimum conformance with the regulations.

The Connecticut state legislature in 1979 further reinforced the state's extension of service policies by adopting, in P.A. No. 79-533, a requirement that companies serve the "primary franchise area" originally specified in the certificate of public convenience and necessity before extending into new franchise areas. The same legislation also prohibited a company from refusing to construct in any part of its franchise area on the sole basis that it can only be served by underground facilities.

Connecticut's extension of service formula is similar to the first such policy, which the Vermont Public Service Board devised in 1975. Although the Board already had the necessary jurisdiction, the Vermont legislature in 1976 adopted a law *mandating* that the Board adopt extension and disconnection policies. The Board then began revising the policy and, as of April 1980, had developed a proposal similar to Connecticut's adopted policy, except that the Vermont formula uses a variable rather than fixed saturation level (subscribers per mile).

In Nevada, the Public Service Commission in August 1978, established a policy that the rate payers had to fund service extension at one dollar per foot of cable, to prevent the need for subsidization by other rate payers. A company has to request the PSC to allow it to extend service.

New Jersey's Office of Cable Television has developed a totally unique approach to interconnection. The state statute is imprecise, instructing the agency to consider interconnection questions in reviewing municipal consents, i.e., franchises. The state Board of Public Utilities may amend a system's state certificate to direct that areas covered in the application be included. Despite difficulties in the case-by-case approach, some of which are described in the Harvard study, the OCT now has developed a model interconnection project. If the plan is fully implemented, the result will be the nation's largest microwave-interconnected system, which includes all of the state's cable systems.

The New Jersey interconnect plan establishes four distribution points from which programming can be provided, with four channels and two-way capability along the backbone of the system. The project involves many state government and educational interests. Partially funded by a federal grant administered by the National Telecommunications and Information Administration, the project's use of preexisting towers and other equipment has helped to keep costs low. The future role of the state is to hire a coordinator for the project and to serve as a clearinghouse for scheduling, recruitment, and further funding. The project continues to attract widespread attention both within New Jersey and in other states.

Rate Regulation

In the history of state involvement in the regulation of cable television, the single most difficult and resource-consuming concern for both states and municipalities has been, and continues to be, rates. Methods of regulating rates vary widely—from arbitration to rate-base rate of return. For even the most experienced rate regulators—the public utility commissions—cable television has presented challenges to traditional rate-setting methodology and has necessitated the formulation of new approaches, such as those developed in Connecticut, Hawaii, and New Jersey. A growing number of states are considering and adopting deregulatory measures. Many cities are reconsidering and deregulating rates in light of new service offerings. For example, in late 1979, a cable television advisory committee in Lansing, Michigan, recommended a rate increase and rate deregulation in return for a proposed new "Lifeline Service" of eight channels. Some of the significant turning points in state rate regulation are discussed in this section.

States are involved in rate regulation to varying degrees. Among the states which regulate cable through state agencies, only Minnesota and Rhode Island have not decided rate cases, due to lack of statutory authority to do so. Massachusetts and New York have appeals procedures; localities there set the rates, guided by some state standards, but companies can approach the state to set rates if a municipality refuses or the rates it sets are disagreeable to the company. In Massachusetts, the procedure has resulted in at least one case where subscribers in two municipalities with identical cable services are being charged different rates. Not surprisingly, the Massachusetts and New York cable commissions have broad inquiries pending (as of spring 1980) concerning rate regulation.

As some utility commissions and independent commissions have gained experience in regulating rates, they have found competition to be a significant factor. One measure of competitiveness is penetration—the lower the penetration, i.e., the fewer subscribers per total number of homes passed by the cable, the more competetive the system in relation to alternative sources of video entertainment. In Hawaii, for example, if the system attains 80 percent penetration, there is little incentive to add new services. Rate increases, however, can be justified only for the addition of new services to noncompetitive systems. Hawaii, perhaps more than any other state which starts with a straight rate-base rate-of-return approach, considers the unique qualities of cable television which distinguish it from traditional public utilities. Connecticut, Massachusetts, and New Jersey also have considered competitiveness in rate proceedings conducted by their state commissions.

Table 3-2: Rate Regulation in the States

State	Method	Proposed Modifications or Problems
Alaska	rate of return	Problem: jurisdiction with regard to pay cable separation in rate base
California	total deregulation under certain conditions	
Connecticut	rate of return	
Delaware	PSC must approve or disapprove increases exceeding 5% in any 1 year.(very little state involvement)	Problem: overlapping jurisdictions; cities and state both setting rates as dictated by the statute
Hawaii	modified rate of return (18-20% approx.)	
Massachusetts	appeals only; modified rate of return	*Notice of Inquiry in Docket No. R-4*, Competitive Standard Inquiry proposes deregulation where competitive alternatives exist
Minnesota	none standards for franchising	
Nevada	rate of return	
New Jersey	common tariff	
New York	none; standards for franchises; approval authority for rates contained in franchise agreements	*Notice of Inquiry in Docket No. 90172*, 79-142, June 14, 1979, to develop standard for analyzing rates and how to segregate pay cable
Rhode Island	none	Statute unclear as to PUC's authority
Vermont	rate of return (20% approx.)	Problem: how to separate out pay TV

Examination of each of these states's methods provides further insight into distinguishing features. In Hawaii, rate regulation is the most active area of regulation by the Division of Cable Television. The state has been using a modified rate-base rate-of-return approach, allowing a return of approximately 18 to 20 percent. By the state's method, rates are set based on two main criteria not typically included in determining the rate base for a traditional utility: (1) the extent to which the system has been completed and, (2) the quality and quantity of services offered. These subjective criteria are used most frequently in setting the rates in areas where large sections are unconstructed; to monitor this, the state obtains monthly construction reports from companies. If a company does not follow the preset construction plan, additional fees collected from approved rate increases are held in escrow until construction is completed. Rate of return is projected for the company for a year following a requested rate increase.

Through specific investigations rather than elaborate regulations, Hawaii has adopted its policy on rate regulation—one more complicated than straight rate-base rate of return. Once a system has been completed, with no additional plant being built, straight rate of return may be used.

In Connecticut, the experience with rate regulation likewise differs from a traditional approach. The DPUC issued a policy statement (July 26, 1978) on the proper method to be used in arriving at a fair rate of return on investment. The agency decided that the "use of the 'original cost' investment of equity capital is the most straightforward and will produce maximum customer and investor understanding of the computations on invested capital." The basis of the decision was consideration that the infant nature of the industry created a unique operating environment and a concomitant expectation that companies may lose money in their formative years. The use of original cost investment as the basis of rate of return will allow companies a reasonable chance to recover early losses. Connecticut cable regulators believe that this policy has proved workable for cable in Connecticut. They observe that statewide control has the advantage of being uniformly applicable among companies, avoiding the probability of different rates for the same service in two towns. Market pressures have also kept rates down in Connecticut. A law adopted in 1979, containing a provision allowing an unlimited franchise term in Connecticut, may have repercussions for rate regulation. The rate-of-return policy is geared to a 15-year franchise term, to allow companies rapid recovery of start-up losses. Consumer advocates have questioned the need for such quick return in light of the perpetual franchise duration.

Since April 1978, New Jersey has applied a "common tariff" approach to rate regulation, a method in which 64 percent of the state's cable systems participate, or 32 of 50 total operating systems as of January 1, 1980. According to the state's regulation, a system may choose either traditional rate-making procedures or the common tariff approach.

Systems are placed in one of six categories, depending upon the following variables: (1) competitiveness, defined as within or outside of the contours of signals from at least the three major networks; (2) density, meaning greater or fewer than 200 subscribers per system mile; and (3) channel capacity, either fewer or more than 12 channels. Based on its classification, a company is allowed to raise its rates in incremental steps, once per year, up to the maximum level established for the class. The maximum levels may be modified by the OCT with the approval of the BPU after full public hearing.

Most of the companies participating in the common tariff have reached their maximum rates, or will reach them in 1980. Consistent with its plan in 1978, the state OCT is evaluating the common tariff and expects to hold hearings in 1980 to consider raising the maximum rates. As predicted, the common tariff method has reduced the expense of rate cases, which was often passed on to the companies's subscribers. Furthermore, a subscriber growth rate three times the national average virtually eliminates speculation that the common tariff could be a negative factor in cable's development in the state.

The Massachusetts experience with rate regulation is perhaps even more significant. The Commission had been applying a modified rate-base rate-of-return method, but has taken major steps to reduce its involvement in rate setting. First, in a manner similar to the "common tariff" approach in New Jersey, the MCC proposed dividing cable television into four distinct classes for rate-setting purposes: urban competitive systems, rural, classic, and noncompetitive systems, each being further subdivided on the basis of channel capacity. On May 20, 1977, the MCC decided *not* to adopt the proposal due to the difficulty in setting equitable statewide rates which could account for the wide variances in densities among system locations, cable technologies employed, and services offered. No party had submitted comments supportive of the proposed classification scheme. The state reiterated an interest in adopting a regulatory structure that would allow it "to regulate more effectively and efficiently the rates of profitable systems and to reduce the regulation, but not oversight, of clearly unprofitable systems."

The next phase in rate deregulation in Massachusetts was the Revere case in 1978, in which two commissioners dissented strongly from the majority's decision to set a cable system's rates lower than the requested rate in a competitive market. The dissenters suggested that government interference in the form of more traditional utility-type regulation is justified only where there are inadequate competitive alternatives to cable service, so that if a cable company were to show that it operates in a competitive market, a requested rate would be permitted. One commissioner, who strongly supports rate regulation for utility industries where effective competition is absent, does not see cable in Massachusetts fitting that pattern. In dissenting, he stated:

> Very generally, the public receives good to excellent over-the-air TV service, either with or without outdoor antennas, without incurring any monthly charge. So long as such competition exists, and unless cable introduces new communication services without close substitutes, the justification for governmental price control seems hollow.

Since the Revere case, the state has been proceeding on a deregulatory course. Later in 1978, the commissioners were split 3-2 in a decision to permit another company to increase its rates less than requested. In dissenting, another commissioner stated that the majority decision failed to protect the subscriber taxpayers because it was not cost-effective, considering the unreasonable delay in deciding the case. She proposed that "where adequate off-air signals exist (four grade A signals), the existing degree of competition be used to decrease the burden of proof required of the company to obtain its requested rate." In 1979, the governor approved Chapter 249, amending the state law to allow the MCC, after due hearing and investigation, to suspend regulation of rates and charges for any cable TV system "upon a finding that adequate competitive alternatives exist to the provision of services offered by cable television systems. In the event of such a suspension, the commission shall, by oversight and surveillance, review periodically any facts or standards employed in determining the presence of said competition." The MCC has issued an inquiry on competitive standards to define conditions under which rate regulation will be suspended. The state commission is also revising its uniform reporting system, which would serve the following three regulatory functions: (1) periodic review of the financial status of cable companies operating within the state; (2) rate regulation; and (3) reporting for purposes of transfer and assignment of licenses. The Commission will develop new forms containing greater detail and clearer definitions in line with its new legislative authority to suspend rate regulation.

In New York, state law authorizes the NYCC to approve or disapprove rates set by municipalities and to establish rates when existing rates are found to be "discriminatory or preferential," when service is inadequate, when the municipal franchise has failed to include rates, or when a municipality and a cable company are unable to agree upon rates. State regulations have always required municipal control, providing that a municipality include rates in the franchise, to be adopted only after holding a public hearing. A municipality may change rates only by franchise amendment after holding a public hearing. The state commission applied a "range of reasonableness" standard, reviewing rates only in those cases where the proposed rates were "out of line" with rates of other cable companies. More recently the Commission has considered automatically adjusting the "range of reasonableness" and has provided more assistance to municipal governments in effective rate negotiation. Although the NYCC has set rates in a number of cases, the "comparable rates" standard is not defined more specifically than the statutory language.

In an effort to develop more precise standards and regulations, the state initiated three rate-related rule making proceedings in 1979. In one of them, the Commission revised the regulations so as to permit parties to negotiate franchises which require the resolution of rate disputes by the state commission. A municipality's choice of this course of action then invokes certain procedural standards. This rule change was responsive to the desire among many municipalities and cable companies to allow the state to set rates, thereby avoiding local disputes.

The state also concluded a proceeding investigating discriminatory subscriber rates for facilities installed underground as opposed to above ground. Due to the complexity of the problem, the commission decided not to adopt rules but to conduct ad hoc reviews.

The broader questions are yet to be resolved in New York. In June 1979 the Commission began a proceeding (Docket No. 90172) to determine standards for regulating rates, including those which are "discriminatory or preferential." The inquiry also addresses questions on basic jurisdiction, such as "at what governmental level or levels and by what mechanisms should cable television rates be controlled?" As the state faces rate setting in an increasing number of cases, the necessity of resolving these and other questions becomes more apparent.

In deregulating rates, California is again among the avant garde, as it was with pole attachment legislation. A bill, proposed in 1978, to require cities to respond within 90 days to rate increase requests and to hold hearings within 30 days, was vetoed by the governor, due primarily to political pressure from the municipalities. In a statement released concurrently, the governor stated: "This bill unreasonably diminishes the authority of local government without sufficient compensating public benefit. I recognize the need of the industry to obtain expeditious decisions on requests for rate increases and will work with it to achieve this goal in an equitable manner."

Consequently, the industry and the administration in California compromise to produce A.B. 699, uniquely designed to condition the total deregulation of rates on certain competitive characteristics of the system as well as the system's provision of a community services channel program. A cable system may elect to declare exemption from regulation or control of its rates by the city or county if it meets criteria which may be summarized as follows: (1) provision of 20 or more channels; (2) reception of, or plans to receive, signals by satellite earth receive station; (3) penetration rate of less than 70 percent certified by the cable system, subject to review by the franchising authority; (4) location in a county which has available three significantly viewed signals as defined by the FCC, or two significantly viewed and an educational TV station; and, (5) provision of, or agreement to provide, a community services channel program. If the penetration ratio is 70 percent or more, or the system is providing between 12 and 20 channels of television service in a franchise area with fewer than 3,500 subscribers in a community of less than 20,000 (monopoly in a smaller community), but does meet the significantly-viewed signal and community service channel requirements, the system may, by declaration filed with the franchisor, adjust rates up to 75 percent of the percentage increase in the Consumer Price Index since the last previous rate increase, or since December 31, 1975, if rates have not been increased since then. If a system with 12 or fewer channels rebuilds (after January 1, 1980) to 20 or more, the system may raise rates, within 3 years of completion of the rebuild, up to the statewide average rate for systems having 20 or more channels.

The law involves a new type of state agency in cable regulation—the California Public Broadcasting Commission. Systems adjusting rates pursuant to the law must file with the CPBC prior to September 15, 1981, the rates of the system on January 1, 1980, information concerning the number of subscribers and services provided, and all subsequent rate adjustments. After the September 15 filing, systems must "promptly" file any subsequent rate adjustments with the CPBC. The primary reason for the agency's involvement is not regulatory authority but the agency's responsibility to report to the legislature prior to April 15, 1982, concerning "the effect upon subscribers and upon the telecommunications policy of the state of the rate adjustments by cable television systems as a consequence. . .[of the law], including such recommendations for legislative modification as may appear desirable." Unless the legislature extends its operative date, the law terminates on January 1, 1984. Local franchising authorities having rate reduction authority in the franchise cannot reduce rates in effect on that day below the average rate in the state for the class of service provided.

In the first four months after the new law took effect, only two systems deregulated. Most cable operators seem to be interested in working out local plans for deregulating rates. Systems in San Diego and San Jose, for example, are proposing to set up local foundations similar to the state's Foundation for Community Service Channels established by the legislation. The four-year state experiment will be worth the attention of state and local regulators.

Following the track of the 1978 attempt in California, the Florida legislature enacted H.B. 892 in 1979, which attempted to deregulate cable television rate-making authority of local governments. In his veto of the legislation, Governor Bob Graham stated his opinion that the action violated the state's Constitution, which prohibits passage of any law which would render the terms of a contract null and void, i.e., local franchises. Furthermore, he stated that the erosion of powers of local government was undesirable and that local governments were in the best position "to do and determine what is in their citizens's best interests." Stating that any abrogation of agreements between municipalities and cable companies should be determined on the local level, he added that 50 or more communities in the state have voluntarily deregulated already. He also welcomed a study by the legislature on the impact of deregulation on local governments.

Evidence is abundant that rate deregulation among the states is in vogue. Each of the four laws which were enacted in 1979 concerning rates was consistent with the trend. Proposed bills which included rate provisions in Michigan (S.B. 510) and Minnesota (H.F. 1307) also were deregulatory with respect to rates, as well as the Florida proposed bill discussed above. If any single word of advice could be given by all the states involved in rate regulation, it would probably be: either be totally in it or totally out of it. To take an intermediate posture probably results in the least net benefits to all parties.

Taxation

Taxation is important to both the industry and consumers. Some of the effects of tax policies may be similar to overt state regulation, even though state tax policies do not constitute regulation in the form of day-to-day supervision. For the industry, a state's tax methods may affect the cable operators's ability to attract capital. State taxes on competitive services are also important to cable operators. For consumers, the tax policies of a state may affect subscriber rates, increasing them in reaction to the cost of capital.

Taxation is one of the areas affecting cable television which crosses the bounds between "regulating" and "nonregulating" states. Not all states tax cable television systems—some specifically exempt them from certain taxes. States which do tax cable apply various types of taxes, including those primarily on public utilities, property, sales, and business or occupation. The franchise fee is a special tax, usually on the privilege of using public rights of way.

The Harvard study suggests that states are increasingly perceiving cable, as well as other services, as sources of revenue. The study suggests that cable may be in a disadvantageous tax position, compared with other businesses, in that it must pay state and local taxes in addition to business taxes.

Tax methods frequently vary according to definitional differences. Many states have grappled with the definition issues—whether to treat cable as a service subject to sales taxes, a necessity subject to utility taxes, or a new industry subject to specially enacted taxes.

The courts in New York and the Department of Revenue in Illinois have required those states not to place cable television in the same category with telephone service. As a result, sales taxes in New York and a gross receipts tax in Illinois, which are collected from telephone companies, are not applicable to cable television companies. In response to the tax survey in the Harvard study, the Illinois Department of Revenue stated that cable TV was considered to be closer in function to radio and television than to telephone companies. However, a bill pending (as of April 1980) in the Illinois legislature proposes imposition of a gross receipts tax on cable television.

As the cable industry has developed, some states have reduced their assessments on cable companies. For example, since the mid-seventies, the NYCC has collected an annual assessment of two percent of gross receipts. Until 1979, the amount collected has not covered the state commission's expenses. In 1980, a surplus in gross receipts of 1.2 million dollars has enabled the state to assess the companies at .7 percent in April 1980, and perhaps the rate will be only .5 percent in 1981.

Likewise, in Hawaii, an increase in the cable industry's gross receipts prompted the state Department of Regulatory Agencies to lower the state's assessment in 1979 from four percent to two percent.

In only one state—Vermont—has the tax assessment on cable increased; however, it is still applied uniformly to telephone, municipal electric, and cable companies. In 1980 the Vermont legislature adopted Title 30 VSA 22, providing for a tax to finance the Public Service Board at a rate of one half of one percent of gross revenues, with a $25 minimum. That represents an increase over the one quarter of one percent/$20 minimum previously imposed. The Rhode Island PUC also anticipates increasing its annual state fee.

In Connecticut, the DPUC taxes cable as a public utility. The gross receipts tax of eight percent, collected from both cable television and telephone companies, is the functional equivalent of a state franchise fee and in 1974 the state agency received a waiver of the FCC's three percent limit. Municipalities have not always favored the state tax. Bills have been introduced in the Connecticut legislature in every session since 1976 proposing that the state return at least a portion of the revenues it collects from the tax to the municipalities. For example, a 1979 bill proposed to return 25 percent of the state revenues from the tax to localities, divided in proportion to the amount of revenue attributable to cable operations in the given locality.

In December 1978, a Minnesota court upheld the MCCB's fee assessment, over a challenge by the state cable television association. On appeal, however, that decision was reversed, the Minnesota Supreme Court holding the fee unconstitutional because it did not apply uniformly to all cable operators. The court held that the fee was therefore violative of due process requirements and denied equal protection of the laws. The MCCB or the Minnesota legislature may take further action in light of the court's decision, which was issued in February 1980.

Nonregulating states have at least one factor in common—systems do not pay fees to support the cost of regulation. However, systems are frequently taxed in other ways, commonly including corporate income taxes and property taxes. Even more consistently, sales taxes apply to cable television companies.

The industry is now focusing greater attention on the tax field. Legislative activity in this area will probably increase in the 1980s.

Conclusion

The degree of involvement in cable television and other communications technologies varies broadly among the states. It runs the gamut from nonregulatory to regulatory approaches, based on legislatively-mandated or administratively-asserted jurisdiction. Deeper state involvement in the future will depend upon several major factors.

First, the willingness and means for state involvement must be present. Second, preemptive or conflicting federal regulations must not exist. Equally significant, if not most important, is the evolution of the technology involved. If cable television were to evolve into an entity more resembling a common carrier (consistent with popular speculation), the possible regulatory consequences are obvious.

Definite conclusions as to the consequences of state regulations are impossible to draw due to the variety of approaches and varying circumstances among the states. Some useful observations were made in the Harvard study, which addressed political dynamics, legal options, regulatory issues, and economic impacts of state government involvement in cable television. The report on economic impact of state regulation found no difference in penetration rates between regulating and nonregulating states. Therefore, cable's growth is not likely to be affected by state regulation. However, the study found rates to be slightly higher in regulating states.

The chances of reversing federal regulatory trends appear slim. Deregulatory actions at the federal level, however, need not necessarily be replaced at another governmental level without adequate justification. State regulators, as well as states currently studying cable television issues, are developing new, nontraditional approaches to regulation.

Provided that the objective of all involved interests is to provide better telecommunications services, in terms of both quantity and quality, these efforts deserve further attention and analysis.

Resources Mentioned

1. Corwin, Edward S., *The Constitution and What It Means Today*, Princeton U. Press, Princeton, New Jersey (1974).
2. *Case* v. *Bowles*, 327 U.S. 92, 102 (1946).
3. *North Carolina Utilities Commission* v. *FCC*, 56 FCC 2d 593 (1975); 58 FCC 2d 736 (1976) (Docket 19528); 552 F. 2d 1036 (4th Cir. 1977); 434 U.S. 874, 54 L. Ed. 2d 154, 98 S. Ct. 223 (1977).
4. *Notice of Inquiry and Notice of Proposed Rule Making in Docket No. 15971*, FCC 65-334, 1 FCC 2d 453, 4 RR 2d 1679, 30 F.R. 6078 (1965).
5. *Second Report and Order in Dockets Nos. 14895, 15233, and 15971*, FCC 66-220, 2 FCC 2d 725, 6 RR 2d 1717, 31 F.R. 4540 (1966).

6. *U.S.* v. *Southwestern Cable Co.*, 392 U.S. 157 (1968).
7. *Cable Television Report and Order*, FCC 72-108, 36 FCC 2d 143, 24 RR 2d 1501, 37 F.R. 3252 (1972).
8. *TV Pix, Inc.* v. *Taylor*, 304 F. Supp. 459 (D. Nev. 1968), *aff'd*, 396 U.S. 556 (1970).
9. Sheehan, David, Utilities Engineer, Division of Public Utility Control, Department of Business Regulation, State Office Building, 165 Capitol Avenue, Hartford, Connecticut 06115; 203/566-2048.
10. Delaware State Senate, Senate Bill No. 134, introduced March 21, 1979, 130th General Assembly.
11. *Borough of Scottsdale* v. *National Cable Television Corporation*, ____ Pa. ____, 381 A. 2d 859 (1977); Pa. 997 C.D., 1976.
12. *Lower Nazareth Township* v. *Service Electric Cable TV, Inc.*, Court of Common Pleas of Northhampton County, Civil Division, No. 350, October Term, 1975.
13. Pennsylvania State Association of Township Supervisors, P.O. Box 158, 3001 Gettysburg Rd., Camp Hill, Pennsylvania 17011; 717/763-0930.
14. *Brookhaven Cable TV, Inc. et al., FCC and USA* v. *New York State Commission on Cable Television*, 428 F. Supp. 1216 (N.D. N.Y. 1977), *aff'd*, 573 F. 2d 765 (2nd Cir. 1978), *cert. den.* 99 S. Ct., 199 (1979).
15. *Memorandum Opinion, Declaratory Ruling, and Order in the Matter of Orth-O-Vision, Inc. Petition for a Declaratory Ruling*, 69 FCC 2d 657 (1978).
16. *New York State Commission on Cable Television* v. *FCC*, 571 F. 2d 95 (2nd Cir. 1978).
17. *FCC* v. *Midwest Video Corp.*, 440 U.S. 689 (1978).
18. *NARUC* v. *FCC*, 533 F. 2d 601 (D.C. Cir. 1976).
19. Briley, Sharon A., *Cable Television State Regulation—A Survey of Franchising and Other State Law and Regulation*, FCC, Washington, D.C., 1977, 1980.
20. Kalba, Konrad K., *States, Stakeholders and the Cable: The Evolution of Regulatory Policies*, Kalba Bowen Associates, Inc. and the Harvard Program on Information Resources Policy, Publication P-78-11, Cambridge, Massachusetts 02138; December 1978.
21. Virginia Public Telecommunications Council, 902 Ninth Street Office Building, Richmond, Virginia 23219; 804/786-7729.
22. North Carolina Agency for Public Telecommunications, 417 N. Salisbury Street, Raleigh, North Carolina 27611; 919/733-6341.
23. California Public Broadcasting Commission, 921 Eleventh Street, Suite 1200, Sacramento, California 95814.
24. Briley, Sharon A., "State Regulation of Cable TV—Progress and Problems," *The Cable/Broadband Communications Book, 1977-1978*, Mary Louise Hollowell (ed.), Communications Press, Inc. 1977, 1346 Connecticut Avenue, N.W., Washington, D.C. 20036.
25. *Community Communications Co.* v. *City of Boulder*, 485 F. Supp. 1035 (10th Cir. 1980).
26. *Rollins, Inc.* v. *Archie Smith*, No. 76-462-M.P., Rhode Island Superior Court, October 29, 1979, Order filed. *Vision Cable Co. of R.I. Inc.* v. *Archie Smith, Administrator*, C.A. No. 74-3431.
27. *Report and Order in Docket No. R-3*, Licensing Regulations, November 21, 1979 (effective date), Massachusetts 02202; 617/727-6925.
28. *Decision in Docket No. 790914, Request of Greater Hartford CATV, Inc. for Advisory Ruling with Respect to Applicability of Section 16-333(c) of the General Statutes of Connecticut*, February 20, 1980, Department of Busi-

ness Regulation, Division of Public Utility Control, Hartford, Connecticut.

29. *Decision in Docket No. 791003, Investigation into the Suitability of Times Mirror Company as the Owner of a Controlling Interest in Communications Properties, Inc.*, March 7, 1980, Department of Business Regulation, Division of Public Utility Control, Hartford, Connecticut.

30. *Memorandum Opinion and Order in CC Docket No. 78-144*, In the Matter of Adoption of Rules for the Regulation of Cable Television Pole Attachments, 77 FCC 2d 189 (1980).

31. *Notice Of Inquiry and Proposed Rule Making in Docket No. 90174*, In the Matter of Channels and Facilities for Locally Originated Educational and Public Service Programming, adopted December 19, 1979, No. 80-007, New York Commission on Cable Television, Albany, New York.

32. *Decision in Docket No. 770918*, Application of Coastal Cable TV Company to Increase Its Rates and Charges to All Customers, December 21, 1978, Department of Business Regulation, Division of Public Utility Control, Hartford, Connecticut.

33. *Decision in Docket No. 760207*, Invitation to All Concerned Parties to Submit Proposals and Comments Relating to Adoption of a Statewide Extension Policy Applicable to CATV Systems, July 26, 1978. (Rules issued August 4, 1978, effective December 28, 1978.) Department of Business Regulation, Division of Public Utility Control, Hartford, Connecticut.

34. *Notice of Inquiry in Docket No. 90142*, In the Matter of Cable Television Line Extension Practices, January 11, 1980, New York State Commission on Cable Television, Albany, New York.

35. *Report and Order in Docket No. R-1*, In re Rate Regulation Procedures, May 20, 1977, Community Antenna Television Commission, Boston, Massachusetts.

36. *Colonial Cablevision of Revere, Inc.*, Docket No. AFD-37, May 19, 1978, Community Antenna Television Commission, Boston, Massachusetts.

37. *Notice of Inquiry in Docket No. R-4*, Competitive Standards Inquiry, December 21, 1979, Community Antenna Television Commission, Boston, Massachusetts.

38. *Notice of Inquiry in Docket No. 90172*, In the Matter of the Establishment of Rates Charged by Cable Television Companies, No. 79-142, May 16, 1979, New York State Commission on Cable Television, Albany, New York.

39. *Notice of Inquiry in Docket No. 90169*, In the Matter of Rates and Practices of Cable Television Companies Relative to Underground Facilities, No. 79-113, April 18, 1979. *Report and Order in Docket No. 90169*, No. 79-323, November 21, 1979. New York State Commission on Cable Television, Albany, New York.

40. *Notice of Proposed Rule Making and Clarification of Commission Policy in Docket No. 90111A*, In the Matter of Cable Television Franchise Provisions Mandating the Certification of Rule Making to the Commission on Cable Television pursuant to Section 825(5)(e) of the Executive Law, No. 79-129, May 16, 1979. *Order Adopting Regulations in Docket No. 90111A*, January 23, 1980. New York State Commission on Cable Television, Albany, New York.

41. *Notice of Inquiry in Docket No. 90172*, In the Matter of the Establishment of Rates Charged by Cable Television Companies, No. 79-142, May 16, 1979. New York State Commission on Cable Television, Albany, New York.

42. Levine, Larry S., Kalba, Konrad K., and Hochberg, Philip R., *Taxation, Regionalization and Pole Attachments: A Comparison of State Cable*

Television Policies, August 1978, The Harvard Program on Information Resources Policy, Publication P-78-5, Cambridge, Massachusetts.

43. Koenig, Joshua N., Deputy Counsel, New York State Commission on Cable Television, Tower Building, Empire State Plaza, Albany, New York 12223; 518/474-4992.

Other Resources

1. Birinyi, Anne E., *Chronology of State Cable Television Regulation: 1947-1978*, The Harvard Program on Information Resources Policy, Publication P-78-10, Kalba Bowen Associates, Inc. (November 1978).
2. Braunstein, Yale M., Kalba, Konrad K., and Levine, Larry S., *The Economic Impact of State Cable TV Regulation*, The Harvard Program on Information Resources Policy, Publication P-78-7 (October 1978).
3. Hochberg, Philip R., *Federal Preemption of State Regulation in Cable Television*, The Harvard Program on Information Resources Policy, Publication P-78-8 (November 1978).
4. Hochberg, Philip R., *The States Regulate Cable: A Legislative Analysis of Substantive Provisions*, The Harvard Program on Information Resources Policy, Publication P-78-4 (July 1978).
5. Kalba, Konrad K., Levine, Larry S., Braunstein, Yale M., and Hochberg, Philip R., *Executive Summary of Findings of the State Cable Television Regulation Project*, The Harvard Program on Information Resources Policy, Publication P-78-11 (December 1978).
6. Kalba, Konrad K., Levine, Larry S., and Birinyi, Anne E., *Regulatory Politics: State Legislatures and the Cable Television Industry*, The Harvard Program on Information Resources Policy, Publication P-78-2 (August 1978).
7. Levine, Larry S., *The Regulation of Cable Television Subscriber Rates by State Commissions*, The Harvard Program on Information Resources Policy, Publication P-78-6 (July 1978).
8. Mansell, John (ed.), *Cable TV Regulation*, Paul Kagan Associates, Inc., 26386 Carmel Rancho Blvd., Carmel, California 93923. Bimonthly newsletter.
9. National Cable Television Association, *Interaction*, a monthly newsletter. Available by subscription from National Cable Television Association, 918 Sixteenth Street, N.W., Washington, D.C. 20006; 202/457-6700.
10. Rodgers, Paul, *The NARUC Was There: A History*, National Association of Regulatory Utility Commissioners (1979), 1102 Interstate Commerce Commission Building, P.O. Box 684, Washington, D.C. 20044; 202/628-7324.
11. Strzelec, Krystyna, "CATV Regulation Update: A State-by-State Summary," *TVC*, Vol. 12, No. 4, February 20, 1978, Cardiff Publishing Co., Denver, Colorado.

State Commissions (and cable television contacts)

Alaska Public Utilities Commission
    1100 MacKay Building
    338 Denali Street
    Anchorage, Alaska 99501
    907/276-6222
    Ray Wipperman, Chief of Consumer Protection and Information
    John B. Farleigh, Executive Director
Department of Business Regulation
    Division of Public Utility Control
    State Office Building
    165 Capitol Avenue
    Hartford, Connecticut 06115
    203/566-2048
    Robert S. Golden, Assistant Attorney General
    Ralph Reuss, Chief Engineer
    Dave Sheehan, Associate Utilities Engineer
Public Service Commission
    1560 South DuPont Highway
    Dover, Delaware 19901
    302/678-4247
    Mike Tischer, General Counsel
    Leon Ryan, Engineer
Cable Television Division
    Department of Regulatory Agencies
    1010 Richards Street
    P.O. Box 541
    Honolulu, Hawaii 96809
    808/548-6203
    William Milks, Administrator
    Edwin K. Liu, Program Specialist
Massachusetts Cable Commission
    100 Cambridge Street
    Room 1105
    Boston, Massachusetts 02202
    617/727-6925
    Jeffrey R. Forbes, Commissioner
    Margaret A. Sofio, General Counsel
    Jeff Lyman, Financial Analyst
Minnesota Cable Communications Board
    500 Rice Street
    St. Paul, Minnesota 55103
    612/296-2545
    W.D. Donaldson, Executive Director
    Joanne Hinderaker, Special Assistant Attorney General
    Robert R. Nardi, Special Assistant Attorney General
    Anne T. Davis, Cable Television Specialist
Nevada Public Service Commission
    505 East King Street - Kinkead Building
    Carson City, Nevada 89701
    702/885-4180
    Ralph Dishman, Communications Engineer
    Bob Clark, Consumer Director

Office of Cable Television
    Board of Public Utilities
    1100 Raymond Blvd.
    Newark, New Jersey 07102
    201/648-2670
    John P. Cleary, Director
    Joseph J. Fisher, Deputy Director
    Michael A. Doyle, Coordinator, State and Local Planning
Commission on Cable Television
    Tower Building, 21st Floor
    Empire State Plaza
    Albany, New York 12223
    518/474-4992
    George Sincatta, Chairman
    John Harder, General Counsel
    Joshua N. Koenig, Deputy Counsel
    Edward P. Kearse, Executive Director
Division of Public Utilities and Carriers
    Rhode Island Public Utilities Commission
    100 Orange Street
    P.O. Box 2471
    Providence, Rhode Island 02903
    401/277-3500
    Edward F. Burke, Chairman (PUC), Administrator (Div. of Public Utilities)
    Bruce Stevenson, Deputy Administrator
    Patrick Tengwall, Cable TV Research Analyst
Vermont Public Service Board
    125 State Street
    Montpelier, Vermont 05602
    802/828-2325
    Richard Saudek, Chairman
    Robert P. Daino, Telecommunications Auditor
    C.F. Larkin, Telecommunications Engineer

Wilson P. Dizard

4. Direct Broadcast Satellites (DBS): The U.S. Position

Myth and reality have combined to make the future use of direct broadcast satellite technology one of the more difficult issues for the United States in the space field.

The myth is that one day a satellite will appear above the Equator, with a Stars and Stripes decal attached, ready to broadcast *Charlie's Angels,* Coca Cola advertisements, and perhaps even X-rated movies into the rabbit-ears antennas of ordinary television sets down below. The threat is seen as political, economic, and cultural by a large number of countries throughout the world to the point of engendering a decade-old debate on how to protect themselves against a prospect which is foreclosed by the laws of physics.

The reality is that broadcast satellites are a stunning technology whose future, across a broad range of social and economic possibilities, is still not fully understood. After a half-dozen years of active experimen-

Wilson P. Dizard is a professorial lecturer in communications, at George-town University School of Foreign Service, and a foreign service officer in the U.S. International Communications Agency. He was Vice Chairman of the United States Delegation to the 1979 World Administrative Radio Conference (WARC).

This chapter is a slightly edited version of a paper which originally appeared in the April 1980 issue of Journal of Communication. *Copyright 1980 by the Annenburg School of Communications, University of Pennsylvania.*

tation, it is a technology poised on the threshhold of large-scale exploitation. A number of industrialized countries are prepared to sponsor such satellites, under various auspices, for both domestic and regional purposes. More recently, developing nations are considering ways in which broadcast satellite technology can be applied to their economic and social needs. Most countries—developed and underdeveloped—have already agreed to frequency and regulatory standards for operating the satellites, in a series of conferences sponsored by the International Telecommunication Union (ITU), most recently at the general World Administrative Radio Conference (WARC) in 1979.

Meanwhile, the tension between myth and reality continues, threatening the prospects for the orderly application of broadcast satellite technology. In the early years of the debate, the focus of discussion had been on drafting a set of non-binding United Nations principles governing use of the satellites. More recently, the issue has taken on wider implications as one of the factors in the escalating debate over a "New World Information Order," centered around problems of strengthening Third World access to information resources.

This article traces the development of American policy on broadcast satellites from the early sixties to the present. Once the basic technical problem of putting a working geostationary satellite into orbit was solved in 1963, it was clear that their initial use for point-to-point communications services could be expanded to include broadcast services; i.e., transmissions from the satellite to many points. In those heady budget-rich days, NASA had the mandate and the resources to sponsor a relatively wide range of research and experimental projects in this field. The result was to move the technology from the drawing boards to outerspace application within a very few years.

Moreover, the idea captured the American public's fancy. The idea of broadcasting from space quickly entered the Sunday-supplement litany of space-age wonders. It was given the hallmark of legitimacy early on by many experts, including the communication industry's elder statesman, Brig. Gen. David Sarnoff of RCA who predicted in 1965 that satellite-to-home television would be a technical reality within a decade.

The new technology was still in its very early development stage when policy questions at the international level were raised for the first time. This occurred in 1963 at a specialized World Administrative Radio Conference. The meeting was called by the ITU to consider technical and regulatory requirements for communications satellites, shortly after the successful launching of the American Telstar, the first active-repeater satellite. The conference emphasis was on point-to-point (fixed) satellite communications, but the prospect of broadcast satellites was also raised. The physical requirements of the spectrum necessitate some division in frequencies for fixed and broadcast services. Without clear-cut allocations to each service, jamming and other interference could occur. The conference agreed on a definition of broadcast-satellite service as:

> a space service in which signals transmitted or retransmitted by space stations, or retransmitted by reflection from objects in orbit around the earth, are intended for direct reception by the general public.

It was a simple, even simplified, definition which gave the unintended impression to laymen that such satellites could transmit directly to ordinary television sets with no special technical devices and no political control—a misconception that has muddied the political debate ever since.

Another development at the 1963 space communications conference anticipated the later controversy over the kind of controls which might be applied to broadcast satellite transmissions. The issue involved changes, proposed by the French delegation, to existing ITU regulations which prohibited the establishment and use of broadcasting stations on board ships, aircraft "or any other floating or airborne object outside national territories." The French proposed adding the word "satellite" to the list, thus prohibiting in effect broadcast transmissions from space. The United States, supported by the Soviet Union, opposed the change, arguing in favor of specifically *excluding* satellites from the prohibition. After considerable debate, the language of the original regulation was left unchanged. As part of the compromise, an ITU technical consultative body, the International Radio Consultative Committee, was asked to study and submit specific recommendations on the technical requirements for broadcast satellites. The study, completed several years later, was to play an important role in defining the technical framework within which the political debate took place.

This political discussion began to take shape in the late sixties in various United Nations forums. An important early event was the passage in 1967 of the U.N. Outer Space Treaty, defining the rights and obligations of nations in space. Direct satellite broadcasts were not mentioned in the treaty although a number of its provisions have been used to support conflicting sides of the debate. The treaty is, in fact, ambiguous enough to permit varying interpretations of the rights and obligations associated with broadcast satellites. The document is permissive concerning broadcasting, among other space activities, but it also contains what some interpret as at least narrow constraints as to the content of broadcasts.

A fundamental principle cited in the treaty is the freedom of all states to conduct space activities in accordance with international law, including the U.N. charter. Article 55 of the charter commits each member state to promote a "universal respect for, and observance of human rights and fundamental freedom for all. ..." One such right, explicitly stated in the Universal Declaration of Human Rights as well as in other U.N. covenants and resolutions, is the right to receive information regardless of frontiers. This would argue for extending the right to distribute information freely from outer space, in much the same way that radio and television signals move across national boundaries. This reasoning was to become a central point in the American case against proposals for prior-consent requirements, either binding or non-binding, before broadcasts could be transmitted from space.

On the other hand, the Outer Space treaty contains language which can be interpretated as imposing constraints on the content of satellite broadcasts. In its operative paragraphs, the treaty mandates that space activities be carried out for the benefit of all countries and that this be done with due regard to the "corresponding interests of all other States parties." Since a large number of U.N. member states have indicated that they are in favor of some sort of restrictive principles governing the content of space broadcasts, it has been argued that a transmitting state has to respect the "corresponding interests" of the majority.

Finally, the treaty makes reference to previous U.N. resolutions condemning propaganda "designed or likely to provoke or encourage any threat to the peace, breach of the peace or act of aggression" and applies them to space activities. This was an extension of long-standing efforts, actively pressed by the Soviet Union and its allies, to get U.N. sanctions against news and other information which allegedly promoted war, racism, and other evils. The idea of specific sanctions has always been resisted by the United States and other democracies as a threat to freedom of international information flow. Nevertheless the loose formulation which the United States and others finally agreed to was incorporated into the Outer Space Treaty, and eventually into the rhetorical arsenal of those arguing for restrictive principles governing the use of broadcasting satellites.

Meanwhile the broadcast-satellite issue was being added to the agenda of another United Nations element—UNESCO. The Paris-based organization had, in its early years, taken the lead in promulgating and promoting free-flow-of-information ideas put forward largely by the United States. This initiative was specifically extended to include international broadcasting. In 1948, the UNESCO second general conference adopted a resolution recommending that its members "recognize the right of citizens to listen freely to broadcasts from other countries." Although this formulation did not have the legal status of a treaty, it represented a general international consensus (with the predictable exception of the Communist states) on the subject for almost two decades. By the mid-sixties, however, this consensus began to erode as pressures arose, within the UNESCO bureaucracy and from member states, to examine the relationship between the free-flow doctrine and the imbalance in actual information flow favoring the Western industrialized countries. The new prospects for space broadcasting became part of the agenda of these concerns.

In December 1965, UNESCO sponsored an experts meeting on space broadcasting, the first in a series which had the effect of focusing attention on the political and cultural aspects of the subject. As a result, broadcast satellites became a firm (and often emotional) element in the larger debate on the validity of the free-flow-of-information doctrine, and on the need to seek new ways to improve the balance of information flow between the developed and developing countries. At the time, the United States generally relied on a reiteration of its advocacy of the free-flow arguments in responding to challenges about the alleged inadequacies of the concept. Whatever the merits of this position, it proved eventually to be insufficient in meeting the growing pressure for a review of global information policies and practices.

The broadcasting-satellite issue came into sharp focus during the fall of 1972. UNESCO's biennial General Conference and the U.N. General Assembly each took actions which have set the framework for the political debate on the subject since. The sequence of events was indicative of the approaches taken by the contending parties.

In August, the Soviet Union requested that the issue be put on the agenda of the upcoming General Assembly. In October, the Soviets introduced at the United Nations a draft convention or treaty which, among other provisions, would authorize any receiving nation to take "the means at its disposal to counteract illegal television broadcasting of which it is the object. . . ." Although the threat was not spelled out, this was taken as a Soviet warning that it would try to jam or even to destroy any satellites whose transmissions it disapproved. The receiving nation would be the sole judge of the illegality of the offending broadcasts. The Soviet list of illegal programs included, among other prohibitions, those involving interference in a country's domestic affairs, attacks on local culture or traditions, advocacy of violence, and, finally, "misinformation." The United States reacted to the Soviet proposal by describing it as "completely unacceptable and unwise."

At the same time, a UNESCO committee on communications in Paris was discussing the draft of a declaration which, among other provisions, favored a restrictive ban on broadcast satellite transmissions to other countries without their permission. The key paragraph read:

> It is necessary that states, taking into account the principle of information, reach or promote prior agreements concerning direct satellite broadcasting to the population of countries other than the country of origin of the transmission.

This language, with minor variations, set out the major policy problem in the debate over broadcast satellites over the past decade. The committee draft declaration was approved (47 in favor, 9 against, and 13 abstentions) following a heated session in which the chairman refused to allow debate on the text. The United States was able to make clear its opposition, declaring that the resolution was too negative, contrary to the principle of the free-flow of information and ideas, and also unjustifiably assuming that there was a need for additional restrictions, however non-binding, on the new technology.

Meanwhile in New York, the General Assembly's political commit-approved a resolution which in effect rejected the Soviet treaty proposal. The Committee recommended instead that the U.N. Committee on the Peaceful Uses of Outer Space draft "principles" governing the use of broadcasting satellites. The tone of the Third World's support for the resolution was typified by a Colombian delegate's estimate that unrestrained use of broadcasting satellites would bring about "an ideological occupation of the world by the superpowers and their advertising mentality." The resolution was passed by the General Assembly by a vote of 102 to 1, with the United States casting the dissenting vote. Two weeks later the UNESCO General Conference voted a "Declaration of Guiding Principles on Satellite Broadcasting," based on the report approved by its communications committee. The declaration was approved with only the United States and six other states in opposition.

The domestic reaction in the United States to these developments was sharp, with the print and broadcast media taking the lead in pointing out the dangers of international censorship implicit in the two United Nations documents. During the U.N. debates, Frank Stanton, Vice Chairman of CBS, wrote an article (*The New York Times*, October 20, 1972) critizing the State Department for allegedly trying to temporize on the issue:

> What the Department has in mind is an attempt to avoid a head-on confrontation and give everybody a tidy diplomatic out. But I submit that the central issue here transcends that kind of diplomacy. . . . You don't negotiate free speech. The United States must do all within its power to block the path to international censorship.

Although broadcast satellites continued to be discussed in UNESCO forums following the General Conference resolution, the primary focus of debate during the seventies was in the U.N. Committee on the Peaceful Uses of Outer Space. Set up as a permanent standing committee in 1959, the Committee divides its work between a legal subcommittee and a scientific and technical subcommittee. In its early years, the Committee was active in establishing the principles which became the main provisions of the 1967 Outer Space Treaty. In 1969, a special working group on direct broadcast saellites was formed to consider the technical, legal, and political aspects of the new technology. The group concluded that "true" direct broadcasting was neither technically nor economically feasible before the mid-eighties. However, it did not reach a consensus on the need for additional legal instruments for controlling satellite broadcasting. The United States took the lead in arguing against this approach in the working group, insisting that any premature regulation would inhibit rather than promote international cooperation as the technology became operational.

The 1972 UNESCO and General Assembly resolutions gave added emphasis to the working group's activities. It reconvened in June 1973 to begin work on the General Assembly mandate for principles governing broadcast satellites. An important factor in the long, and still unfinished, debate is the Outer Space Committee's practice of consensus decision making, a procedure that was instrumental in its earlier successful work on the Outer Space Treaty. Conflicting positions must be resolved by unanimous agreement or, if not unanimous agreement, by the dissenting member noting or reserving its objections or position on the record.Testifying before a subcommittee of the House of Representatives in September 1979, S. Neil Hosenball, general counsel of NASA, observed that "the process has worked probably because nations have perceived if not unity of interests, at least roughly parallel interests in securing outer space for the peaceful pursuit of its potential benefit for all nations and mankind." The important point is that the consensus principle has been adhered to so far during the committee's long consideration of the broadcast satellite issue. The net result has been to keep the debate within the relatively restrained precincts of the Committee, where the opportunities for some form of compromise and consensus may be possible.

When the Committee's working group on broadcast satellites met after the General Assembly's action, three general positions eventually emerged. The first involved a set of principles which, following the lines of the UNESCO Declaration, called for *a priori* agreement on satellite broadcast transmissions between the transmitting and receiving countries. This position was supported by the Soviet Union and its allies, by most Third World countries and by several Western countries, including the French. (The Soviets continued to press their original idea of a binding international convention for several years, but dropped it when it became clear that the idea had little support.)

The second position, generally identified as a "middle" or compromise approach, was put forward by the Canadian and Swedish governments as a joint proposal. It has gone through a number of changes over a period of years. Essentially, however, on the prior-consent issue, it calls for advance agreement on satellite transmission as such, without reference to the question of the content of the transmissions. The United States has always regarded the Canadian-Swedish initiatives as a constructive attempt to seek compromise on a difficult issue. However, it has not been able to support their proposal on the ground that any prior-consent regime, even the non-binding variety, would set an unfortunate precedent not only for satellites but also in the wider field of world information flow.

The third position was that of the United States and a relatively small number of other democracies, not all of which supported the American case in every particular. In the original General Assembly and

UNESCO debates, the United States questioned the advisability of adopting any principles governing satellite broadcasts. When it became clear that eventually some form of document might emerge from the debate on the subject, the American government muted this theme and sought to influence the debate by submitting its own version of principles in June 1973. The document included, to a considerable degree, language similar to that found in other drafts submitted to the Outer Space Committee. As a result there has been a large measure of agreement by all parties concerned on the text of a non-binding resolution on broadcast satellite principles. The significant exception has been on the prior-consent issue where the U.S.-sponsored draft has been at odds with the differing formulations laid out in the other major drafts before the Committee.

The United States has emphasized four major themes to support its case against adopting a set of principles that were any stronger in language and intent than its own generalized proposals. There have been some adaptations of each theme since 1972 but the basic approach in each has remained more or less constant. They can be summarized as follows:

1. *There has been insufficient experience with broadcast satellites to determine what, if any, political constraints should be placed on their use.* This was certainly true at the time of the UNESCO and General Assembly actions in 1972. Broadcast satellite technology was still very much in the research-and-development stage, with no practical indication of how, or whether, the new technology would work in specific projects. The United States was, in fact, the leading experimenter with the new technology, sponsoring a number of projects designed to demonstrate broadcast satellite capabilities.

The first large-scale broadcast satellite experiment involved transmissions into widely-scattered community receivers, utilizing the NASA ATS-6 satellite. Beginning in 1973, experiments in the United States and India were generally successful in demonstrating the satellite's potential for large-scale educational, health, and other public service programming, particularly in reaching remote areas. The Indian experiments involved transmissions to over 2200 villages. Aside from these practical benefits, the ATS-6 experiments demonstrated that control of programming and of distribution remains firmly with the local government in the receiving country, a point stressed by American officials in the political debates on the broadcast satellite issue. Their purpose was to correct the simplistic assumptions about "cultural imperialism" that underlay much of the argumentation favoring political restrictions on broadcast satellites.

The argument about lack of experience has not been stressed in recent years, in part because of the development of higher-powered satellites capable of transmissions into smaller earth terminals. The experience to date, and the even greater experience which will be accumulated in the next few years, should lay to rest fears about uncontrolled intrusive satellite broadcasting which would justify the kind of prior-consent arrangements being advocated in United Nations and other forums, in the opinion of American experts.

2. *Enactment of a set of political principles governing broadcast satellite transmission could have the effect of inhibiting the technology before its potential is fully tested.* With most of the basic technical problems of broadcast satellites already solved or within reach, the practical questions now revolve around decisions on how to configure future satellites to carry out specific broadcasting tasks. Economic considerations become more important in establishing the trade-offs between satellite transmissions and more conventional means of broadcasting. Politically-motivated restrictions could place an added inhibiting burden on decisions to proceed with innovative satellite development, particularly in adapting the technology to the economic and social needs of developing countries, in the view of American experts.

3. *Existing ITU regulations provide sufficient safeguards against unauthorized broadcast satellite transmissions.* The United States contention is that, in effect, a form of prior-consent, based on the need for technical coordination, has already been agreed to by the 154 ITU member-states. These restraints were initially the result of the study of broadcast-satellite technical requirements initiated by the first "Space WARC" in 1963. The study laid the groundwork for key technical decisions on broadcast satellites at a second specialized WARC dealing with space communications in 1971. The 1971 conference treated two aspects of broadcast satellites: (1) it refined the definition of the service and (2) it authorized the first allocations of frequencies for its use. Both decisions had important implications for the political debate on the satellites' future.

On definitions, the conference went beyond the simple definition about "direct" broadcasting agreed to at the 1963 WARC. A clear distinction was made between "community" and "individual" reception. The latter involves transmission received by a home receiver equipped to process the signal. The former is transmission into some form of communally-controlled receiving equipment either for direct access at one location or for redistribution over a limited area. The distinction between the two types of reception served to clarify some of the fuzziness inherent in the use of the adjective "direct" in both the UNESCO and General Assembly resolutions on satellite broadcasting. Both technology and economics support the fact that most so-called direct broadcasting for the near-term will be indirect community-type reception, fully capable of being regulated or otherwise controlled technically and by other methods by local authorities. As broadcast technology advances, however, there will be a new blurring of the distinction between community and individual reception. Both can be received by small "dishes," and it is probable that a broadcast satellite service (like the one proposed by Comsat) will serve both types. Whatever the case, in any country, including the United States, domestic satellite broadcasting would be regulated in some way.

The ITU's new definitions reinforced the American unwillingness to accept the premise that any set of principles were necessarily applicable to all potential modes of satellite broadcasting. The argument was a logical one, supported by technical facts of life. Its force was dissipated, however, against the persistently incorrect perceptions about "direct" broadcasting held by many of the politically-oriented officials who represent their countries in the debates on the subject at the United Nations and other forums. The mythology of direct broadcasting into rabbit-ear antennas dies hard.

The 1971 conference also allocated broadcast satellite frequencies in four frequency bands. These decisions set the stage for bringing this type of satellite out of the research stage into actual experimental use. The only negative note as far as the United States was concerned was a conference decision recommending follow-on specialized ITU conferences to plan broadcast-satellite frequencies and the geostationary orbital positions of the satellites. The American reluctance was based on the possiblity that such planning might restrict flexible use of both frequencies and orbital slots. This concern proved to be well-founded, since this is what happened at a 1977 specialized WARC to plan the important 12 GHz band for satellite broadcasting and other services. (The conference decisions did not immediately affect the United States and other Western Hemisphere nations, which will meet in a specialized conference in 1983 to make regional arrangements on these issues.) The third ITU conference affecting broadcast satellites was the 1979 general World Administrative Radio Conference which further clarified technical requirements for such satellites as part of its overall review of frequency and regulatory needs in the years leading up to the end of the century.

The three ITU conferences were important not only in establishing the global technical and regulatory framework for broadcast satellites, but also in influencing the political debate on their use. The United States and its supporters argued that the technical and regulatory limitations placed on broadcast satellite use had, in effect, overtaken the need for political principles. In this view, the ITU procedures were in themselves proper and sufficient safeguards against any misuse of the new technology. This did not, however, end the debate. The counterargument, supported by many of the countries involved in the Outer Space Committee discussions on the subject, was that the ITU decisions, dealing with the physical transmission of a satellite signal, did not address the need for principles dealing with a country's right to prior approval of message content. Since 1972, these differing perceptions of the issue have affected the central unresolved issue in the Outer Space Committee's debates on the political factors involved in satellite broadcasting. Throughout the discussion the United States has consistently supported the right to broadcast messages freely, once ITU technical and regulatory standards have been complied with. It is a subject which the U.S. has viewed as part of the larger issue of defending the principle of open information channels, to wit:

4. *The prior-consent principle, applied to the program concept of satellite broadcasts, undermines the concept of international free flow of information and the free exchange of ideas.* In articulating this position, U.S. officials have cited chapter and verse from the extensive series of U.N. resolutions defending the free-flow princple. They have reinforced this ideological position with the pragmatic suggestion that a prior-consent regime would probably be unworkable in practice.

The reason for this lies largely in the technical characteristics of satellite broadcasting itself. As a practical matter, it is probable that very little broadcasting would take place if the prior-consent of every receiving state were required, with the possible exception of domestic broadcasts within very large countries. Even with sophisticated beam-shaping techniques limiting the satellite's "footprint," regional broadcasts in most areas of the world would be receivable in many countries. Given the harsh realities of international politics, there are few areas of the world with sufficient political compatibility that all states in a region would give their consent. The net result is that the benefits of satellite broadcasting would not be attainable, even if they were desired by a majority of states and population in the area.

The United States took a major step in attempting to break the deadlock on the prior-consent issue in 1975. This involved a proposal that any system for direct television broadcasting by satellite should include provisions for "full consultations" by the countries concerned. First suggested in August 1975 by Secretary of State Henry Kissinger in a speech before the American Bar Association, the proposal was elaborated by W. Tapley Bennett, Jr., U.S. Ambassador to the United Nations, in October 1975. Since the statement was an important American initiative which has not changed substantially since then, it is useful to quote it in full:

> In particular we are proposing that before direct television broadcasting is undertaken, states within the reception area should be notified of the intention to broadcast. Those who broadcast should be prepared, on a reciprocal basis, to assume an obligation to give formal notification to states within the likely broadcast area. In addition, those who broadcast should agree to consult fully with the governments of the states in the in-

tended reception area if the latter so request, with the intention of making good faith efforts to reconcile problems which may be raised.

We believe that this approach would offer protection for any state which has legitimate concerns about direct television broadcasting into its territory, without establishing an international scheme based on prior consent. We do not envisage establishment through these procedures of a right of any state to prohibit others from undertaking broadcasting. We do envisage that such notification and consultation requirements would go substantively beyond the technical consultations now provided for within the ITU.

It is our belief that the actual process of consultations, which would cause the parties to deal expressly with problems which may arise, would go very far to reconcile differences. The very process of bona fide consultations would give the broadcaster considerable incentive to work out mutually satisfactory solutions, and would guarantee those in the reception area a full opportunity to resolve problems they may foresee. Broadcasters would clearly not wish to alienate prospective audiences, and hence would desire to reconcile differences. The natural dynamic of the dialogue would work in favor of reconciliation.

However reasonable this proposal may have seemed to American policy makers, it did not substantially change attitudes among the majority of the 43 countries represented on the Outer Space Committee. If anything, positions held by a number of Third World countries favoring the prior-consent principle may have hardened as a result of their new sensitivity to information issues raised by the call for a "New World Information Order."

The prior-consent principle remains the major obstacle preventing a resolution by consensus of the broadcast satellite issue in the Outer Space Committee. In recent years, the U.S. Government has considered various other formulations on this subject which might have gained consensus support within the Committee. However, there has been no change in basic policy on prior-consent, beyond the "full consultations" proposal made by Secretary Kissinger in 1975. Attempts by Sweden and Canada to modify their original proposal in ways which would meet objections from both sides proved to be unavailing.

Meanwhile the satellite broadcast issue is still on the Outer Space Committee's agenda. A March 1980 meeting of the Committee's legal subcommittee failed to resolve the outstanding issue of prior-consent. As long as the Committee's consensus principle holds, the subject will continue to be debated, with a maximum of recycled arguments, within the Committee itself. The alternative is a possible breach in the consensus rule which could put the issue before a U.N. General Assembly session. A resolution on satellite broadcast principles incorporating a prior-consent provision would probably be overwhelmingly approved in that forum. Whether this will happen sometime in the next few years is problematical.

There is increasing evidence that the political debate on the subject is being overtaken, and perhaps rendered academic, by events outside U.N. committee rooms. There are strong indications that broadcast satellite projects for both domestic and regional use will become more common in all regions of the world during the 1980s. Whether or not agreement is reached in the United Nations on general principles governing their use, it seems probable that both transmitting and receiving countries will make their own arrangements, based on their own interests and needs. The "natural dynamic" of their consultations, as suggested in the 1975 U.S. proposal for prior consultations, will probably be more effective in resolving any differences over satellite use than will declarations coming out of Turtle Bay.

Resources

1. "Satellite-to-home TV in decade," *Broadcasting*, May 31, 1965.
2. The ITU regulation prohibiting the establishment and use of broadcasting stations on board ships, aircraft, "or any other floating or airborne object outside national territories" is contained in Article 422 of the ITU Radio Regulations approved by the 1959 World Administrative Radio Conference.
3. For an account of one of the early Soviet attempts to press the issue of sanctions against news and other information which allegedly promoted war, racism, and other evils, see "UN efforts are revived on information codes," *Editor & Publisher*, November 15, 1953.
4. "Right to destroy satellites sought by Soviets in UN," *Aviation Week & Space Technology*, October 22, 1972.
5. "Curb on satellite broadcasts voted," *The Washington Post*, November 3, 1972.
6. The text of the 1972 resolution which in effect rejected the Soviet proposal for a convention or treaty is given in U.N. General Assembly document A/RES/2916 (XXVII), November 14, 1972.
7. Stanton, Frank, "Will they stop our satellites?" *The New York Times*, October 20, 1972.
8. For a discussion of the U.N. Outer Space Committee's consensus practices, see Galloway, Eileen, "Consensus decisionmaking by the United Nations committee on the peaceful use of outer space," *Journal of Space Law*, Spring 1979, pp. 3-13.
9. General statement of S. Neil Hosenball, general counsel of NASA, in testimony before the subcommittee on space science and applications, Committee on Science and Technology, U.S. House of Representatives, September 6, 1979.
10. For a summary of early positions taken on the broadcast satellite principles debate, see "Report of the Working Group on Direct Broadcast Satellites on the work of its fifth session," Committee on the Peaceful Uses of Outer Space, U.N. General Assembly document A/AC. 105/127, April 1, 1974.

11. Statement by Ambassador W. Tapley Bennett, Jr., Press Release USUN 116 (75) October 13, 1975, U.S. Mission to the United Nations, New York. The United States submitted a formal text reflecting these views at the 1979 meeting of the legal subcommittee of the Outer Space Committee.

12. "Era of direct broadcast satellites underway," *BM/E World Broadcast News*, October 1979. The article documents the intense activity in this field in Japan, the United States, and Canada, as well as plans for broadcast satellite services in other parts of the world.

13. Rice, David M., *Direct Broadcast Satellites: Legal and Policy Options*, consultant report for the Network Inquiry Special Staff to the Federal Communications Commission, March 1980. Printed as an Appendix to the *Preliminary Report on Prospects for Additional Networks*, a report from the Network Inquiry Staff, FCC.

Tom Wolfsohn and Peg Kay

5. Ascertainment of Community Needs: Proposing a Systems Approach

Ascertainment of community needs or needs assessment is an activity commonly associated with human services and health planning. Often, before public monies can be spent on a project, a needs assessment must have been carried out. While ascertainment studies are required of radio and television broadcasters by the Federal Communications Commission (FCC), their widespread use in other areas of telecommunications is relatively new.

Recent changes in the regulatory and economic environments surrounding cable television have rekindled the franchising fire which

Tom Wolfsohn is Vice President, Corporate Development, Telecommunications Management Corporation, and has served as a consultant to a number of organizations, companies, and cable TV systems. He is a former staff member of the National Cable Television Association and the Cable Television Information Center.

Peg Kay is the Management Scientist, Institute for Computer Sciences and Technology, National Bureau of Standards. At the time this paper was written, she was Director of Special Projects, National Rural Center. Prior to that time she was associated with the Cable Television Information Center, the Program Evaluation Group of The Urban Institute, and was a fellow-in-residence at the Office of Telecommunications Policy, Executive Office of the President.

sputtered in 1974. Harold Horn, executive director of the Cable Television Information Center (CTIC), notes that increasing numbers of cities are asking franchise competitors to perform ascertainments. In fact, the Center, a nonprofit organization which assists local and state officials, encourages franchising authorities to include an ascertainment study as a bid item in their requests for proposals. Though some cable companies ignore it, Horn observes that those cable operators who have undertaken conscientious and sophisticated ascertainment approaches have had better track records in recent franchising contests. And in one state, Minnesota, the cable TV commission requires needs studies in every franchising situation.

Why Do An Ascertainment?

Ascertainment studies can be of value to cable operators, telephone companies, local governments, and community groups.

In the cable context, most franchising authorities are interested in selecting a franchisee that is both financially sound and responsive to needs of the community. For the cable operator, an ascertainment study can represent a marketing tool. First, it can "sell" the company as a responsible franchise applicant. Second, properly done, an ascertainment suggests potential services which can be sold to business, institutional, and residential subscribers—and this applies to existing franchise holders as well as franchise applicants.

The authors have managed a number of telecommunications needs assessments carried out for cable TV operators and public agencies, in urban, suburban, small town, and agricultural areas. In this paper, we will review several ascertainment approaches. We will also present a general methodology called Community Needs Analysis (CNA) which we have adapted for different situations, and describe the findings of some of these ascertainment studies.

Commonly Used Ascertainment Methods

Many readers are probably familiar with the nature of ascertainment studies carried out by broadcasters to meet FCC requirements. Typically, a broadcast ascertainment report has three components.

One component consists of demographic data pertaining to the city of license. These data include the total population, the numbers and proportions of males and females, of minorities, of those 17 and under, of those 65 and older, and so forth. The second component consists of two surveys. The first survey is of "community leaders" selected from 18 "institutions and elements commonly found in a community" such as agriculture; business; charities; civic, neighborhood, and fraternal organizations; and so on. The second survey is usually of a probablistic sample of members of the general public. The sampling may be taken from a telephone directory, done on a geographical distribution basis by means of "man-on-the-street" interviews, accomplished by questionnaire responses collected by the licensee, or carried out by other survey techniques. Third, every year the broadcaster must place in the station's public inspection file a list of no more than 10 of the significant problems, needs, or interests identified during the preceding 12 months.

There are several basic flaws in this whole process. First, examination of a number of these studies, which are available for inspection at every TV and radio station and in the FCC's public reference room, reveals that many of the problems identified are too general in nature to be evaluated. "Apathy" is a typical example of state-of-the- art generality. Second, the broadcaster has extremely limited tools with which to solve even the most concrete of the ascertained problems. For the most part, the available tools are confined to TV or radio news or public service programs, spot announcements, and editorials. Third, most of the methodologies employed in broadcast ascertainments to identify telecommunications-soluble problems are not appropriate for that purpose.

Another ascertainment approach utilizes both random and stratified sampling techniques, and resembles the marketing strategies used by some cable TV companies. Known as the "laundry list" approach, respondents are asked "if" a service were available would they pay for it or utilize it. Results end up being presented as thus: "68 percent of the respondents interviewed stated they would pay $2 per month for a comparative shopping guide if it were offered" or "The League of Women Voters, Urban League, YMCA, Gray Panthers, and Chamber of Commerce stated that they would use a public access channel if one existed." There are several weaknesses in this type of polling. To begin with, a recitation of potential services may raise expectations and in turn produce disenchantment if the services are not immediately forthcoming. Next, a natural tendency of people to say "yes" to what sounds like a good idea (especially if they don't have to commit to it on the spot) tends to skew the sample upward. And finally, this method of ascertainment does not define problems.

Apparently we are not alone in our skepticism. Implementing its overall policy of deregulation, in September 1979 the FCC issued a *Notice of Inquiry and Proposed Rule Making* which would eliminate the ascertainment requirement for radio stations. As of April 1980, the matter was still pending. And the requirement has gained attention in Congress as well, in proposals for rewriting the Communications Act. While the 1979 rewrite bill in the House has been shelved, with no further action planned on it as of April 1980, in the Senate the issue was still pending (S.611 and S.622).

Community Needs Analysis—A Systems Approach

Community Needs Analysis was developed to identify the stakeholders and define the stakes when a technological, social, or administrative innovation, such as a cable communications system, is introduced into society.

Whenever an innovation is successfully introduced (i.e., adopted), changes occur in the environment. These changes (which are, in themselves, innovations) lead to other changes, and so on, so that the initial innovation many eventually result in extensive "ripple effects." The economic and social ripples caused by the mass production of automobiles over the past 60 years is an obvious and pervasive example of this phenomenon. The people and institutions expected to be affected by the innovation and its ripples are the stakeholders. The expected social and economic gains and losses are the stakes.

In developing the methodology, a "systems approach" was adopted. That is, society is assumed to be a system and, by definition, all parts of a system are linked. Therefore, in order to identify ripple effects (and thereby to identify stakeholders and stakes) we can start with the first-order (*directly* affected) stakeholders and, fanning out from there, trace the potential ripples through society. In this way, it is possible to discover latent "consortia" of users who have a positive stake in particular services or technologies (e.g., a security alarm system or a microwave distribution system). It is also possible to discover secondary beneficiaries of a given system who might "chip in" to make it go. For instance, certain local businesses or industries might help pay for an educational loop on the cable system if the technical school would use it to provide some on-the-job instruction to employees.

The Sampling

The technique used for selecting people to interview is called "snowball" sampling, a technique which has been used primarily in communications research and in the study of the diffusion of innovation. The snowball is begun by carefully choosing a "seed" organization in which *everyone* is interviewed (a "saturation" sample). The seed organization chosen will vary from community to community and the final selection will often depend on which appropriate organization is willing to be saturated.

There are two reasons for interviewing everyone in the seed organization. First, this provides a fairly sizable pool of their contacts from which to select succeeding interviews. Second, by interviewing everyone top to bottom, the pool will contain the names of people at all levels in the organizations and institutions which deal with the seed organization as well as a vertical sample of members of the public who have contact with the seed organization. For instance, if the seed organization were the community's information and referral service, the initial pool would probably contain both social workers and the Director of Human Services, both welfare recipients and civic leaders.

Once the saturation sampling of the seed organization has been completed, the interview team has a pool of potential interviews from which to select subjects to begin the "snowball." The selection of respondents is made on the basis of their connections with problems identified within the seed organization. As the snowball rolls, it picks up increasing numbers of people and organizations affected by any given problem.

There are two distinct parts of the interview questionnaire. The first part asks the respondents about their own jobs and about the institution which employs them. The questions are designed to determine: What tasks they perform; what problems they have in doing each task; and what they perceive to be the function of their institution or organization. The second part of the interview consists of questions asked about the *referring* organization. For instance, if an interview in the Police Department led the interviewer to someone in the District Attorney's office, the latter person first would be queried about the District Attorney's office; in the second part of the interview the questions would be about the Police Department. By using this approach, the analyst can examine a problem from several perspectives. The method also permits the analyst to trace a problem through the community and thus avoid confusing symptoms with causes.

To illustrate, if the Court Clerk's Office were the seed organization, it is likely that employees would be shown to deal with attorneys, human service agencies, police, etc. A problem uncovered in the Clerk's Office might lead the interviewer to the Police Department, from there to insurance companies, then to the hospital, from there to the mental health clinic, and so on. As the interviews snowball through a community, the impact of a problem is traced through institutions and organizations; stakeholders in the ripple effects are noted; and causes can often be attributed. It is important to note that the interviews also identify (where invasion-of-privacy is not threatened) *individuals* who deal with the organizations. This provides a sample of the population affected by the institution and who will therefore have a stake in changes made—a much more pertinent sample than one derived from statistical techniques.

As mentioned above, both policymakers and people who do the work are interviewed, the former to get "official" views, and the latter to determine how intentions are translated into action. When a telecommunications system changes the way things are done, the decision makers will be the ones who decide if and when the changes will be initiated. But the people who implement policy will determine whether the changes are really adopted in practice. It is therefore necessary to get their input in order to determine whether the system will not only be installed, but *used.* It is a sad fact that the storerooms in countless schools are filled with audio-visual equipment gathering dust.

The Analysis

Properly analyzed, the material gathered in the interview process will describe how a community "works." It is, in effect, a communications roadmap showing who communicates with whom and for what purposes.

The primary job of the analyst is to reveal how telecommunications services can help the community work better. The solution to a particular problem might involve a mix of two technologies such as telephone and two-way radio for instance, or a particular telesolution might lie in the shared use of a service or technology—e.g., a data network or broadband channel.

Telesolutions of the shared-use variety can be the hardest to identify, requiring ingenuity on the part of the analyst. Their discovery can also be very rewarding—for the analyst, who gains a sense of professional accomplishment; for the sponsor, who can open up a new area of service; and for the community, which not only alleviates a problem but moves closer together because of the cooperative endeavor.

A major focus of the analysis should be the identification of groups and institutions with problems that can be eased by the same telecommunications service.

The End Product

The end product of a Community Needs Analysis contains several elements. Most important is a narrative analysis of each of the problems ascertained and.a proposed telesolution. The format should stress the technological alternatives and the individual aspects of the problem. Where appropriate, resources available to the community from outside sources (e.g., grants, programs) should be cited.

The creation of a matrix for each problem can be a graphic illustration of how a given problem affects a community. Such a matrix should contain those institutions which share a generic problem (e.g., the inability to provide and/or receive off-site instruction or consultation) plus all of the other institutions which the interviews have revealed as being linked in a functional way to those with the problem (e.g., businesses which habitually get robbed are functionally linked to the Police Department and have a stake in upgrading police training). It demonstrates the extent to which a problem pervades the community, as the problem is likely to affect the way in which the primary institution functions in relation to the secondary entities it deals with—that is, how the stakeholders interact.

... Options for Inclusion

There are a couple of optional products which can be produced to accompany the narrative analysis. A cluster analysis is the output of a computer program which reflects the communications pattern of a community. Simply, the computer counts and compares repetitive patterns, thus grouping the community's institutions so that those with similar communications patterns are placed near one another. The more similar the patterns, the closer together the clusters are. The proximate positions often reveal overlapping potential consortia of users, pinpointing institutions that have multiple stakes in a given technological system. Beyond its application to the ascertainment, a cable operator or telephone company may find this analysis useful as a system design tool.

Another option is a map of the community which shows all existing telecommunications facilities uncovered during the survey process. Such a map may be of use both in forward planning and in those cases where it is determined that some problems may be solved through sharing facilities; also, the study sponsor may be the catalyst in enabling some major local institutions to form a user's consortium (e.g., data network via cable system), and it will be necessary to define physical locations in reference to the system's headend.

The Payoffs

For community groups and local governments the payoffs from a Community Needs Analysis include: (1) the realistic identification of local problems; (2) the definition of the scope of the problems in terms of whom they affect; and (3) the proposed solutions.

For private companies, we have already noted one practical application—the winning of a cable TV franchise. But for cable operators and telephone companies, a Community Needs Analysis can also identify potential revenue producing services, and shed some light on who can use the service and how they might pay for it. And a Community Needs Analysis can be a useful planning tool in setting out system configuration, i.e., putting services where the users are, running dedicated lines to where those users are. For a new system especially, it is better to have this information before the cable is laid since it could be very expensive news after the fact.

Experiences in Using the CNA Methodology

A. The first needs analysis we shall describe was carried out by the National Rural Center under contract to the Rural Electrification Administration (REA), a federal agency which provides financial and management assistance to rural telephone companies and cooperatives.

REA has an interest in developing an effective ascertainment methodology for two reasons. First, while REA is not currently directly involved with traditional cable services, it is possible that its congressional mandate will, in the near future, be expanded to include them. As a "banker," REA wants to ensure that, if and when it makes broadband loans, those loans will be as financially sound as its narrowband (telephone) loans have been. Some REA officials feel that the agency's current methodology might not be adequate to analyze the potential of a broadband system. Second, it was expected that the Community Needs Analysis would identify many problems that could be ameliorated by upgraded telephone systems alone. Given the current trend toward increased competition among telecommunications carriers, it may become necessary for rural telephone companies to sell a wider range of services than previously in order to both remain financially stable and maintain an affordable basic rate structure.

Specifically, REA undertook the project in order to develop a process which would lead to (1) the identification of aggregated potential users of telecommunications systems and facilities, and (2) the identification of communications patterns in any given community served by an REA telephone company.

The test site chosen by REA was the service area of a middle size independent telephone company. The telephone system covers one full county and portions of two others—an area which includes a county seat, several hamlets, and an agricultural expanse.

In the course of 94 interviews among about 60 entities in industry, business, public agencies, and nonprofit organizations, interactions among 164 institutions and groups as well as their interactions with the public were articulated. Aggregated usage was identified and analyzed for both broadband and narrowband systems.

In small town and agricultural areas, a problem in utilizing telecommunications systems has been the difficulty in aggregating sufficient users to provide a sound economic base. While it may not be necessary to identify every potential beneficiary of, for instance, a business information system in order to create a successful system in a big city, a town of 20,000 may need everyone it can get. It is interesting to note that the ascertainment in this case identified 21 primary local entities and over 100 secondary local institutions that might benefit from a telecommunications-assisted business information system designed to reduce repetitive paperwork.

An add-on to such a system was suggested when the analysis disclosed that about 25 groups and institutions were affected by the community's inability to accurately project its economic growth. These institutions included not only the community's businesses but such essential-service organizations, as the fire and sanitation departments. The shared use of a dynamic economic model would clearly be of benefit.

Both of those uses are well within the capability of a narrowband system. Certain other problems, such as the inability to provide off-site instruction by institutions like the Police Department and the vocational school would more effectively be addressed through the use of broadband.

A second important facet of this needs assessment process is the identification of communications p-tterns within a community. While a traffic study will reveal how much traffic emanates from a given telephone station, it does not indicate who talks to whom. This latter information can be of particular importance to the forward planning of telephone companies in areas experiencing a high rate of growth and development. In growth areas one would expect not only that total communications carried by telephone lines (versus face-to-face) will grow as the tempo of life grows. People tend to become too busy to drop in to someone else's office, for instance. This aspect of an assessment is still more important when broadband is considered since even small mistakes in constructing a fixed path system, such as a traditional cable system, can be costly to correct.

B. The second example is an ascertainment which was carried out for an applicant for the cable television franchise of a suburban community of over 100,000 population in one of the 10 largest TV markets, and the study was included as part of the application.

The cable operator had two basic goals for the ascertainment. First, the company wanted to construct a separate institutional network or "B" cable in addition to the regular subscriber network. The cable company wanted to utilize the findings of the study to determine the configuration of such a networking arrangement, which institutions or organizations should be selected as terminal points in the network, and how these entities might utilize the institutional net.

The second purpose was to develop information about the various institutions and organizations in the community and to uncover issues of importance to its citizens. This intelligence–gathering was to be used in developing priorities in choosing institutional network participants.

The scope of this study then was narrower than that of the REA assessment. Hence in this suburban community, interview respondents were largely limited to municipal agencies and departments, private human service organizations and other nonprofit agencies, schools, neighborhood associations, and others. After completing nearly 80 interviews the project team was satisfied that it had collected sufficient data to meet the sponsor's needs (whereas a general Community Needs Analysis might have required more than twice that number of interviews for a community of this size). From these interviews, interactions among about 140 groups and institutions were identified.

In approaching the task of developing a configuration for an institutional network, the project team had four basic considerations:

• Which agencies and institutions, in the ascertainment, expressed a *need* to communicate with other entities in the course of their work;

• Which of those agencies and institutions had functions that *could* be carried out via telecommunications;

• Which suggested uses had *actually* been successfully implemented in other places; and

• The levels of service in that City's cable television ordinance, and the system capacity which might reasonably be expected initially given the cable operator's financial projections.

Utilizing the data gathered in the ascertainment process and the recommendations of the project team, the franchise applicant designed a hub-type system with an institutional network interconnecting 30 different public buildings.

An interesting concomitant of this approach is the feedback component. When an interview takes place, the respondent is asked not only about his or her own organization, but also about the organization which supplied the respondent's name. This feedback allows the analyst to assess both how organizations see themselves, and how they are seen by others. It has been our observation that in each community there is at least one public agency which, deservedly or not, has a generally negative image. In one place it might be the Department of Social Services, in another the CETA office, and so on. In a general Community Needs Analysis this information can show where necessary public support for a given telesolution is lacking; more positively, it might demonstrate to a particular agency how its function is misperceived and offer valuable clues toward improving its relationship with the citizenry. In this cable TV franchising case, it helped the cable operator decide which agencies not to include in the institutional network.

In the narrative portion of the study, the project team emphasized problems which had been ascertained and how they might be solved or ameliorated with the application of telecommunications technology.

For example, during the interviews it was found that in certain locations in the community, communication between a hospital emergency room and the rescue squad was completely cut off, and the physician on duty could not monitor or give instructions regarding the victim being transported. The proposed solution was to place satellite radio receivers at various locations in the community, based upon a technical survey. When communication was disrupted, the rescue vehicle's signal could be picked up by the nearest receiver and transmitted via the institutional network back to the hospital and the physician could respond via the same route.

C. The third example is an ascertainment of community needs

study which was also done for a cable TV operator who was seeking the franchise in a city of nearly 200,000 located in the "second fifty" television markets.

In this situation, the time period in which interviewing, analysis, and writing of the report took place was limited. Thus only 75 interviews were taken. (Here, interaction among some 215 entities was articulated.) The effort was further circumscribed by a provision in the request for proposals (RFP) which called for applicants to describe how specific institutions, agencies, and public buildings might be included in an institutional networking arrangement.

While the thrust of the ascertainment was the identification of problems which could be addressed by the sponsor's cable TV system, the identification of resources within the community was also emphasized. For example: pinpointing potential contributions from the computing center of a large university located in the city, such as the generation of computional and high quality instructional systems; consulting on the selection of home and business terminals; and obtaining grant monies.

Of the problems treated in the study, one of the more interesting was the inability of the city's information and referral system to meet local demands combined with coordination problems among state, local, and private human service agencies. The project team described this problem and outlined a proposed solution utilizing dedicated channels on an institutional network.

D. The fourth example is a pilot project which has been ongoing since the winter of 1978. Under the direction of the National Telecommunications and Information Administration (NTIA), the Rural Communities Federal Assistance project was instituted to make it possible for rural communities to ascertain their own telecommunications needs.

The project employs three site directors who were trained to carry out Community Needs Analyses in rural counties in California, New Mexico, and North Carolina. Their mandate is to evaluate how existing telecommunications facilities are meeting community needs, and to produce both short- and long-term improvements in problem areas they uncover.

When problems are identified and solutions proposed, NTIA will aid the site directors in finding federal programs to assist them, e.g., with federal loan programs. NTIA will track these particular requests through "the system," and may eventually recommend changes in procedures which would facilitate the process for rural communities.

In California, the county site has an 80 percent Hispanic population. The project team determined that the local media was not reaching that population, especially farm workers whose major source of information is radio. A local community group has been encouraged to apply for a radio license in order to broadcast in the major dialect of the area, a combination of Spanish and English. Major funding would be expected to come from a Public Telecommunications Facilities grant. The group is also planning a 24-hour bilingual telephone "hot line" service which would advise local residents of available services.

The New Mexico site is a 5800 square mile county approximately the size of Rhode Island. The local telephone company suffers major outages and frequent disconnects, and has a high proportion of partyline service.

Physicians in the county often spend up to three hours per day on the road, out of contact with their clinics. In addition, maintenance problems with repeaters and the nature of the terrain result in "dead spots" along the highways, and ambulances can be without radio communication for up to 30 minutes at a time. A group there is working with the state board which coordinates emergency radio services to solve these problems.

In the North Carolina county, that group is working to create a computerized human services system which would cross reference agencies and services and would make enrollment in various programs more efficient. At present, some services in the county are underutilized, while in other instances persons are applying for the same program in different agencies.

NTIA is operating from the premise that in most rural communities there are a lot of small problems that can be solved by readily obtainable and inexpensive applications of telecommunications technologies. The agency forsees a program of aiding rural needs assessments which would entail direction of a local community leader who would spend the equivalent of six months of a year-long period surveying local communications media, telephone, emergency medical services, and the like, as well as users. NTIA experts are to issue a report on the experiences in the three pilot sites sometime in mid-1980. It may also produce a guide to communications-related programs.

Summary and Conclusions

The four studies described show uses of the methodology which represents progressive divergence from the original intent of the methodology's developers. The REA study was a genuine technology–last process. That is, the focus of the interviews was to uncover problems, whatever they were and wherever in the community they existed. It was only during the analysis that appropriate problems were placed in the "telesoluble" category. Analysts suggested other means and other agencies to help with the remainder of the problems.

In the first cable-franchise assessment described, the technology was predetermined, i.e., cable television. The Community Needs Analysis revealed the potential *uses* and *users.* The methodology worked extremely well in both of these cases—somewhat more efficiently in the first.

In the second cable-franchise assessment, both the technology (cable) and the bulk of the users were predetermined. The ascertainment was for the purpose of defining the *uses.* For this purpose, the methodology should probably be considerably refined since, as it stands, it casts a very wide net to catch relatively few fish.

The NTIA program is particularly interested in preselected uses and technologies (e.g., those which are currently supported by federal programs) and, to some extent, preselected users (e.g., minorities). In this, it resembles a traditional demonstration program and it is likely that a more traditional assessment methodology would have served the agency better.

To summarize, the Community Needs Analysis is most efficient and effective when the study proceeds from problem discovery to stakeholders to general telesolutions to specific appropriate technologies. It is least efficient and effective when the study proceeds from a preset cluster of stakeholder/solution/technology to appropriate problems. Between the two extremes, the methodology is useful but requires some degree of adaptation.

Resources

1. "Ascertainment of Community Problems by Broadcast Applicants," *Federal Register,* January 7, 1976. Federal Communications Commission, 1919 M Street, N.W., Washington, D.C. 20554.
2. Harold Horn, Executive Director, Cable Television Information Center, 2100 M Street, N.W., Washington, D.C. 20554.
3. Minnesota Cable Communications Board, 500 Rice Street, St. Paul, MN 55103.
4. House Subcommittee on Communications, Room B-333, Rayburn House Office Building, Washington, D.C. 20515.
5. Frank Norris, Chief, Loans and Management Branch, TOSD, U.S.D.A., Rural Electrification Administration, Washington, D.C. 20250.
6. Ted Schwalbe, Telecommunications Policy Analyst, National Telecommunications and Information Administration, 1325 G Street, N.W., Washington, D.C. 20005.

Jean Rice

6. Cable Access: Promise of the Eighties

Cable access has developed into a community communications system in municipalities across the country. Despite major obstacles to the growth of cable access, the seventies saw the blossoming of this localized, often community responsive medium. New trends in business, technology, and regulation will have a profound impact on the availability of access to the cable medium.

The cable television industry is no longer primarily comprised of small firms organized for the cable market. Increased possibilities for lucrative returns have attracted new multiple system owners, including multinational corporations such as American Express, General Electric, Times-Mirror, and Time, Inc. (See Chapter 1 for detailed information on cable TV ownership and structure.) The credit climate has also changed with banks and insurance companies, which once declined cable loans, making large loans available. Concurrently, cable system prices and

At the time this paper was prepared, Jean Rice was a Senior Municipal Consultant, Division of Municipal Assistance and Policy Development, New York State Commission on Cable Television. Currently she is a Program Officer in non-broadcast technologies, National Telecommunications and Information Administration (NTIA). She also serves on the Board of the National Federation of Local Cable Programmers (NFLCP).

stock values are increasing rapidly. These business trends have stimulated increased bidding for municipal franchises and increased access package offerings, however questions of oliopolistic competition and concentration of media ownership are raised. Another major new development in the industry is the franchising and cabling of major urban areas. While sections of Manhattan and Los Angeles have had cable TV for years, most urban areas have not been wired. Late seventies economic conditions, coupled with ownership consolidation and pay TV revenues, have primed the industry to undertake the wiring of virtually all metropolitan areas. Cable access in the cities offers new promise of providing access to the television medium for persons who traditionally have not had access, and for meeting specialized urban information needs.

Technological innovations of a few years ago are becoming the mainstay of the cable industry. Twelve channel systems are outmoded by systems of 35, 54, or more. One of the bidders for the franchise in the Queens borough of New York City has offered to bring 125 channels to subscriber homes. Two-way polling and audio-video capability, once only offered on flagship systems, is a common part of today's urban franchise proposals. Satellite promise has become a reality as over 1,200 cable systems now receive multiple channels through low-cost satellite receive stations. These technological trends bring added channel capacity for entertainment, news, and access programming, and the capability for more interactive programming.

New regulatory trends have also surfaced in 1979. In April, the Supreme Court's *Midwest Video* decision held that the Federal Communications Commission (FCC) did not have the jurisdiction to mandate access to cable television. This ruling ended federal regulation that had been in existence since 1972. Most municipalities franchising during that time period had relied, in some way, on those rules to further the public interest by requiring the allocation of access channels for public sector use. The rescinding of this regulation has placed the burden of ensuring access on states and municipalities. Only two states have regulations regarding access and one other is presently proposing adoption of such regulations. Municipalities, which have varying levels of knowledge about cable television and sophistication in negotiating contracts, are now the prime regulatory entities. (See Chapter 3 for more detailed discussion of state regulatory activity.)

Cable access regulation has been one of the issues focused on during congressional efforts to rewrite the 1934 Communications Act. Several bills, which were under discussion in 1979, proposed changes to the 1934 Act, but none of them placed regulatory responsibility for cable access within the FCC's jurisdiction. In the Senate, Senator Hollings introduced S.611, under which state and local governments would continue to have their present right to require access. Senator Goldwater's S.622 and subsequent drafts proposed prohibiting state and local government regulation of access. In the House, Representative Van Deerlin's Bill, HR3333, would have prohibited state and local governments from requiring access without compensation to the cable operator. Municipalities and access programmers participated in congressional hearings to voice concern about the restrictive access provisions of the various bills. Given the intent of these bills, the public interest in public access may best be served by congressional inaction. This may be the outcome in 1980 since the House and Senate Subcommittees on Communication are focusing their attention on common carrier amendments to the Communications Act. In the near future cable access regulatory responsibility is likely to remain in the hands of state and municipal governments.

The legacy of new business, technological, and regulatory trends, in conjunction with obstacles cable access faced in the seventies, will have a dramatic impact on access of the eighties. Presented here is an overview of the development of access; discussion of the *Midwest Video* decision and the national, state, and local response to it; and description of the new developments which will expand the scope of access.

Development of Access

The FCC launched the cable access experiment in 1972 by requiring cable operators, in certain locations, to provide the public sector with access channels and five minutes of free production time. These modest beginnings offered only a soapbox. Today with additional equipment, staff, financing, and community involvement, cable access offers a unique intra-community communications system. What makes cable access unique is its accessibility, that anyone in the community may produce a program; its lack of gatekeepers, that each person has control over the message he/she produces; and its availability, that it offers the capacity to narrowcast programs to a specialized local audience. While the public has little if any involvement in the content or production of broadcast television programming, cable access provides a refreshing alternative.

This local alternative is far more widespread than many decision makers, industry experts, and local programmers realize. The National Cable Television Association's 1978–79 *Cable Services Report* surveyed its membership, and 919 cable systems responded. Of those systems, 400, or 43 percent, provided an average of 1.4 access channels, or 566 channels total.

A wide variety of organizations have been involved in establishing access centers. Libraries, schools, consortiums of local organizations and institutions, nonprofit access groups, or the cable companies themselves often administer use of the access channels. In some areas an individual agency or organization will catalyze use of the access channel. For example, in Brookhaven, New York, the Youth Bureau began facilitating access use in 1978 with high school students involved in program production. By 1979 they cablecast an average of seven and one-half hours per week. In Sunnyside, Washington, the Migrant Education Support Services Project operates an access channel and cablecasts 18 hours per week of local programming. The Arkansas Legal Services was instrumental in forming the nonprofit Open Channel organization that will operate the access channel in Fayetteville, Arkansas.

Nonprofit, tax-exempt, community-based organizations like the one in Fayetteville, which are established solely to operate the access channels, have become the predominant organizational structure for access centers. (For more information on community video center operations see "The Public Access Experiment" in the 1977–1978 volume of the *Cable/Broadband Communications Book*.)

The involvement of a wide variety of organizations in facilitating access use, and the formation of nonprofit access centers around the country, is indeed remarkable when one considers the lack of consumer knowledge about the public's right of access to cable television. No nationwide publicity campaign heralded this new form of access to the television medium. The responsibility for informing citizens of their rights and how cable access could serve their needs, and in financing and promoting use of the channels, lay with the community itself. Word of cable access and the promise it held was largely spread by word of mouth.

While diversity and localism are the strength of community access, communities have a considerable amount of information to share with each other on center structures, operation, and programming. In 1977 the National Federation of Local Cable Programmers (NFLCP) was formed by persons involved in cable access to facilitate the exchange of information between communities, to assist municipalities interested in local cable programming, and to provide direction on state and national policy. The NFLCP is a volunteer-run organization that is supported on membership dollars. Over 600 individuals and organizations from 40 states belong to the organization. Members include community organizations, access centers, librarians, educators, cities, and a cross-section of access users. Through its national and regional conferences, quarterly newsletter (the *Community Television Review*), and committee activities, the NFLCP is helping overcome the obstacles of isolation and lack of information. This exchange, stimulated by the NFLCP, has been a vital element in increasing the success rate of access centers and in the development of new access facilities across the country.

Federal regulatory mandates which required the reservation of channel capacity stimulated access development, but, at the same time, the preemptory nature of the rules severely impeded its growth. In-

Samplings of Amount and Types
of Cable Access Programming

Cable access provides the local alternative to normal television fare. Following is a sampling of the amount of programming shown on cable access channels around the country: In 1978, in Rome, Georgia, the Tri-County Regional Library cablecast 2,626 hours of programming; on Cape Cod, Massachusetts, Cape Cod Cablevision Access Channel 11 cablecast 1,300 hours;and the St. Johnsbury, Vermont, Co-op cablecast 200 hours. In 1980, WELM Public Access in East Lansing, Michigan, produces 110 programs per month; the Video Action Center in Columbus, Indiana, produces 235 hours per month; York Community Access TV in York, Pennsylvania, cablecasts 24 hours per month; the Miami Valley Cable Television Council in Centerville, Ohio, cablecasts 60 hours per month; and the Schenectady Access Council in cooperation with the Schenectady, New York, cable company, cablecasts 60 hours per month.

To illustrate the various types of programs offered to viewers in a particular community, below are descriptions of some of the programming in Rome, Georgia; Schenectady, New York; and Madison, Wisconsin.

In Rome, cable subscribers can view:
Check-Up, a weekly series where doctors discuss various medical problems and concerns such as heart disease and cosmetic surgery;
Birthdays, weekly celebrations of area residents's birthdays;
Discoveries, featuring people and places, and hosted by the local museum curator;
Folk Art, focusing on folk artists living in the North Georgia region;
Legislative Report, state legislators answering questions posed by reporters from the local media;
Happily Ever After, a daily children's program;
Know and Tell, a quiz program for fourth graders;
Look Into Our World, a program that promotes public awareness of the needs and public concerns of handicapped people;

itially, the FCC precluded local governments from utilizing the franchise fee, which they received from cable operators for using the public's right of way, for local programming. Other federal preemptions also stopped many municipal officials from seeking cable contracts that would enhance the public's access to the cable television medium by providing equipment, facilities, and technical assistance. In 1976 the FCC revised its access regulations and began allowing special access package agreements to be made in conjunction with franchise agreements. The FCC also granted waivers which allowed a portion of the franchise fee money to be used in support of local programming. Unfortunately, this

Readers Theatre, local actors reading scripts of area writers;
Spotlight on Business, discussing various local businesses and how they work, and hosted by the president of a local industrial corporation;
Tour of Homes, a documentary tour of historic homes in the area; and
What Will You Be? A career information series.

In Schenectady, some of the programs produced for the access channel include:
County Advocate, focusing on county agencies;
Schenectady, a daily community affairs program;
Dominick Lecie Speaks Out, an individual editorial;
City Council Meeting, live coverage by high school students;
Cala Page Presents, a weekly program featuring music, dance, drama, and poetry from local guests;
WAGIT(Women Are Getting It Together), program produced by women, featuring topics of interest to women;
Apostolic Pentacostal Church, religious program hosted by the Reverend of the Schenectady Pentacostal Church;
Electric City Forum, discussion program with local officials; and
Panorama, a series presented by the cooperative extension service, focusing on nutrition.

Among the many local programs that Madison, Wisconsin, cable viewers have been able to see are the following:
ERA, a call-in program about the equal rights amendment;
Studio None, long-running series by local video artists;
Art Exchange, series on local artists, art galleries, and sidewalk art fairs;
Warzagrass, a children's play written by area students;
The Oriental Art of Bonsai, a how-to program;
Dr. Acharya on Cancer, a controversial researcher's opinions on cancer;
Reynolds and Hynes, local musical group;
Visit to the Methodist Retirement Center, beginning of a series for Madison's senior citizens;
Off the Wall, skate-boarding demonstrations;
Tennis Player, weekly call-in instructions with a tennis pro;
The Myth of Epilepsy, call-in program on epilepsy; and
Madison Review of Books, discussion and book reviews.

came four years after the FCC began the cable access experiment and the change in policy was not widely publicized. Today, hundreds of cable programmers are bound by 15-year franchise agreements that have no provision for the financial support of access programming.

The amount of funding available to support access use is a determining factor in the utilization of access channels. For example, the Tri-County Regional Library in Rome, Georgia, supports access and it cablecast 2,626 hours of programming in 1979. In East Lansing, Michigan, WELM 70, the public access channel, supported by the cable company franchise fees, in 1979 cablecast approximately 1,600 hours of programming. This is in addition to programming cablecast on four educational channels, one municipal channel, and one library channel. In a recently franchised area, Cape Cod, Massachusetts, the cable operator financially supports access and 1,300 hours of programming were shown in 1979. Many communities, like St. Johnsbury, Vermont, have no city or operator funding, and the number of hours of access programming produced is correspondingly limited. It is a tribute to local initiative that even without ongoing financial support from the city or the cable company, these communities, with an all volunteer effort, have raised funds, from a variety of sources, for the necessary personnel and facilities. In fact, some access centers that have been operating for several years have found sources within the community to financially support a large-scale access effort. In these communities access usage has grown slowly but steadily.

The growth of access despite widespread lack of consumer knowledge and the pervasive obstacle of federal preemptions on primary sources for funding can be attributed to the public's desire for access to the television medium, growing sophistication on how to operate access centers, the fact that many access programs address the needs, interests, and concerns of the community, and the formation by cable programmers of a national service organization.

Midwest Video

Communities that do or would like to utilize cable access confronted a new obstacle to the growth of the dedicated use of cable access channels in April 1979. At that time the U.S. Supreme Court in a 6-to-3 decision ruled that the FCC did not have the jurisdiction, derived from the 1934 Communications Act, to require channel capacity, mandatory dedication of access channels, or access equipment obligations. Thus ended seven years of federally-mandated access to cable television.

The Supreme Court's decision was the culmination of a suit brought by the Midwest Video (Cable) Corporation against the FCC. A major ruling in the case, which contested the FCC's ability to promulgate access rules, was handed down by the U.S. Court of Appeals for the Eighth Circuit. On February 21, 1978, the Court of Appeals ruled in favor of Midwest Video on the basis that the access requirements were not "reasonably ancillary" to existing broadcast regulation. The court found that no similar requirements were made of broadcasters and further that, based on the Communications Act of 1934, the FCC had no grounds for requiring "common carrier" like obligations on cable systems because the Communications Act of 1934 states that "a person engaged in radio broadcasting shall not ... be decreed common carrier." The dissenting opinion on the case takes issue with the conclusion that the 1934 Act forbids the FCC from imposing common carrier regulation on broadcasters. The dissenting justices pointed out that the section mentioned is in a definitional section of the Act and was not meant to be jurisdictional in nature. The FCC argued that it had the jurisdictional grounds to establish access regulations and that the access rules did not treat cable systems as common carriers. While the court's ruling was based on jurisdictional issues, in its decision it discussed the constitutional issues raised by the case on First and Fifth Amendment rights (whether the First Amendment's free speech and free press protections and the Fifth Amendment's "due process" protections should be applied to cable operators as they are to newspapers).

The American Civil Liberties Union (ACLU) also challenged the FCC's 1976 access rule making, but from an entirely different point of view than that of *Midwest Video*. ACLU's suit contended that the 1976 rule making weakened access rules and was therefore not in the public interest. The Eighth Circuit Court's decision settled this case as well as the Midwest Video suit.

On appeal, the case was taken to the Supreme Court. Midwest Video's petition was supported by Teleprompter Corp., the largest cable TV multiple systems operator, while the FCC was supported by the American Civil Liberties Union, Citizens for Cable Awareness of Pennsylvania, Philadelphia Community Cable Coalition, and the National Black Media Coalition.On April 2, 1979, the Supreme Court upheld the Eighth Circuit Court of Appeals' decision that the FCC lacked the statutory authority to issue access regulation requiring the provision of access to the cable television medium by the public. This leaves open the possibility of legislative changes which would provide the FCC with the statutory authority to mandate access. (While the Supreme Court did not rule on the constitutional issues raised, it did note that such concerns were not frivolous.)

This decision presents a severe blow to the public's right of access to the cable medium. Throughout the country, local governments, educators, and the general public have relied on the FCC regulations. Many franchising authorities did not include franchise provisions regarding access channel allocations or equipment requirements, because they felt the FCC rules obviated them from needing to include them in their contracts. Others included access requirements in their franchises with the proviso, "as required by the FCC." Seven out of seven franchises in communities around Albany, New York, contained such provisos, which, of course, are no longer valid. The decision also circumvents the FCC's stated purpose of providing access to the medium by all citizens. Even though supporters of access across the country criticized the preemptive nature of the FCC's access rules, they supported the FCC's right to serve the public interest by mandating access to a communications medium that is a virtual monopoly.

The *Midwest Video* case elicited considerable national, state, and local concern and response. On the national level, the FCC received requests from over 40 access organizations from around the country to appeal the Eighth Circuit Court's decision on *Midwest Video*. Public interest groups like the ACLU, the National Federation of Local Cable Programmers, and the United Church of Christ, to name a few, have expressed their concern about the impact that the Supreme Court's decision will have on current and future access to cable television.

The FCC, while restricted from mandating access to cable television, did retain the authority to require mandatory program origination on the part of cable companies. In an effort to ensure that some local programming was available on cable systems, the Consumer Federation of America and The United Church of Christ petitioned the FCC in August of 1979 to reinstate its 1972 local origination rules giving local operators the option to comply with regulations by providing access channels. Many supporters of this petition see it as one way of ensuring a minimum level of locally originated programming and some opportunity for local expression. By April 1980, the FCC had not acted on this petition.

On the state level, two states have adopted access regulations and three are considering promulgation. The Minnesota Cable Communications Board, one of 11 state cable regulatory bodies, is retaining the access rules it has held concurrently with FCC access regulations. The rules basically track the FCC's 1976 access regulations. The rules basically track the FCC's 1976 access regulations. The New York State Cable Commission is the only state body which has formally proposed new statewide access regulations. The New York State Cable Commission is the only state body which has formally proposed new statewide access regulations in response to the *Midwest Video* decision. In Connecticut, the Office of Consumer Affairs has requested that the state's Public Utility Commission, which is the state cable regulatory body, promulgate access regulations. The Rhode Island Public Utilities Commission is in the process of setting statewide standards and access will be a part of those regulations. In California, a state without a state cable regulatory structure, the state legislature in 1979 passed a bill that permits voluntary rate deregulation for the cable industry. Individual companies, which meet specific eligibility criteria, may regulate their own rates if the companies provide channel capacity for access programming and support that programming by providing fifty cents per subscriber, per year, to a newly created Cable Foundation. Specifically mentioned in the California bill, the Cable Foundation was established by the state's cable industry and includes public, industry, and NFLCP representation.

Considering the loss of all federal access regulations because of the *Midwest Video* decision, the lack of access rules in all but two states by the end of 1979, and the denial by many cable systems of public sector access unless mandated by law, municipalities are recognizing the importance of local action. As the 1980s begin, including access provisions in local franchises is the only way to insure access to the medium by educators, the public, and the local governments themselves.

Providing Fully for Access Through Local Regulation

Cable operators have been predicting that in the next three to five years the majority of cities in the United States will be franchised. The franchising boom that has been underway since the end of 1978 has been characterized as the "last landgrab." Competition for franchise rights has never been more pitched. This increased competitive atmosphere can result in higher "stakes" in the community access package offerings. Mandating access channel capacity itself is becoming increasingly important. In 1972, cable television was heralded for its virtually unlimited channel capacity. Today, those channels are rapidly being filled by imported programming. The responsibility for ensuring that access channels are available for public, educational, and governmental use, that access packages meet community needs, and that compliance in these areas is enforceable, lies with the local government.

Municipalities initiating the franchising process usually establish a cable advisory board. This board serves at the pleasure of the town and city council and performs the following tasks: (1) informing itself and the community about cable television and what it has to offer; (2) ascertaining community needs; (3) preparing the request for proposals; (4) reviewing proposals and negotiating with cable companies; and (5) advising the council on which applicant offers the best service. The citizens advisory board plays an essential role in defining the community's needs in terms of access channel allocation, staff, facilities, and equipment, and in ensuring that the final franchise document reflects those needs.

Joint franchising, where several contiguous municipalities have franchises together, is a fast-growing trend. Through joint franchising each participating municipality can benefit from the knowledge and expertise of the citizens and staff of the others, can be sure that they receive an integrated system that would allow from the interconnection of access channels and institutional loops, and are often in a better position during negotiations with potential cable operators. For example, six cities near Dayton, Ohio, formed the Miami Valley Cable Television Council and granted a joint franchise. They boast a fully activated institutional loop and soon to be completed, two-way cable systems. Obviously, the larger the population in close proximity, the greater the probability of being able to negotiate a good access package.

Aside from the initial franchising process, there are several opportunities for access provisions to be included in local franchises: renewal and rate increase negotiations; five-year reviews; transfer proceedings; and, since the franchise is a two-party contract, any time both parties agree to amend the franchise.

Some cities are considering municipal ownership as an alternative to granting a franchise to a private company. One of the primary advantages to a municipally-owned system besides low rates, is the opportunity to use the revenues generated from cable television for additional services for local residents.

Whenever access provisions are being considered, whether for a privately- or municipally-owned system, the following items should be considered: (1) the community's communication and social needs; (2) ways the cable system can meet those needs (e.g., system design, two-way capacity, institutional loops, channel allocation, origination points, community viewing centers); (3) what ways the municipality, the community, and the cable operator can foster access (e.g., facilities, equipment, staff, training, outreach, financing); and (4) ensuring that the language of the access provision details each component of the requirement (e.g., equipment, penalty fees for non-compliance).

The increased compeitition for franchises and the growing sophistication of municipalities and their advisory boards has resulted in communities receiving better community access packages. Franchises granted in New York State since 1978 illustrate this trend. In Rensselaer, New York, the cable system serving 4,200 subscribers with a 57 percent rate of penetration, provides a color access studio and a full-time access coordinator. (Note, the Rensselaer franchise included the "As the FCC requires" provision on its access rules.)

In White Plains, New York, a community of approximately 20,000 persons, the city conducted shrewd negotiations in 1979 that led to the award of a franchise that is a model for cities its size. The White Plains franchise was the final component of a company countrywide system and has franchise provisions requiring dual trunk and upstream capability from at least 20 locations. The two-way system will have four access channels and a city school district institutional loop that allows for dissemination either to the schools alone or to the general public. An additional feature is a requirement that the cable system interconnect with any other cable system serving an adjoining municipality.

Nonprofit community production groups, named in the franchise, will encourage public access usage and be financed by payments from the company totaling $60,000, an additional $5,000 per month for 23 months, and a sixth of the franchise fee. The payments are conditional on the production of at least two hours of locally originated programming per week. The company also agreed to pay the school district an initial sum of $20,000 and $1,250 per month for 11 months with the school district agreeing to produce an average of one and one-half hours per week of locally originated programming for access cablecasting. The company has also agreed to originate 15 hours per week of local programming for the first year and 42 hours per week thereafter. The types of locally originated programming to be produced are specified in the franchise with minimum requirement for 20 percent local news and public affairs, 20 percent local and regional programming, 15 percent educational programming, and 15 percent entertainment programming. The automated programming is enumerated including an alphanumeric origination cablecasting of the tape origination and access programming. Staff and training, as well as a list of equipment for a fixed and a mobile studio, are required.

In Rochester, New York, the company that received the franchise agreed to provide $110,000 worth of equipment for company originated programming, $100,000 for access equipment, and a $40,000 mobile van for use by the company and access users. The company will also provide for an access staff, with a budget between $63,500 and $83,100 a year for the first five years and a total of $511,700 for years 6-10.

The Syracuse, New York, franchise requires the cable company to provide public access, local origination, local government, medical and health, and municipal training channels, and free channels for the development of interactive services. In this case the franchise requires the company to provide an access studio, a mobile van, and a minimum staff of three persons for the administration and operation of the central access studio. The company is also required to increase the minimum staff to at least six persons when the system achieves 40 percent penetration and to spend a minimum of $600,000 for local origination and access programming during the first 21 months of operation and $125,000 per year thereafter.

As one can see from the New York State franchises mentioned, a cable channel and equipment are only part of the components needed to make access channels a viable community communications system. Franchise agreements also need to include staff, training outreach, financing, and provisions for community involvement in decision making. Since the burden of access regulation lies with the states and municipalities, it is important for interested citizens to become politically sophisticated in dealing with governments and cable companies. It is also important for states and municipalities to draw on the experiences of the past and work through regulation and the contractual processes to see that the communications and social needs that can be met through cable access are indeed met. This includes regulatory mandates as well as ongoing supervision for compliance.

New Developments

New developments in the cable industry, increased interest in non-broadcast technology by the Congress and federal agencies, and new initiatives by local cable programmers indicate that cable access will be growing component of the media picture of the eighties.

Big City Cable

A major new development in the growth of the cable television industry is the wiring of large urban areas. New pay services and advertiser-supported programming offered through satellite distribution and new trends in cable ownership, have reshaped the economic viability of bringing cable service to the cities. Houston, Minneapolis, and Pittsburgh recently granted cable franchises and many other cities, such as Boston and Washington, D.C., are in the franchising process.

Cable access provisions are an extremely competitive component of the bidding for these franchises. Cable companies are offering multiple channels and studios, hub technical designs that allow programming to be cablecast to the entire city or to specified neighborhoods within it, two-way capability, training, large programming staffs, and adequate financing. Some companies are even offering to provide the access channels to any resident who pays a one-time installation fee. As these systems are constructed, a quantum leap will be taken in the number of persons who receive access channels.

Rural Communications

Rural America will also see a dramatic increase in the availability of multiple-channel services. Federal agencies, including the Small Business Administration, Community Services Administration, Farmers Home Administration , and the National Telecommunications and Information Administration (NTIA), are aware of the services cable can provide to rural residents and have either provided loans or grants to nonprofit telecommunications entities to cable rural areas. For example, the Western Wisconsin Communications Cooperative in Trempealeau County, received a Rural Electrification Administration loan to build a cable system that serves 8 school districts, 11 communities, and 3,600 rural homes. This cable system provides two-way capacity between the schools for in-service training and an exchange of course offerings; educational, cultural, and municipal programming for the public; and entertainment services. An NTIA grant has provided production capability from the county seat. Mississippi, Washington, and North Carolina are some of the other states that have rural cable systems underway. Federal agency initiatives prompted by congressional action, coupled with the telephone companies' ability to provide service to rural areas will bring multiple television channels and local access programming that can address specific rural needs, to a much larger proportion of rural residents. (A report of the Office of Technology Assessment (OTA) on Communications and Rural America is excerpted in the 1977-1978 volume of *The Cable/Broadband Communications Book*, providing some understanding of major concerns, costs, and services involved.

Two-Way Interactive Cable

Two-way cable technology provides innovative programming opportunities, but, as pointed out in Chapter 12 of this book, possible threats to individual liberty as well. Chapter 12 provides detailed discussion of three innovative experiments: one commercial—the QUBE system in Columbus, Ohio; and two in the area of public service—in Reading, Pennsylvania, and in certain localities in Japan. The Reading experience will be briefly described here.

Approximately 20 hours of live, two-way audio and video community programming is cablecast in Reading each week. A variety of programs is offered, including discussions of local issues with city officials, public hearings, sing-alongs, and discussions between senior citizens and high school students. Through use of a split screen, participants at two senior citizen centers, a community center, and up to four mobile locations can be visual participants of local programs that can also be seen in subscriber homes. Home viewers often participate in program discussions by telephone. The interactive programming was initiated by the Alternate Media Center, through a grant from the National Science Foundation, to utilize two-way cable television to deliver social service information to senior citizens. The inactive programming proved popular and this access project is now operated and financed by the community and the scope of programming has been broadened to be of interest to all city residents. The Reading experience clearly illustrates the benefits of two-way cable in promoting intra-community communications.

Two-way capacity is also being offered on a number of new systems. In Westchester County, New York, all of the municipalities in the entire county will be double wired, allowing origination from any point on the system. Older systems also have the potential of providing two-way services if, when they rebuild, they utilize the old cable to form an upstream loop as was done in Reading. While considerable community effort is required to sustain two-way cable programming, the benefits are exceptional. (For questions on privacy, see Chapter 12.) Cable capacity and local initiative will determine the growth of innovative interactive programming and services.

Multiple Technologies and Networking

Cable coupled with other technologies such as Instructional Television Fixed Service (ITFS), satellites, and broadcast stations, can provide new opportunities to serve community needs. Kirkwood Community College in Iowa is constructing the first phase of a region-wide interactive system that will utilize four ITFS channels, two-way microwave links, and access channels on existing cable systems. The first use of the system will be educational, with plans to expand to municipal and public programming. A few communities, like Reading, Pennsylvania, are proposing cooperative arrangements between cable access centers and broadcast licensees who see the need for local programming in areas served by translators. In another cooperative venture, cable access centers are utilizing satellite feeds of national programming in conjunction with local programs. In the future, cable access centers will use satellite to send programs of more than local interest to the entire county on a long-term basis. The use of multiple technologies will further expand the use and distribution of access programming.

County, state, and regional cable networks have been and are being formed around the country, through the use of hard wire, microwave, and translator interconnects. The cable systems for 15 cities in and around Dayton, Ohio (including the 6 mentioned earlier, in the Miami Valley, who franchised jointly), are interconnected to distribute access programming. A cable interconnect for the delivery of educational programs was initiated by the University of Pennsylvania and now provides programming to 283,000 subscribers and microwave interconnects with other systems are under construction. The cable office of the New Jersey Public Utilities Commission is conducting an engineering study for the interconnection of the state's cable systems. These are just a few examples of the trend to interconnect cable systems to distribute municipal, educational, and public programming of more than local interest. Further discussion of public services, particularly via satellite, is provided in Chapter 10.)

Government Programming

Due to regulatory and financial constraints, the development of specialized governmental uses of cable channels has proceeded slowly. While a majority of access channels carry city council meetings live, few cities in the past seven years have utilized access channels specifically designated for governmental purposes. Tulsa, Oklahoma, and Madison, Wisconsin, were among the first cities to program a governmental access channel. However, in the last two years more municipalities have begun similar services. In Albany, The New York State Commission on Cable Television operates a government access channel that reaches 13 municipalities and 550,000 subscribers. In Manhattan (New York City), the Municipal Access Channel L reaches 150,000 subscribers on two cable systems. Telephone call-ins are a standard feature of Manhattan municipal programming which includes *Manhat-*

tan At Large, discussions of city problems including "The Reorganization of the Poverty Programs," "The City Can Meet the Budget Without Cutting Services," and "Community Board," where each week one of the nine community boards leads the discussion on topics in the district. On the federal level, coverage of floor sessions of the U.S. House of Representatives is available to cable subscribers all over the country through C-SPAN, the Cable Satellite Public Affairs Network (described in Chapter 10).

Educational Access

While many educational institutions provide programming for public access channels, only a few specially designated educational access channels have been developed. For example, in Spokane, Washington, a consortium of 13 junior and senior high schools, 2 state universities and the local PBS station program 5 educational access channels, and 1 medical education channel. While these and a few other models of specialized channels have been developed, widespread development has just begun to surface. As the number of cable systems with 35 channels or more are constructed, the more opportunity there will be for the development of specialized programming. Specialized channels of the next few years could include foreign language, women's, minority, captioned programming, mental health, and "how to" channels.

Federal Aid

Congress illustrated its interest in developing public uses of non-broadcast technologies in 1978 when it changed the name of the Public Broadcasting Financing Act to the Public Telecommunications Financing Act. The new legislation authorized the Public Telecommunications Facilities Program of NTIA to support planning and construction grants, for the extension of non-commercial educational and public programming, and for the provision of services to specialized audiences, through broadcast and non-broadcast means. In 1979, the first year of the authorization, 17 non-broadcast grants were awarded. This attention to the potential of non-broadcast technologies may be the first step in congressional recognition and financial support for access programming that utilizes the developing technologies.

Access in the Eighties

Prospects for growth in the eighties have a solid grounding in the lessons learned and obstacles overcome in the last decade. Cable programmers have become more sophisticated in generating community responsive programming, access organizations have become increasingly able facilitators of community use of the access channels, and many municipalities are now ascertaining community information needs and negotiating strong franchise standards. The National Federation of Local Cable Programmers will continue to play a vital role in informing municipalities about access and facilitating information exchanges between access programmers. Access has continued to grow even though great obstacles were presented by a lack of consumer knowledge about access and preemptive federal requirements which restricted the funding base for access operations. It is the need for access to a communications medium and local pressure to have and use it, that has stimulated access despite impediments.

The *Midwest Video* decision places the responsibility for access regulation and its maintenance in the hands of state and municipal authorities. It is incumbent on them to learn what access can offer and ensure the public's right of access. It is the responsibility of interested citizens to make their desire to use these channels known at the state and local level. There is still a vast consumer education need for informing state and municipal governments, and local residents about the opportunities offered by access and how to obtain them.

New developments open new avenues for cable access. Urban and rural expansion, if coupled with clear access directives, will extend the reach of access channels and will afford the development of programming that meets distinct communications and social needs. Two-way technological advances and cable access coupled with other technologies will offer the possibility of new programming initiatives. Cable networks and specialized channel use are on the increase and will provide continued diversity in cable access offerings.

These developments in conjunction with congressional attention, effective regulation, and a lion's share of local initiative make the "blue sky" promises of cable access a reality in the eighties.

Resources

1. Austin Community Television, Box 1076, Austin, Texas 78767; 512/478-8600.
2. Berks Community Television, 1112 Muhlenberg, Reading, Pennsylvania 19602; 215/374-3065.
3. Brookhaven Youth Bureau, Town of Brookhaven, 227 Main Street, Port Jefferson, New York 11777.
4. Cable Channel 10, 224 Clinton Street, Frankfort, Kentucky 40601; 502/277-4480.
5. Cape Cod Access, 28 White's Path, South Yarmouth, Massachusetts 02669; 617/771-3700.
6. Community Access Channel 7, Monroe Public Library, 303 East Kirkwood Drive, Bloomington, Indiana 47401; 812/339-2271.
7. Community Services Directory, National Cable Television Association, 918 16th Street, N.W., Washington, D.C. 20006; 202/457-6772.

8. Community Television Review, Newsletter of the National Federation of Local Cable Programmers, P.O. Box 832, Dubuque, Iowa 52001; 802/229-4508.
9. City of Syracuse, Office of Special Projects, Rm. 225, City Hall, Syracuse, New York 13202; 315/473-5690.
10. East Lansing Public Access Center, 1070 Trowbridge Road, P.O. Box 918, East Lansing, Michigan 48823; 517/351-0214.
11. Fayetteville Open Channel, N.W. Arkansas Legal Services, 530 N. College Street, Fayetteville, Arkansas 72701.
12. Kids Alive, P.O. Box 142, Sun Prairie, Wisconsin 53590; 608/837-6775.
13. Kirkwood Community College, P.O. Box 2068, 6301 Kirkwood Blvd., S.W., Cedar Rapids, Iowa 52406; 319/398-5481.
14. Migrant Support Services, Sunnyside, Washington 98944.
15. Madison Community Access Center, 1024 Regent Street, Madison, Wisconsin 53715; 608/266-9060.
16. Manhattan Channel L, 49 East 68th Street, New York, New York 10021.
17. Miami Valley Cable Television Council, 100 West Spring Valley Road, Centerville, Ohio 45459; 513/434-2053.
18. Pennorama, The Worthington Scranton Campus, 120 Ridge View Drive, Dunmore, Pennsylvania 18512; 814/863-1984.
19. Public Telecommunications Facilities Program, National Telecommunications and Information Administration, 608 13th Street, N.W., Washington, D.C. 20005; 202/724-3307.
20. National Federation of Local Cable Programmers, P.O. Box 832, Dubuque, Iowa 52001; 215/374-3065.
21. New York State Commission on Cable Television, Tower Building, Empire State Plaza, Albany, New York; 518/472-4992.
22. Rensselaer County Access, P.O. Box 439, Rensselaer, New York 12144; 518/283-6159.
23. Schenectady Access Cable Council, 830 McClellan Street, Schenectady, New York 12304; 518/370-3955.
24. Spokane Cable Project, KSPS, 3911 S. Regal Street, Spokane, Washington; 509/455-3709.
25. State of Minnesota Cable Communications Board, 500 Rice Street, St. Paul, Minnesota 55103; 612/296-2545.
26. State of New Jersey Cable Office, Dept. of Energy, 1100 Raymand Blvd., Newark, New Jersey 07102; 201/648-4009.
27. St. Johnsbury Television Co-operative, Box 333, St. Johnsbury, Vermont 05818; 413/748-9653.
28. Tri-County Regional Library, 606 West First Street, P.O. Box 277, Rome, Georgia 30161; 404/291-9360.
29. Western Wisconsin Communications Co-operative, 205 Osseo Road, P.O. Box 326, Independence, Wisconsin 54747.

Lynne E. Bradley

7. Libraries and Cable: Access to Information

Why are libraries involved with cable television? One of the main reasons is to increase the public's access to information. It should be common knowledge by now that libraries provide more than just books. The main service of libraries is information, regardless of the format. Films, videotapes, computerized data bases, and community information files have been developed and produced by public libraries as well as by libraries in schools, colleges, corporations, and other institutions. "New" materials, coupled with traditional library items such as books, magazines, and other print materials, are tremendous sources of information. This abundance of resources cries out for broad accessibility to the widest audience. Libraries embrace the use of cable television as an opportunity to extend their information services to the largest clientele. Cable has offered libraries the opportunity to reach not only traditional library users but also many non-library users, including non-readers.

One factor which encourages libraries to utilize cable is that cable TV allows narrowcasting of unique programming and information services that do not necessarily appeal to large audiences served by "mass media." Cable provides libraries with a distribution system for a variety

Lynne E. Bradley is the Video Librarian at the District of Columbia Public Library, and formerly Chairperson of the Video and Cable Communications Section, American Library Association. She is a contributing editor to CableLibraries *newsletter.*

of live and taped aural and visual programs. Cable programming can serve those interested in stamp collecting or romantic novels or bilingual children's stories or local consumer complaint procedures or discussions of local history and current events. Cable's technical capabilities can provide distribution of electronic data bases and information files including entire "card catalogs" into individual homes. With the advent of two-way, interactive cable capability, users will have more individualized access to information. An individual will be able to sit down at his/her own video terminal and access information on an individual basis not unlike someone reading a textbook or novel at his/her own speed.

There are many variables affecting how libraries have initiated involvement with cable television. Local needs and resources in any particular community determine the different cable activities. Long before libraries purchase video equipment or have access to a local cable system, library staff members have been able to provide information about cable television and to facilitate the development of local knowledge about cable issues. For example, many libraries have started by providing books, pamphlets, magazines, bibliographies, etc., about cable communications; libraries have sponsored panel discussions, workshops, and other programs educating and informing their communities about cable; and libraries continue to provide information about local, state, regional, and national sources for additional information about cable and video resources.

Even without a cable system, libraries utilize video programming to broaden their services to readers and non-readers alike. Prior experience with video programming as an information tool helps the community and library staff gain technical and programming experience that encourages appreciation for electronic communications and visual resources. By the time many new cable systems are operational or new franchises negotiated, libraries are there with information about cable opportunities and with video resources to facilitate the development of cable programming.

Levels of Involvement

Library involvement with cable television can be illustrated as a spectrum of activities starting with basic information about cable TV and the ordinance/franchising process. This should be a continual function for libraries regardless of any other video and cable commitments. Subsequent levels of involvement lead to video playback services, production of video programming, use of cable access channels and ultimately, though still infrequently, programming via two-way cable.

Table 7-1: Levels of Library Involvement in Cable TV

Level I: Basic Information Services About Cable	Level II: Video Playback Service	Level III: Video Production Capability	Level IV: Use of Cable Channel on Shared, Cooperative or Dedicated Basis	Level V: Two-way Cable Capability
*Information available on the ordinance and franchising process.	*Library provides video programming and equipment for playback in the library.	*Library produces video programming either in cooperation with other local groups or in-the-library.	*Cable system constructed and operational.	*Library provides on-line data bases, video programming, while using two-way capability.
*Information available on the local, regional, state, and national resources including software sources, maintenance and repair information, consultants, producers, and activities of other communities already involved with cable and video.	*Video collection from local and national sources may include adult education, consumer information, local TV documentaries, school productions, video as art, etc.	*Provides workshops on the production and utilization of video programming.	*Library programs all or part of a cable access channel either through a combined municipal access channel, a cooperative educational access channel, or a dedicated library channel.	
*Information available on cable's economic, social, and educational issues through books and other media, workshops, panel discussions, etc.	*Promotes the use of video both for library-sponsored programs and for other community programs.	*Continues to provide access to video programming through playback decks, closed circuit systems, etc.	*Facilitates public access by community groups, including information for productions as well as training on use of equipment.	
*Organization of programs and workshops on video and cable, and work with other community groups and agencies to educate the public.			*Facilitates getting video "experts" together with local groups.	
			*Provides cable channel viewing in library branches for those citizens without cable service and for other programming purposes.	
			*Develops in-library origination points.	

Types of Activities

Level I—Basic Information Services About Cable & Video

The library function of providing information about cable television and video programming helps local officials and citizens become more aware and informed about the potentials of cable, especially during the ordinance-writing and franchising processes.

For example, the Baltimore County Public Library pulled together information for its county council about municipal regulation of cable during a critical post-franchising debate over the cable operator's performance. In the District of Columbia, during its long ordinance-writing process, the D.C. Public Library is the only nonprofit or public agency which has participated in all of the public hearings on the ordinance held since 1970. And in Baltimore City, the Enoch Pratt Free Library has provided its cable coalition and other community groups with lists of speakers, referrals to other sources of information, access to its meeting rooms, and a bibliography on its cable materials and other resources to help educate and keep the community informed about the pending ordinance legislation and subsequent franchising process.

The Rockford (Illinois) Public Library demonstrates how providing information about cable and video services is one way to facilitate the development of community access. The Rockford library staff members continue to make their patrons more aware of the possibilities of video though the library has never purchased a videotape. "All" it offers is information. The Rockford library has worked with the local chapter of the National Federation of Local Cable Programmers (NFLCP) and co-sponsored a workshop on "Cable Access—Use It or Lose It." (A comprehensive picture of cable access—applications and issues—is presented in Chapter 6 of this book.) The library also cosponsored a workshop with the Rockford Women's TV Coalition on "Making Media Work for You." The purpose of these programs was to encourage community groups and agencies to utilize cable and media to inform and promote. The Women's TV Coalition then worked with the library to produce a program about the library's "Reading Is Fundamental" (RIF) program that encourages children to read and enjoy books. This TV program publicized the RIF project and gave the library additional experience at producing televised programming.

Meanwhile the library also worked with Northern Illinois University on the use of video as an intervention tool. As part of "Project Interact" the library has been making "soapbox" tapes of citizens' opinions about library services, recent proposed budgets and cutbacks, etc. Students from the University trained the library staff and other people from the community and helped with the productions. These tapes focused on people with conflicting opinions; the tapes were then shown to the library's board of trustees to provide them feedback about community interests and to resolve conflict.

Now the library is working with a committee developing a combined public television station and community access cable channel. When WPTR comes on-air sometime in the early 1980s the Rockford Public Library will continue to provide information and research to help with productions as well as develop its own library-related programming.

A truly service-oriented library will develop and maintain a basic information service about cable regulatory and programming issues regardless of any other involvement the library may have with cable resources. Such basic information services must be maintained and respond to community needs as cable evolves in its community.

Level II—Video Playback Services

A second level of involvement includes video information for patron and staff use since video materials are becoming a legitimate reference and information tool. The Donnell Branch of the New York Public Library has a Video/Film Study Center which presents regular video screenings and sponsors forums with local video and film producers. Its collection includes an extensive and unique group of video-as-art tapes. In California, the Los Angeles County Public Library System has six viewing centers located in its regional branches as well as a van with video, film, and audio playback capability to provide mobile media service. Like many libraries that are collecting video, the Los Angeles County Library includes in its collection materials on consumer information, how-to-fix-it, music, sports, and travel, as well as library staff training tapes. PBS Video (formerly Public Television Library) of the Public Broadcasting Service (PBS), reports that it has sold such programming to almost 400 different public libraries.

The George Washington University Library can be added to the list of academic libraries providing video reference. It has become the Regional Television News Study Center for the Vanderbilt University Television News Archives. Together these two universities provide unique resources for television news research. With Vanderbilt's publication *Television News Index*, videotapes of network news programs are now accessible to scholars and researchers; such programs can now be documented as true "original sources."

Libraries of the University of Maryland-College Park, the University of Wisconsin-Milwaukee, and the University of Tennessee, like many school and academic libraries across the country, continue to provide instructional programming on video. Their video collections can be used by teachers and students for specific class assignments in all academic areas as well as for information sources for individual research.

The use of video and other media as an important research tool is underscored in the Library of Congress which has reorganized and expanded its Motion Picture Section into the Motion Picture, Broadcast and Recorded Sound Division. In 1979 the Library of Congress's Cataloguing Department started including video materials in its media cataloguing services.

Such sources for video cataloguing are important to public, academic, and school libraries which must continually organize and catalog video materials in order to make them accessible to the public. The computerized bibliographic service of the Ohio College Library Center now includes video cataloguing from Library of Congress and Ohio College Library Center member libraries. Libraries are not mere storehouses of information; accessibility to library collections is based on cataloguing information. It is important that video materials are included in such sources of bibliographic data so that video can be as accessible as other library materials.

Cooperative cataloguing is not the only area where libraries can share. State libraries in California, Connecticut, and Texas have established circulating video collections. Some cooperative projects have been able to deposit video playback equipment at the participating libraries to facilitate video activities. Regional projects in Los Angeles and Chicago have also been established to work on selecting, cataloguing, and distributing video collections. The Suburban Audio Visual Service, supported by several suburban Chicago library systems, provides home format video programs to its participating members. In Los Angeles a regional collection emphasizes signed and captioned programs for the deaf and hearing impaired.

The Gallaudet College Library, a four-year liberal arts school for the deaf in Washington, D.C., continues to help identify captioned and signed video materials both for its own students and for librarians and others serving the deaf in local communities. Video is a unique tool for providing information to the deaf and such captioned/signed programs have been a featured part of the collection at the San Francisco Public Library's Communications Center.

San Francisco Public Library and the Cherry Hill (New Jersey) Public Library, like the Suburban Audio Visual Service outside Chicago, have been purchasing and circulating VHS and Betamax format videotapes for patrons to checkout. A few, such as the Seattle Public Library and the Enoch Pratt Free Library in Baltimore, are experimenting with videodisc. While the majority of libraries are still purchasing programs on three-fourths inch videocassettes, increasing numbers of libraries are collecting programs on VHS and Betamax one-half inch videocassettes. More will join the video ranks when videodisc becomes more widely available.

Much video programming is available from distributors. Most 16mm film distributors now make the majority of their titles available in video formats. Many public television programs are available on video from

PBS Video, as well as from agencies such as the Maryland Center for Public Broadcasting, WGHB-Boston, and the Great Plains National Television Library. Many independent video producers make their programs available through groups like Electronic Arts Intermix in New York City. Libraries also obtain programming when possible from local video producers and television stations. Such local documentaries are unique and prized additions to video collections since they are not available from any other kind of national source or producer.

The availability of so much video material means that most libraries are able to develop video collections on many subject areas and for all age levels. Collections usually include materials on high school equivalency, children's literature, storytelling, folklore, music, art, drama, consumer information, Black studies, job hunting, and reading improvement. Academic libraries can find programming for courses on Shakespeare, math, science, study skills, and much, much more. School libraries have access to videotapes from most of the traditional instructional television sources as well as the types of distributors listed above.

To help librarians and others identify and select video programming, the American Library Association publishes video reviews in *Booklist* magazine on a monthly basis. Other magazines like *CableLibraries* and *Sightlines* also identify video programs. The Video and Cable Communications Section of the American Library Association has published a bibliography of video sources and reviews to assist colleagues in the collection development process.

A basic video playback service can start with just one video player and television set or monitor. Library patrons can come into library, select a video program from a catalog, and view the program immediately. Many libraries utilize such equipment and tapes for public programs and video series. Libraries are also developing closed circuit television systems to distribute programming within their libraries. For example, the Seattle Public Library recently included an extensive media distribution system in the remodeling of its main library building; Hennepin County (Minnesota) Public Library has had a multi-media distribution system since 1975; and the University of Maryland-College Park has operated a dial-access closed circuit system since 1973 utilizing three-fourths inch videocassettes and having an eight-channel video capacity.

Video information and reference services are an important and unique tool for libraries and library users. Video playback services have also been valuable in providing library staffs with more technical experience, while getting feedback from library patrons on their programming interests and needs as well. Regardless of a library's involvement with cable, video activities have become a legitimate information function of libraries.

Level III—Video Production Capability

"Librarians don't write books—so librarians shouldn't produce videotapes." That's a statement frequently debated when librarians and others discuss the issue of library productions. And that statement is also a misconception about what librarians really do. A librarian may not author a book but library staff must catalog and organize collections, develop "finding aids" and bibliographies, and provide instruction on the use of library and information services. Libraries have developed extensive community information files to serve as central referral points to local services and activities—information not available in any book.

The key to all this is accessibility to information. A bibliography, a library catalog, a program on the use of the library, or a community information file are library-created communication tools that increase users' access to information. Considered in that light, the production of video programming is just another communications vehicle to increase accessibility to certain kinds of information.

Many libraries have started producing their own video programs though they have no cable system for distribution. The preliminary stages of this Level in Rockford (Illinois) Public Library and other libraries described earlier provide examples. Another, more fully developed, example is that of the Tucson (Arizona) Public Library, which is heavily involved in production as well as video playback services. The library produces its own programs on the Southwest environment, Southwest gardening, solar energy, and a unique series for children of bilingual (Spanish and English) stories based on traditional Southwestern folk tales.

The Tucson programs, which are in color and of broadcast quality, are the types of programs that the library obviously could not find from any other source. The tapes are on special topics that speak to the needs and interests of the library's patrons. While cable is anticipated in Tucson, the programs are presently available in the main library through a closed circuit distribution system to several areas, and in eight branch libraries which have video playback capability.

The Baltimore County Public Library also has its own color, broadcast quality studio from which it produces public service announcements for the library and other county agencies. For example, a special BCPL production, *Generations*, is a magazine format program for senior citizens which focuses on local history, special events for seniors, and other topics. The tapes, with playback equipment, are loaned for weekly periods for use in nursing homes and senior citizen centers.

Frequently cooperation with other agencies facilitates libraries initiating video productions. The Monroe County Library System, headquartered in Rochester, New York, worked with a local community video center to provide an eight-week video course for a dozen library staff members. The library staff, including audiovisual, young adult, and children's librarians, became familiar with video equipment and the potentials of production. In turn, the library sponsored the local video group as visiting artists, to bring a concert of locally produced video programs to the library. The young adult librarians, again working with the same video center, sponsored a series for teenagers who then made their own documentaries and video-as-art tapes. Now the library hopes to invest in its own recording equipment, both for the intrinsic value of video and in anticipation of cable opportunities as Rochester comes closer to being wired.

Elsewhere in upstate New York, the Clinton-Essex-Franklin Library System has used its video portapaks to tape children's storytelling and in-service training programs. It has also circulated its portapaks to other municipal agencies. For example, the local sewer department used the portapak with an electronic "bug" to snake down through the city's sewers so that engineers could make their sewer inspection via videotape.

The Port Washington Public Library on Long Island has been a pioneer on the use of video with the public. Now called "Media Port," the library's video project started in 1971 with a grant from the New York State Council on the Arts. The goals of the project were to train local citizens to make their own tapes, to encourage more awareness about community issues through video, and to make it possible for people to use video to exchange information and personal viewpoints. The library has now trained over 1,900 people to use its portable video equipment; over 700 tapes are in the library's collection which has a special emphasis on oral history tapes and interviews and discussions with local residents, including photographers and independent filmmakers.

Some libraries start doing video productions for staff training and library instruction. In San Jose, California, the public library has developed many tapes for staff development. Its programs have included training on the use of a computerized cataloguing network and bibliotherapy, as well as tapes for the public on how to use the library. A consortium of libraries in Milwaukee, Wisconsin, produced training tapes on the reference interview, emphasizing body language and the role of nonverbal communication between library staff and patrons. Baltimore County Public Library has produced a special program on the "nitty-gritty" problems for reference librarians such as how to deal with problem patrons, how long to spend on a reference question, and how to manage extremely busy periods.

Baltimore County Public Library will also serve as a headquarters for a Maryland State Library Video Network which will help member public library systems develop video services and produce public service announcements and staff training programs for each system. The West Virginia State Library fills a similar role for its entire state from its headquarters in Charleston.

Libraries are using everything from black and white portapaks to elaborate broadcast-quality studios to produce programming. These programs typically utilize video to speak to local and specialized needs and resources; this is video information that cannot be purchased from national or commercial sources and can best be made on a local basis. With the availability of low cost video recording equipment libraries have realized that the development of video collections includes library produced videotapes as an important service to which patrons respond. Whether building their own studios, cooperating with other agencies with production capability, or receiving grants to contract productions, libraries are increasingly engaged in video production even without cable television as a distribution system.

Level IV—Programming on Cable

Considering the library's information function and the experience that librarians have gained using video as an information tool and production medium, it is no wonder that with increasing frequency libraries are anxious, excited, and reasonably well prepared when cable television finally comes to a community. Some libraries still borrow, rent, and cooperate with other agencies to produce programming but as soon as they are ready, libraries utilize the distribution potentials of their cable systems. As more cable systems are franchised, libraries are negotiating and receiving cable drops, including origination points, or headends, to allow programs to go out from a library building onto the cable systems. In Ithaca, New York, the Tompkins County Public Library convinced the cable operator to have headend equipment installed in the library so that the library and public access programs can be distributed into the cable system from the main library. In Iowa City the library will be participating in a community access studio with its own origination point from which the programs can go into the cable. This kind of capability is an important consideration for libraries during the franchising process.

Experiences in a number of cities—for example, Memphis, Tennessee; Rome, Georgia; Altoona, Pennsylvania; and Bloomington, Indiana—demonstrate that libraries are not just superficially getting into cable activities but are maintaining and improving their cable services all the time. The Monroe County Library in Bloomington reports that it is now producing 40 new programs each month and involving about 20 community groups and 30 to 40 local residents in the productions. In addition to checking out portable equipment to local residents, the library also responds to specific requests for programs on the library's channel between 9a.m. and 5p.m. daily.

The Tri-County Regional Library in Rome, Georgia, has been cablecasting since 1974. It started with a 15-minute children's story series in January 1974, and by 1976 the local cable operator had turned over the entire daytime programming of the local access channel to the library. Now the library programs over 40 hours per week from its own productions; there are frequent special programs produced in the evening hours, such as city council meetings and citizen forums, to bring the average number of cable library hours to over 50 hours per week.

The Brunswick-Glynn County Regional Library, also in Georgia, uses its full color production facility in the library as well as a mobile van also with color production capability. The library has been recording local commission meetings and other political/government activities both for use on the cable channel and for later research and viewing purposes in the library's video department. The Brunswick-Glynn County staff check out video cameras and recorders to the public and provide training on the use of the equipment, especially for cable access purposes. So much was going on in the state of Georgia, that Brunswick-Glynn County Library and Tri-County Regional Library joined with other regional libraries in their state to coordinate and exchange information and video programming in hopes of softening some of the financial problems.

The Altoona Area Public Library in Pennsylvania is still very active. Its downtown Media Center provides citizens with access to video and other media of all kinds. Its mobile video van can do color, broadcast quality productions. Coupled with other productions from its studio the library continues to coordinate municipal and public access programming in Altoona. The library's service started from a single video portapak purchased with federal money from Library Services and Construction Act grant.

The Memphis-Shelby County Public Library in Tennessee provides another lively example of how libraries are pursuing cable activities. The Memphis library, which began cablecasting in 1973, is now programming five days a week from 9a.m. to 9p.m. with 95 percent of its programming being produced in-house. Some of its most popular series are *Talk with Authors*, a genealogy workshop series, and a local music series with jazz and bluegrass artists. A wine tasting series was also popularly received. Over 60 percent of the library's productions are done in its studio with the remainder being done on location. With its own headend at the main library building, the library staff has complete control of its own scheduling and programming arrangements.

The East Brunswick (New Jersey) Public Library does several weekly cable programs: *East Brunswick Live* features interviews with local officials, heads of organizations, and "personalities." There is a call-in portion on each show, which has turned out to be the library's most popular cable program. *Sessions* is another production featuring contemporary music composed and performed by local musicians. Children's programming has included puppet shows, penny theaters, a talent show, and regular library story hours.

Similar types of programs have been produced at the Tompkins County Public Library in Ithaca, New York, where one of its series, called *Top Shelf*, promotes library materials and services, and another series, *Community Information Services*, shares information about local agencies and activities and how citizens can make use of other local community services. The Steele Memorial Library in Elmira, New York, started cablecasting in 1975 and has produced programs on community affairs, crafts, and local artists and performers, as well as library-related programs on reading for children and adults. Construction of a new main library building will incorporate video throughout the building and provide studio space for continued cablecasting. And at the Pocatello (Idaho) Public Library has produced over 100 video programs and cablecasts for half of every hour from 8a.m. to 7p.m., Mondays through Fridays. Like libraries in Port Washington, New York, Utica, New York, and Bainbridge, Georgia, the Pocatello library loans video equipment and continues to provide backup and training on its use.

Space does not permit a listing here of all the libraries and all the programming they are doing on cable. *CableLibraries* in its monthly "Reports from the Field" column presents reports from new libraries that are getting into cable programming. The reports also indicate that those libraries that don't have access to a cable service want it. Those libraries that are not yet using an available cable system, want to start using it. And those libraries already cablecasting look forward to improved cable systems with two-way capability. The situation is always in flux, but the trend is that as more and more cable systems become operational more libraries are utilizing cable communications.

Level V—Two-Way Capability

Two-way capabilities should mean a lot to libraries and their use of cable television. Coupled with computer technology, cable can mean even greater accessibility to the information in libraries. Few libraries have had the opportunity to use more than telephones to approximate two-way services.

The main exception has been the Public Library of Columbus and Franklin County (Ohio), which has used Warner Cable's QUBE system. (Chapter 12 of this book presents a detailed discussion of two-way interactive cable, including QUBE.) The library has produced a monthly television program, *Home Book Club*, which allows viewers to talk back and provide their responses to discussions of current bestsellers. At the end of each show, readers/viewers may participate in selecting the next book for discussion. Through the same QUBE system, viewers can also request that the next book be mailed to their homes: using their home consoles, viewers can instruct a computer to print out the mailing addresses and the library then mails viewers paperback copies of the next selection.

The Columbus library staff hopes that these experiences with QUBE will make way for the library to provide home reference services via cable. Plans are underway to computerize dictionaries, reference tools, and community information files, which should enable QUBE subscribers to access this information through their QUBE consoles. Similarly, the Columbus staff hopes to put its catalog of library materials on-line via cable.

The Lexington Public Library in Kentucky received as part of the local franchising agreement, $260,000 from the successful cable applicant to purchase an automated circulation system that can be linked up to the cable. By 1981 both Columbus and Lexington libraries hope to have such systems operational utilizing the two-way capacity in their respective systems. Their colleagues at other libraries look to these two pioneers to help forge the way on such applications.

The opportunities for two-way cable to distribute other forms of data are exciting. Chapters 11, 12, and 13 of this book treat the computer-cable connection; libraries, already participating in several regional and national computerized bibliographic data networks, look to the commercial services described in those chapters as models of what could happen to library information presently available. Though none of these data services are offered at this time via cable from libraries, application of such technology to library services is a logical extension of existing cable and library activities.

Lacking two-way cable, many libraries are utilizing the telephone for direct talkback between homes and libraries. For example, in Rome, Georgia, the Tri-County library has a daily reference hour when viewers are given an opportunity to call up and request that any book, map, or other reference material be televised. Individuals wishing to see the exact reference source or a specific map can have these brought into their home via cable. While this application is hardly as sophisticated as QUBE, the Rome staff members report that this has been a unique service, especially for homebound library users. But using the telephone during call-in talk shows or discussions does not take the place of real two-way cable capability—a capability that is anxiously awaited.

Professional Activities

While libraries are waiting for two-way cable, many are still waiting for a cable system of any kind to come to their communities. Until cable, including two-way systems, are more widely available, librarians are helping each other and their communities to develop their knowledge of cable television. The American Library Association's Video and Cable Communications Section has published a handbook entitled *Video and Cable Communications: Guidelines for Librarians*, which is still available from ALA in Chicago. Until a second edition of the *Guidelines* is published in late 1980, the VCCS group has an information packet to supplement the original guidelines, including a bibliography on "Video Review Sources" and another on "Sources of Cable Information." VCCS continues to sponsor programs at ALA Conferences including discussions of the ordinance/franchising process, video fundamentals, the use of video and cable for research and reference, and applications of video and film materials. Since 1975 the same group has sponsored an annual *Video Showcase of Library Produced Videotapes* at ALA's summer conferences. The number and quality of library productions have continued to increase as more and more libraries become involved with video and cable. Initial efforts to establish an exchange between libraries of their own productions is one outgrowth of these annual showcases.

Since 1976 ALA's Video and Cable Communications Section has periodically surveyed library video/cable activities. During the original 1976 survey over 360 libraries responded; 190 of these were participating in some level of video production. A subsequent VCCS survey used a smaller sampling with more detailed descriptions of specific library activities for inclusion in the second edition of the VCCS guidelines to be published in 1980. Mirroring the decline and then spurt in growth of cable systems, these libraries report a gigantic boom in involvement with video service since 1976, including increased levels of video production and cablecasting. Summaries from the VCCS information are the basis for the "Reports from the Field" column in CableLibraries and a source for this article as well.

The American Library Association was also among the many groups participating in the first White House Conference on Library and Information Services (WHCLIS) held in Washington, D.C., in November 1979. Over 600 conference delegates (two-thirds laypersons; one-third library professionals) were joined by 3,000 alternates, observers, and volunteers to discuss and debate the future of library services. The application of many new information technologies including computers, satellite communications, and cable television were discussed and demonstrated during the meetings and caucuses, and in the exhibits. Major themes repeated in many of the final conference resolutions adopted by the delegates emphasized equal and full *access* to information. The development of a national information policy and the use of networks for many kinds of services and information formats were also endorsed by the conference. Included in the final report sent to President Carter in March 1980 was a special resolution on telecommunications:

> Whereas, we seek to maintain diversity and autonomy of libraries and their collections, and to provide a suitable communications system which will facilitate equal access to information for all citizens and eliminate the inequities created by physical barriers of time and distance, and to encourage a diversity of facilities and services,

Therefore be it resolved, that our national information policy encourage:

1) interconnecting all networks, fostering service in all States and Territories, and inviting the cooperation of all telecommunication industries to provide distributed access broadband common carrier service to homes, businesses, agencies and all libraries.

2) the integration of broadcast, conference, and private communications and document delivery of audio, data, and image transmissions and

3) provision of lower rates for libraries and educational services.

Many librarians supporting the development of telecommunications applications within the profession, as well as representatives from groups such as the National Federation of Local Cable Programmers and the National Citizens Committee for Broadcasting (who were also represented at the WHCLIS) supported this resolution as a way to demonstrate a national interest in the utilization of telecommunications in libraries.

The American Library Association and other library groups keep involved with telecommunications issues in other ways. ALA is a member of the Joint Council on Educational Telecommunications and the AdHoc Committee on Copyright; ALA works with these groups on issues such as off-air taping and funding for library telecommunications projects. Librarians also have voiced their opinions and concerns in efforts to rewrite the Communications Act; in fact, during the 1979 ALA Midwinter meeting in Washington, D.C., staff from the U.S. House of Representatives Subcommittee on Communications provided an open hearing on the rewrite proposal it was then considering, so that library interests could be heard. That bill has been shelved, and as of April 1980, no further action was planned; in the Senate, however, two rewrite bills remained under consideration. It is likely that librarians will be active in any ongoing efforts to update the Communications Act.

Many VCCS members and other cable librarians have worked on the local and national levels with the National Federation of Local Cable Programmers (NFLCP). A librarians' panel participated in the 1979 NFLCP national conference, while on the local level librarians have worked with NFLCP chapters in New York, Connecticut, Illinois and the MidAtlantic. VCCS has established a network of librarian-contacts to encourage communications both among librarians and with other cable programmers. The VCCS network regions were made the same as those of the regions of the NFLCP to facilitate exchange between the two groups.

National activities within the ALA are only part of the professional activities. State library associations in New York, California, Texas, Georgia, and Maryland have recently offered programs for their members on video and cable communications. Library schools at Syracuse University and Mankato State University (Minnesota) offer courses on cable technology; other library schools incorporate cable communications into their curriculums on new technologies and audiovisual services. Many library school students and practicing librarians are taking courses in communications, broadcasting, and other information sciences. Through such professional activities librarians are keeping up-to-date on the quickly changing developments in cable television.

The Realities of Funding

While it is easy to find many positive examples of cable-library activities the picture is not always rosy. Funding for library cable programming, which does not always come easily, is a persistent problem in light of severe budgetary constraints felt in every community across the country. Most libraries have funded their activities from a mixture of funding sources. For example, federal money from the Department of Education has been distributed on a state basis as Library Services and Construction Act monies. LSCA has been responsible for the startup of many library video programs in New York, Maryland, Washington, D.C., and California.

Several libraries have been successful at getting grants from state and national arts and humanities endowments. The Friends of Library groups have also helped raise outside money in other communities. In some instances, cable operators have offered equipment and assistance for local access. Many libraries are now reporting increasingly good relationships with local cable operators, while others continue to report uncooperative cable operators.

Active libraries in Rome, Georgia, and Memphis, Tennessee, would like to see reasonable methods for completing access channel audience ratings as one way of demonstrating their performance to funding authorities. Most libraries are so busy actually cablecasting and working with video that it is difficult to do audience surveys.

Developing new services and technologies such as the application of computers to local community information data and the interface of these and other computerized bibliographic data bases to cable systems has not been extensively tried by libraries. Simple as well as exotic uses of character generators for the display of print or bibliographic data via cable is an area that will see increased library applications but it will take funding and skill to develop these services. There is still much to do.

*   *   *   *   *   *

Experience is showing that libraries are keeping their commitments to cable by dedicating staff, equipment, and funding for cable and video programming. Libraries with their giant sources of information, are demonstrating that cable systems can effectively be used as true communication vehicles. The various levels of involvement reflected in library video and cable activities all reveal a consistent commitment to provide information. From information about cable TV to video playback and production services to cablecasting, libraries across the country are dedicated to making information *accessible* to all.

Resources

1. *American Libraries.* A monthly membership publication of the American Library Association, 50 E. Huron St., Chicago, IL. Recent articles have discussed such topics as selection of video equipment, video software, library video networks, etc.
2. Bahr, Alice Harrison, *Video in Libraries—a Status Report 1979-80* (White Plains, NY: Knowledge Industry Publications, Inc., 1979).
3. Boyle, Deirdre, ed., *Expanding Media* (Phoenix: Oryx Press, 1977). Reprints various articles discussing cable TV applications, guerilla television, and video as community information.
4. *Cablelibraries.* C.S. Tepfer Co., Ridgefield, CT. A monthly newsletter reporting on many video-cable issues including recent legislation, video software sources, and reports on library applications of cable and video technologies.
5. "CATV and Circulation Hookup Will Provide Online Catalog," *Library Journal,* December 1, 1979, pp. 2508-2509.
6. *Community Television Review.* Quarterly. National Federation of Local Cable Programmers, P.O. Box 832, Dubuque, IA. 52001.
7. "Direct Access via Cable Television," *Wilson Library Bulletin,* January 1980, p. 280.
8. Genova, B.K.L., "Video, Cable Television and Public Libraries," *Catholic Library World,* March 1978, pp. 328-331.
9. Katz, R. M., "Communication Technologies and Issues: the Librarian's Need to Know," *Catholic Library World,* April 1979, pp. 374-379.
10. Kenney, Brigitte, and Esteves, Roberto, *Video and Cable Communications: Guidelines for Libraries* (Chicago: American Library Association, 1975).
11. Norwood, F. W., "Telecommunications and Public Broadcasting," *A.L.A. Yearbook, 1979* (Chicago: American Library Association, 1979), pp. 279-284.
12. "Open Hearing on the Communications Act" (at the A.L.A. Midwinter Conference, 1979), *Journal of Library Automation,* March 1979, pp. 53-79.

John R. Barrington

8. Pay TV: Now a Staple on the Cable "Menu"

As the 1980s began, there were almost 6.5 million pay TV subscribers in the United States, the number having approximately doubled in each of the previous 2 years. Prospects were for an increase of another 3 million in 1980, and observers predict that every home in the nation will have access to some form of pay TV by the end of the decade.

Clearly, the concept of viewer-supported television has struck a responsive chord. In the summer of '77, when a pay TV chapter was prepared for the 1977-1978 volume of the *Cable/Broadband Communications Book (C/BCB)*, subscribers to all forms of premium television were 1.25 million—the harvest from almost five years of plowing, planting, and pruning since the first pay cable system had turned on. The number of locations where a subscription service could be had was below 600, and fewer than a third of those received their programs by domestic satellite.

In the intervening months, both subscriber totals and the number of viewing localities have increased five fold. Viewers may reside in any of the 50 states, Puerto Rico, or the U.S. Virgin Islands—or, while traveling, find pay TV a guest amenity in hundreds of hotels. The spread of

---

John R. Barrington is an independent public relations consultant, who has been Vice President, Public Relations, for both Teleprompter Corporation and Home Box Office. He is a member of C-TAM and Cable TV Pioneers.

satellite receivers has been even more dramatic, with substantially over two-thirds of all pay TV markets feeding off earth stations. While both over-the-air subscription television (STV) and multipoint distribution service (MDS) microwave systems have become established means of pay TV delivery, about 90 percent of all pay TV subscribers are served by cable TV systems.

Growth figures are only part of a pay TV progress report. Satellite transmission, beginning September 30, 1975, provided pay TV's most important impetus (and changed the face of the cable TV industry as well). However, a number of other milestones are noteworthy:

- The Federal Communications Commission's approval in December 1976 of 4.5-meter antenna dishes for receive–only earth stations put pay cable within reach of the very smallest cable systems. Over half of systems now offering a pay channel have fewer than 5,000 subscribers. (The Commission's 1979 removal of all regulation of receive stations creates new questions of direct-to-home transmission to be discussed elsewhere in this paper.)

- Broader program choices, particularly in the cases of motion pictures and sports, were created by the overturning of FCC pay cable rules protective of broadcast television. (A March 1977 U.S. Court of Appeals decision was left standing when the Supreme Court declined to review. The decision is described in Chapter 2 of this book.)

- As the public became aware of this programming phenomenon, acceptance mounted faster than almost anyone would have anticipated. In 1977, *C/BCB* reported that between 20 and 25 percent of cable subscribers where pay TV was offered, and about 12 percent of all homes passed, were taking the additional service. By spring 1980, both those figures have almost exactly doubled, to 41.3 and 22.3 percent, according to pay TV census taker Paul Kagan.

- Although programming has improved significantly in both quality and quantity, pay cable charges have increased less than the rate of inflation. The average monthly charge has gone up only from $6 to $8.25. Increasing numbers of cable operators are offering more than one pay cable service on the same system and making "combination sales" at $20 to $30 a month (including the basic cable charge). This "tiering" trend will be discussed in the marketing section of this paper.

For all of its lusty growth, pay TV (and especially pay cable) retains characteristics reminiscent of a seven-year-old human child—a bit cocky, perhaps, not always totally sure of itself, much richer in promise than in performance. To examine the industry's present and future, it is useful first to sketch in some background.

Some Definitions

What are the prevailing forms of pay TV? How do they interrelate? What is the distinction between cable TV and pay cable? At some risk of over-simplication, here are a few definitions:

Cable TV—Cable TV systems are broadband communications systems, capable of delivering multiple channels of entertainment programming and non-entertainment information, generally by coaxial cable. Some systems integrate microwave links into their overall design. Fiber optics are being tested and may, in the future, become a primary part of more technically advanced cable/broadband systems. "Basic" cable service generally is sold for a flat monthly fee, the purchaser receiving superior reception of off-air TV channels and, more and more frequently, a package of additional services such as imported distant stations, locally originated programming, public access channels, and government and institutional information channels.

Pay Cable—Using one or more available cable TV channels for an optional "pay" service (or services) has been a happy marriage that has made both pay TV and cable TV prosperous. Like other forms of pay TV, the cable system's pay channel is an alternative for which the subscriber pays an additional fee. Understandably, "pay cable" seems redundant and confusing to many prospective purchasers, especially since "basic" service often is considered purely as a necessity for obtaining the pay TV films, entertainment specials, and sports programs. The practice of "tiered marketing" tends to blur the basic/pay distinction still further.

Subscription TV—Known as STV, this form of pay service is delivered over the air by scrambling a UHF signal. Specially licensed by the FCC, STV services share air time with stations that function during the daytime as conventional local UHF outlets. At the beginning of 1980, 8 STV stations had approximately 400,000 subscribers in New York, Los Angeles, Detroit, Cincinnati, Phoenix, Boston, and Miami-Fort Lauderdale markets. STV charges generally are higher than those for pay cable, ranging from $19 to $23 monthly after an installation charge of as much as $90. STV and pay cable are viewed as more likely to be complementary than competitive when multi-channel cable systems spread through major markets.

Multipoint Distribution Service—Originally authorized by the FCC as a business communications service, MDS provides an omnidirectional microwave signal in the 2150-2162 Mhz frequency range that has proved to be an effective pay TV delivery system. Originally employed to feed apartment house master antenna systems, MDS has been able to make some inroads into single-family dwellings due to dramatic reductions in the cost of receiving equipment. MDS signals have an effective radius of approximately 30 miles from their transmitter but, due to their straight-line path, may be blocked by buildings or even a leafy tree. At the beginning of 1980, approximately 50 MDS operations served 278,000 subscribers. Wherever cable TV becomes available, it is thought that MDS operations will be absorbed or phased out. Bruce Merrill, a veteran cable operator, who is marketing both MDS and a new cable system in Phoenix, Ariz., says that MDS, introduced earlier at $18.95 a month, serves to pre-sell his cable when it becomes available a bit later with six tiers of service ranging from $3.95 to $25.95.

The Historical Perspective

When television—"radio with pictures"—began to be discussed prior to World War II, there were at least three options. It might have been a pay TV service from the outset, with viewers charged a monthly subscription fee or program-by-program. It might have emerged with viewers buying an annual license for their sets, as is the case in Great Britain and many other countries. Or, with radio broadcasters in the forefront of its shaping and testing, it could—and did—follow radio's example of commercial sponsorship.

As early as 1931, Zenith Radio Corporation was working on its Phonevision pay TV system, but not until 16 years later—after World War II—did the FCC authorize a three-months test of the system in Chicago. Three hundred households were selected by the National Opinion Research Center of the University of Chicago to provide a demographically balanced sample. An over-the-air signal was unscrambled upon receipt of a telephoned request for one of three film choices. The charge per showing was $1, and the average family expenditure was $1.73 a week, even though the most recent film had been in distribution for 27 months and all had been through numerous theatrical runs. Eleven years were to pass before Phonevision was tried again in a Hartford, Connecticut, experiment that set the stage for FCC authorization of pay TV on a very limited basis.

With opposition strong from both broadcasters and theater operators, several other ambitious over-the-air proposals failed to get started in the years prior to the Hartford test. Meanwhile, at least in part because cable TV was not then regulated, four wired experiments did take place:

Palm Springs, California—International Telemeter Corp. (of which Paramount Pictures was the majority owner) offered a selection of feature films, using a coin box attachment to TV sets, for five months in 1953.

Bartlesville, Oklahoma—Jerrold Electronics Corp. and Video Independent Theatres, Inc. (a motion picture theatre chain that owned all of

Bartlesville's movie houses) offered films for a monthly charge from September 1957 until June 1958.

Etobicoke, Canada—International Telemeter, through Famous Players Canadian Corporation, offered two channels of movies and one of sports and other attractions in a Toronto suburb from February 1960 through April 1965, again using a coin box attachment to TV sets.

Los Angeles, California—Subscription Television Inc., an offspring of the Skiatron Electronics system, launched service in May 1964 using an IBM-card billing device. Headed by former NBC President Sylvester L. (Pat) Weaver, the expensive project featured baseball games of the Dodgers and Giants, who had been lured westward from New York in part by the prospect of pay TV money. It had first–run movies and generated tremendous promotion and publicity fanfare. It also generated opposition from a well-organized "Crusade for Free TV" bankrolled by the National Association of Theatre Owners. The "Crusade" succeeded in winning a voter referendum to outlaw pay TV. Although the referendum later was ruled unconstitutional by the California courts, STI had declared bankruptcy and did not resume operation. In five months, it had acquired 6,000 subscribers among 100,000 homes passed.

The FCC Acts

The test that shaped the FCC's eventual STV and pay cable rules coexisted in part with both the Etobicoke and Los Angeles experiments. It began in June 1962, under a three-year FCC authorization that was twice extended, and lasted until January 1969. Zenith, through a subsidiary, Television Entertainment Company (TECO), operated an updated version of its long dormant Phonevision system over a Hartford, UHF station, WHCT.

TECO had major handicaps. Its system was not color compatible, so that all pay programming was in black and white. FCC restrictions were tight, and cooperation by motion picture suppliers was grudging at best. In six and a half years, the venture never achieved the 20,000 subscribers, or 10 percent penetration, projected for breaking even.

Nevertheless, the FCC relied heavily on Hartford data when it issued its *Fourth Report and Order* in 1968 authorizing token over-the-air subscription service in markets already well served by commercial TV. Immediately challenged in the courts, the rules did not become effective until 1970, when the Supreme Court refused to review a lower court decision upholding the FCC. Seven years later, STV service finally got underway in Los Angeles and in suburbs of New York City. These two stations now have about 250,000 and 75,000 subscribers, respectively.

Meanwhile, in its *First Report and Order* on cable regulation, in 1969, the FCC appeared to be inviting unrestricted pay TV experimentation on cable systems "unless and until experience gives some indication of a trend calling for action in the public interest." Eight months later, although there had as yet been no experimentation, and thus no "experience," the Commission reacted to broadcaster predictions of calamity with a memorandum extending the STV rules to cable (with minor variations).

In July 1972, the Commission issued a *Notice of Proposed Rule Making* that resulted almost three years later, in April 1975, in "final" pay cable rules. These extended the initial period of film availability for pay TV from two to three years after the start of theatrical ditribution, but they virtually eliminated use of sports events that ever previously had been on commercial TV. Challenged by cable and pay cable interests, the rule making was set aside on March 25, 1977, by the U.S. Court of Appeals. Subsequently, the Supreme Court refused to review the decision.

Getting Started

Although wired distribution systems figured in several early experiments, the cable TV industry's primary involvement was that of Jerrold Electronics' system in the Bartlesville, Oklahoma, test. In 1959, Teleprompter Corporation acquired its first cable TV system with the thought that its founders, Irving B. Kahn and H. J. Schlafly, could test a proposed pay TV system, Key TV. While Key TV, a push-button "answer back" system, never advanced beyond early feasibility tests, Teleprompter remained in cable TV to become the nation's largest multiple system operator (MSO).

Another early concept that failed to take off, Gridtronics, was previewed at the 1968 National Cable Television Association Convention by Alfred R. Stern, founder of TeleVision Communications Corporation, since acquired by Warner Communications. A four-channel service, some vestiges of Gridtronics survived in Warner's Star Channel motion picture service, and later in its QUBE system at Columbus, Ohio.

By the dawn of the 1970s, cable TV had attracted a flock of pay TV suitors. Warner announced its Star Channel plans. Hughes Aircraft Company was separately involved with Teleprompter and with Time, Inc. in pay TV development projects. Optical Systems demonstrated a "black box" that would accept plastic credit cards. Theatre Vision, Inc., headed by producer and playwright Dore Schary, featured a home terminal that "chewed up" cardboard tickets.

What most of these concepts, and others, had in common was the belief that pay TV, when it arrived, would be sold on a program-by-program basis. When the pay cable era actually began, it involved a company called Home Box Office—and a monthly subscription format. The first night's programming, transmitted to fewer than 400 homes at

Wilkes-Barre, Pennsylvania, consisted of a National Hockey League game and a film memorable only for its prophetic title, "Sometimes a Great Notion."

Home Box Office, Inc., had been developed primarily by Charles F. Dolan, founder of Sterling Communications, the cable TV franchisee in New York City's lower Manhattan, and Gerald M. Levin, a young attorney and management consultant. Begun as a potential revenue–producing program service for the Sterling Manhattan system, HBO became instead a programming and marketing middleman for the cable industry.

HBO had four basic precepts that differed, in whole or in part, from all other early pay planners: (1) the monthly fee; (2) an "affiliation" arrangement with cable operators rather than channel leasing; (3) a commitment to live sports and "special interest" entertainment, instructional and informational programming as well as feature films, and (4) in order to accommodate its live shows, transmission by common-carrier microwave and long lines.

Appropriately enough, one of the cable industry's original pioneers, John Walson, became a trail-blazer again as HBO's first affiliate. Transmission to his Wilkes-Barre system began on November 8, 1972, and within the next few months Star Channel, Schary's Theatre Vision, Optical's Channel 100, and several others followed HBO into operation. Today, none of those systems, except HBO, remains a force in pay TV, although Star Channel's parent company, Warner Communications, is very much involved, both with its multi-channel QUBE experiment in Columbus, Ohio, and with its new corporate partner, American Express, in the 24-hour Star Channel successor, The Movie Channel.

The Satellite Connection

Just prior to the annual National Cable Television Association Convention in April 1975, nearly two and a half years after Wilkes-Barre received its first transmission, the pay cable picture remained cloudy. Piecing together its microwave "network" like a jigsaw puzzle, HBO had not quite 100,000 subscribers in four Northeastern states. Optical Systems claimed 52,000 viewer homes in scattered parts of the country. There were perhaps 40,000 additional home pay TV subscribers, mostly in "standalone" cable systems, so-called because they chose to program their own pay channels with the assistance of film bookers such as Telemation Program Services and Cinemerica.

On April 10, three days before the NCTA Convention, Gerald Levin, who had succeeded Charles Dolan early in 1973 as president of HBO, announced that its parent, Time, Inc., would make a 5–year, $6.5 million commitment to lease 2 channels for 12 hours a day on the yet-to-be-launched RCA American Communications' Satcom I domestic satellite. Two cable TV operators with reputations for somewhat conservative management, UA-Columbia Cablevision and American Television and Communications, completed the equation by agreeing to install earth stations—then an approximately $100,000 investment with the FCC willing to authorize only antenna dishes with a 9-meter or larger diameter. Pay cable distribution by satellite began on September 30, 1975, to receiving stations serving UA-Columbia systems at Fort Pierce and Vero Beach, Florida, and ATC's system at Jackson, Mississippi.

"Rarely does a simple business decision by one company affect so many," wrote Paul Kagan, publisher of the *Pay TV Newsletter*. "In deciding to gamble on the leasing of satellite TV channels, Time, Inc. took the one catalytic step needed for the creation of a new national television network designed to provide pay TV programs.

"As a result, it has altered the business plans of cable TV system operators, equipment manufacturers, communications common-carriers, the performing arts, sports promoters, and private investors. To name just a few."

Many companies and individuals figured directly in the satellite decision, including Robert Rosencrans, president of UA-Columbia; Monroe M. Rifkin, president of ATC; J. Richard Munro, vice–president in charge of Time, Inc.'s Video Group; H. J. Schlafly and Robert Button of TransCommunications Corp., satellite communications consultants to HBO, and key members of the HBO staff. Kagan, however, quite rightly singled out Gerald Levin for an unusual tribute. A "special page in pay TV history," he wrote, must be reserved for Levin, "whose perception tied up all the loose ends and fired the imagination of so many others."

(Munro has since become executive vice-president of Time, Inc., and Levin has succeeded him to the helm of the Video Group, which is rapidly becoming the dominant influence in a company long identified most closely with magazine and book publishing.)

Cable TV Puts It Together

The domestic satellite, insensitive to distance, and therefore to time and cost, offered instant interconnection. Cable TV systems previously formed a loose, amorphous "industry" at best. Even major MSOs were usually remote administrators of scattered individual systems. There even was growing antagonism between large operators and small ones, who felt their interests frequently conflicted. Satellite interconnection knitted systems together with common programming and marketing interests, and authorization in 1976 of small earth stations meant that the small community could have the same television fare—first, pay TV, and then more than 30 other satellite-delivered services—that large cable systems offered. In fact, the viewer in Thief River Falls, Minnesota, had a lot more options than his counterpart in Detroit, Boston, or Chicago where cable TV did not yet exist. (Chapter 9 of this book describes the many programming choices available now through the cable/satellite connection.)

For more than two years, Home Box Office had the satellite to itself among pay TV services, and during that period it gained a huge lead in the race for subscribers. By early 1980, however, the number had grown to four "maxi-" and four "mini-" services and HBO, among others, had indicated it was contemplating a new "compatible" service to be marketed in combination with its own or other maxis. In addition, PRISM, a Philadelphia-based microwave network offering motion pictures and regional sports, is closing in on 100,000 subscribers, and a variety of standalone or special-situation systems account for more than a half million viewer homes.

Here, briefly, is a rundown of the pay cable networks:

Home Box Office—Oldest and largest, it began operations November 8, 1972, and had attained four million subscribers by the end of 1979. A wholly-owned subsidiary of Time, Inc., it occupies RCA Satcom I transponders 22 (Pacific and mountain time zones) and 24 (eastern and central) and also feeds a substantial number of Northeastern systems by microwave. In a typical month, April 1980, HBO programmed 12 new movies, 7 new entertainment and 7 sports specials. Holdover and return engagement movies and specials brought its total of features to 44 for the month.

Showtime—Viacom International, a major cable TV MSO as well as a leading syndicator of broadcast programming, formed Showtime in 1976 and began satellite distribution early in 1978. In that year, it also sold half of the pay TV company to Teleprompter Corporation, which shifted some 300,000 pay cable connections from HBO to Showtime at the beginning of 1979. Showtime had reached one million subscribers by early 1980, and its "catch-up" strategy has been to position itself as a "second service" to be offered in addition to HBO. Occupying transponders 10 (west) and 12 (east), Showtime restructured its service in April 1980 to accentuate differences between it and HBO. Its schedule for that month included 42 features, among them 13 new films and 5 new specials.

The Movie Channel—A 24-hour service on transponder 5, The Movie Channel was introduced by Warner Amex Satellite Entertainment in the fall of 1979, building upon the established framework of Warner's original Star Channel. During the April period under examination, 26 feature films were shown, including 18 new offerings, 5 previous month's holdovers, and 3 encores from earlier months. With approximately 12 program slots to fill each day, The Movie Channel repeats each title more often than either HBO or Showtime and stresses the viewer convenience of availability at a number of different times.

GalaVision—Introduced early in 1980, GalaVision has an all-Spanish language format. It transmits 9 hours during the week, 12 on weekends using transponder 18.

Home Theatre Network—Conceived as an economy "family" service by cable operator Peter Kendrick of Portland, Maine, Home Theatre Network offers one G or PG movie nightly, six nights a week. Using Southern Satellite Systems transponder 21 since September 1978, HTN has about 45,000 subscribers.

Front Row—Offered by Showtime in response to interest in the mini-pay concept, Front Row is a cherrypicking service maintained by blacking out portions of the regular Showtime feeds on transponders 10 and 12. It has very limited acceptance, and Showtime has discussed other mini-possibilities.

Take 2—HBO introduced a G/PG film and entertainment special mini-pay service in April 1979—somewhat reluctantly in response to requests by some HBO affiliates. Fully programmed on transponder 23, its differences apparently have not been sufficient to distinguish it from the HBO foundation service, and it has had mixed success. HBO's plan to introduce a new Satcom I maxi-pay package would mean dropping Take 2 or shifting it to a channel leased by RCA Americom from AT&T (following the loss late in 1979 of its newly-launched Satcom III).

Showtime Plus Sports—In Southwestern states, Showtime provides a package of Southwest Conference college sports in addition to regular Showtime service. The additional rights were acquired when another regional pay TV packager, Fanfare, suspended operations.

Tiering and Multi-pay

Charles F. Dolan, the originator of Home Box Office in 1972, left the company within a few months and began to develop a large complex of cable systems in New York City bedroom communities on Long Island. Off-air reception was no problem in these areas, and to lure customers Dolan pioneered the concept of "tiered" marketing—different packages of programs and services for different prices. The concept worked well for Dolan's Cablevision Systems Development Co., and his systems were projecting almost 200,000 subscribers by the end of 1980 on Long Island and in Westchester County, New York, New Jersey, and Chicago suburban areas.

Elsewhere, tiering has caught on to become almost an industry standard for sophisticated marketing. While effective, it alters the distinction between "pay" and "non-pay" services by combining both into levels of pricing. For example, here's how Cablevision presents its tiers in a sales approach called "Rainbow Programming":

- *Purple Service*—28 channels for $9.50, not including sports, HBO, action movies, or weather/commuter information channel.
- *Blue Service*—adds HBO for $16.50 total.
- *Green Service*—adds sports, but not HBO, also for $16.50.
- *Yellow Service*—30 channels for $19.50, including both HBO and sports.
- *Orange Service*—34 channels for $26.50, including action movies, art films, weather/commuter info, Satellite Program Network; excluding sports.
- *Red Service*—34 channels for $26.50, substituting sports for HBO.
- *Rainbow Service*—35 channels (the works) for $29.50.

From that sort of tiering, it is a short hop, step, and jump to maxi-mini, dual-maxi, or even maxi-maxi-mini, or maxi-maxi-maxi pay TV alignments. Given HBO's long lead in affiliates, Showtime and The Movie Channel have been understandably enthusiastic about the idea of moving into their rivals' markets as an "additional" or "compatible" service. HBO, considerably less pleased with the prospect, announced in April 1980, that it would introduce its own second maxi service—one that, presumably, would wrap around or fill gaps in the programming of the fundamental HBO service.

Within the cable industry, there was a pronounced "jury's still out" attitude on the part of marketing experts, who would be studying early results carefully to see if the surprisingly large numbers of persons accepting more than one monthly pay TV charge would remain true to both services, or drop back to one.

Upon one point there was general agreement, among suppliers and cable TV operators who must retail the package. The service must be "differentiated."

Vive La Difference!

In March 1980, subscribers to all three major pay TV services received program guides on which a cartoon poster from *Animal House* served as cover art. In April, all three featured artwork from Warren Beatty's *Heaven Can Wait*. In May, *Grease* would get similar treatment.

In short, a scarcity of outstanding film product threatened the goal of differentiation—and spotlighted one of the major factors that will shape future development of pay TV.

"Differentiation does not just mean scheduling on different days and at different hours," warned HBO Chairman N. J. Nicholas in discussing HBO's new service. "That's just a one-night stand. It won't suffice over a period of months any more than cosmetic differentiation—different program groupings, different graphics, different promotion and advertising, different names for features and series. ...

"Like it or not, pay TV suppliers are dependent upon movies. The pool of good, current movies is not large, with a narrow exhibition 'window' that almost guarantees parallel showings over a one- or two-month period. And no matter how much the undercard differs, how much you juggle percentages to make differentiation apparent, if the main events are the same, the illusion as well as the reality of compatibility is destroyed."

How pervasive is duplication—or non-differentiation? A survey of the April 1980 period already mentioned showed that six movies were duplicated by HBO, Showtime, and The Movie Channel: *Heaven Can Wait, Animal House, Moment by Moment, The Promise, Oliver's Story,* and *All the President's Men.* Same day duplication with *Heaven Can Wait* among all three services occurred on one date and among two of the networks on four other dates. *Animal House, Oliver's Story,* and *The Promise* had same-day duplication by two networks on four occasions.

The Future: Some Questions and Answers

The question of "competition" or "compatibility" raised by the duplication of film product really is a symptom of a much bigger issue for the pay TV industry—namely, its unquestioned dependence upon films originally made for theatrical distribution. Both HBO and Showtime have moved in two ways to lessen this dependence—first, by increasing emphasis in production or acquisition of their own non-theatrical entertainment specials, series, and motion pictures, and, second, by pre-production investment in theatrical films.

Such investments stimulate the production of more films and, to some degree, may influence their quality and content toward acceptibility for home viewing. They also gave the pay TV companies some slight measure of control over the production and releasing peaks and valleys that have been characteristic of major motion picture distribution in the past.

No pay TV distributor denies, however, that theatrical publicity and exploitation are essential to make pay TV viewers value a picture and want to see it. As a largely passive means of improving TV reception for most of three decades, the cable TV industry is only beginning to acquire the kind of marketing sophistication that has long been second nature to both broadcast television networks and movie producers.

In late 1979 and early 1980, all three pay cable networks became clients of major advertising agencies with plans for national campaigns. Ted Bates & Co., Inc., unveiled a $6 million HBO campaign built around the Unique Selling Proposition, "HBO People Don't Miss Out." Compton Advertising, Inc., for Showtime, and Ogilvy & Mather Inc. for Warner Amex Satellite Entertainment, each were reported to be budgeting $3 million expenditures. In all three cases, affiliates are expected to spend comparable amounts locally. Pay TV advertising is going major league.

Film distribution patterns will change, too—drastically, perhaps, as videocassettes, videodiscs, and other forms of pay TV (such as STV and direct-to-home satellite broadcast) scramble for places in the sequence of distribution. Will this put pay cable suppliers at a competitive disadvantage? More likely, say most of the industry's leaders, it will work favorably by stimulating program production and by shifting control away from theatrically-oriented distributors to home marketers.

Looming also on the to-be-addressed list is the direct satellite broadcast issue, which became highly visible in late 1979. Nieman-Marcus, the Dallas department store, featured a backyard earth station in its Christmas catalog. About the same time, Comsat, the international satellite common carrier company, announced that it would file with the FCC a proposal to provide several channels of programming direct to American homes via its own domestic satellite.

Highly explosive in many ways, the issue already is beginning to get wide attention. An FCC report released in April 1980 stated that adequate technology is now at hand "or soon will be, to provide direct satellite broadcasting in the United States," and "considerations of law and policy may grow increasingly important in determining the structure of domestic regulatory policy." Direct satellite broadcasting is seen as a threat by a large number of countries throughout the world; Chapter 4 of this book traces the development of United States policy on this issue within the international community.

Best estimates are that it will be late in the decade before the issues come to resolution. By that time, cable TV leaders assume, a majority of homes will have gained the option of subscribing to a multiplicity of cable channels for about the cost of the much more limited satellite system.

In that case, the "marketplace" will be the deciding factor, and the momentum that began building in Wilkes-Barre, Pennsylvania, on November 8, 1972, and in Fort Pierce/Vero Beach, Florida, and Jackson, Mississippi, on September 20, 1975, should continue to favor cable/broadband systems.

Resources

1. *Pay TV Census*, Paul Kagan Associates, Inc., 26386 Carmel Rancho Blvd., Carmel, CA 93923.
2. *Cable/Broadband Communications Book, Vol. 1, 1977-1978*, Pay TV chapter.
3. Federal Communications Commission, December 1976 decision licensing small-aperture receive earth stations.
4. U.S. Court of Appeals, *Home Box Office* v. *FCC*, March 25, 1977.

5. Home Box Office, Inc., Time & Life Bldg., Rockefeller Center, New York, NY 10020, Robbin Ahrold, Director of Public Relations.
6. Showtime Entertainment, Inc., 1211 Avenue of the Americas, New York, NY 10036, Sue Denison, Director of Marketing and Public Relations.
7. Warner Amex Satellite Entertainment Corp., 1211 Avenue of the Americas, New York, NY 10036, Margaret Wade, Director of Public Relations.
8. PRISM, 1516 Locust Street, Philadelphia, PA 19102, Jack Williams, President.
9. GalaVision, 250 Park Avenue, New York, NY 10017, Fred Landman, Executive Vice President.
10. Home Theatre Network, Inc., 465 Congress Street, Portland, ME 04101, Peter M. Kendrick, President.
11. Charles F. Dolan, Cablevision Systems Development Co., 33 Media Crossways Drive, Woodbury, NY 11797.
12. National Cable Television Association, Inc., 918 16th Street, N.W., Washington, D.C. 20006, Andrew Litsky, Director of Public Affairs.

John P. Taylor

9. Non-Pay Programming Distributed by Satellite: Explosive Growth

The number of cable programs "on the satellite" is exploding—and this development is changing the face of the cable TV industry. Already satellite distribution has made pay TV programming easily and economically available to cable systems of all sizes, and wherever located. In so doing it has transformed cable from a marginal to a very profitable business. How this happened has been described at length in Chapter 8 of this book.

But pay TV is only one part of the cable/satellite story. The second—and equally important—part is the way in which satellites are making possible and practical the nationwide distribution of a wide range of *non-pay TV* cable services. These are services (other than local) which the cable systems make available as part of their "basic" cable package—and for which the subscribers (usually) do not pay an additional charge.

Most people, even in the industry, do not realize how rapidly the number of these non-pay TV satellite programs is increasing. By April 1980, 25 different regularly-scheduled cable services had begun carriage

---

John P. Taylor is a marketing consultant and free lance writer. He is a contributing editor of Television/Radio Age *magazine for which he has written a widely-acclaimed series of articles on the use of satellites for television program distribution.*

Copyright 1979, 1980 by John P. Taylor.

on the satellite. Only seven of these are pay TV services. All the rest are non-pay TV. No two of them are exactly alike. They include: A full-time, specially-programmed, children's channel—sans advertising, sex, and violence; the full gavel-to-gavel proceedings of the U.S. House of Representatives—live, directly from the floor of the House; a round-the- clock, full-time, all-news video channel; three different all-sports channels; three religious channels; two general entertainment channels; and four "distant signals."

Moreover, this list of already operating services is just the beginning. Recently announced, and scheduled to start within the next six months, are: A full-time national weather channel, another religious channel, a channel programmed for the "over-fifty" generation, a full-time television news channel, four audio channels, and a multi-service data channel.

Looking a little further ahead, cable subscribers probably can expect many more "specialized" programming channels—possibly including things like a Lincoln Center channel, an opera channel, and the like. And, eventually, many innovative services such as data retrieval, interactive games, and various home computer services.

Satellite distribution is the magic genie which has made all of this a reality. Cable operators have talked of diversity, innovation, and specialized programming for two decades—ever since CATV came down out of the mountains and started calling itself Cable TV (instead of Community TV). But "the promise of cable" had little meaning until satellite distribution broke the chicken-and-egg problem of setting up a national cable distribution network.

The breakthrough was first signalled when Home Box Office (HBO) went on the satellite in November 1975. For the first time pay TV programs became easily available to cable systems anywhere in the country. It was truly a "revolutionary" development. But, as with many such developments, the full import was not immediately perceived. And for more than a year HBO was alone in the sky. The cable industry was interested—but hesitant. Installation of the necessary earth stations progressed rather slowly. At the end of the first cable-on-satellite year there were fewer than 80 in operation.

Fortunately there was another entrepreneur with the satellite vision. He was R.E. "Ted" Turner, winner of the America's Cup and owner of WTBS-TV, Channel 17, Atlanta. Turner had bought WTBS (then WTCG) in 1970 and had undertaken a program designed to make the station especially attractive to CATV systems (which were then getting it "off-air" or by microwave relay). By 1976 WTBS had extended its reach to some 300,000 CATV subscribers. But Turner was impatient for a larger audience—and with the satellite he saw a way to get it.

Federal Communications Commission (FCC) regulations preclude broadcasters themselves from putting their station signals on the satellite. But a common carrier can do it. And that is where Southern Satellite Systems came into the picture. Edward L. Taylor, who at the time was Western Union vice-president for WESTAR marketing and development, became interested in the idea. It tied in with his earlier experience as satellite projects engineer at AT&T, and as president of United Video Co. (a microwave carrier). In early 1976 he left Western Union to devote his full time and experience to organizing and operating Southern Satellite Systems as a completely independent common carrier. There are no corporate or financial connections between Southern Satellite and Turner Communications (WTBS). What WTBS gets out of the arrangement is an increased audience — and the prospect of greater advertising revenue.

In December 1976, Southern Satellite put WTBS on the satellite. The synergistic effect was immediate. The availability of the two satellite services was all the convincing most cable operators needed. A rush to install earth stations ensued. As of April 1980 (only 40 months later) more than 2500 cable systems have their own earth receiving stations (TVRO's) and hundreds more are on the way.

The instant accessibility of all these outlets made it easy for other enterprising programmers to launch additional program services. Two did so during 1977. Nine more during 1978. And during 1979 ten more were added — for a total (as of April 1980) of 25 cable services on the satellite. This counts only those actually on the bird. There will be more. At least half a dozen would-be programmers have indicated their intention to go on the satellite. And many in the industry believe that within another few years there will be 40 to 50 cable services on the satellite.

Even the list of cable services already on the satellite represents a cornucopia that cable system operators did not dream of before. These are literally "programs from heaven." The cable operator, having put in an earth station to receive pay TV programs, can install as many receivers as needed and take his choice of programs. In a matter of months he has gone from a lack of program sources to almost more than he knows what to do with. Best of all he can do this with a single antenna (dish).

This happy situation results from an unplanned but fortuitous development. It will be noted that all of the present cable services are on RCA's Satcom I. This is not a coincidence: There are practical reasons. The antenna used with an earth station must be pointed exactly at the satellite to be received. Thus the antenna can pick up signals from only one satellite, unless the dish is rotated (which is possible but awkward). HBO was the first cable programmer on the satellite and it set the pattern. It chose to go with RCA Americom, and, after several early shifts, ended up on transponders 22 and 24 of Satcom I. By December 1976 when Southern Satellite Systems received FCC approval to start its WTBS transmissions, there were already 78 cable system earth stations installed and pointed at Satcom I. Southern Satellite decided it could get started faster if it also went on Satcom I. This also saved its customers money. Most of them needed only to buy an additional receiver at about $3000—rather than putting in a whole new earth station at $25,000.

As a result of this stratagem Southern Satellite was able to grow to about 150 systems served in its first year of operation—and to about 2000 systems (with over 6 million subscribers) by April 1980. The point was not missed by other prospective programmers. Thus, as CBN, MSG (now USA Network), PTL, and others made their plans, they too decided on Satcom I. The result is a sort of de facto standardization which has worked out to the advantage of the cable system operators. With the installation of a single fixed-position antenna they can pick up any of the cable TV services now being offered. All they need do is connect to the antenna one receiver for each satellite service they wish to use.

The cable television program services actually available from the satellite as of April 1980 are listed in Table 9-1. In order for the whole scene to be better visualized, the pay TV services (which were described in detail in Chapter 8 of this book) have been included in this list—as well as the other (non-pay TV) services which have materialized since satellite program distribution became accepted. The general nature of each service is indicated in the Table. Further on each of these services will be described in detail.

From the services listed in Table 9-1, the individual cable system operator can pick and choose to provide his subscribers with a smorgasbord of cable programming which he feels is suited to the local situation. If he chooses well there should be something for almost everyone. Moreover, he can look for a snowballing effect. The more different services he has, the more subscribers he will corral. And the more subscribers he adds, the more program services he can afford to carry.

Who Will Pay for This Programming?

How is all of this programming to be paid for? In a half-dozen different ways—depending mostly on the type of programming involved. In Table 9-1 the 25 services now on the satellite are grouped according to types. The six types, and how they are paid for, are as follows:

Full-Service Pay TV (sometimes called "maxi" service) generally provides 8 to 12 hours a day of continuous programming that includes two or three "first run" movies plus (in some cases) live sports, occasional specials, and short features. The cable system operator puts this programming on a "scrambled" channel and charges subscribers who take this "premium" service an extra $8 to $10 per month. Of this he pays a negotiated amount, usually 40 percent to 50 percent, to the program supplier.

Mini Pay TV services usually consist of just one movie per day, no sports, and only very occasional specials. In most cases the cable operator uses these programs just like the full service, i.e., by putting them on a scrambled pay TV channel. However, his charge to the subscribers is about half as much, as are his payments to the supplier. Many cable systems now offer both maxi and mini pay TV services. Subscribers can take the basic cable service only, or the basic with either pay TV service—or with both.

Paid-For Programming services are those for which the cable system operator pays the program supplier a relatively small fee— usually one cent to 10 cents per subscriber per month (sometimes one cent to 10 cents per event). In addition, most of the suppliers (except C-SPAN and Nickelodeon) sell advertising in these programs—and sometimes provide time slots for insertion of local advertising. Normally the cable systems do not charge subscribers for these programs. They incorporate the programs in their "basic" service and expect to get the cost back from added sign-ups.

Free Programming services of several kinds are offered entirely free to cable systems. These programs come with built-in advertising and with slots into which the local system can insert local commercials. Conceptually, these programs are the same as the barter programs common in radio and TV station programming. They offer cable systems a means of filling channels (especially in daytime hours when most pay TV services are not on)—and of providing some of the diversity so highly sought after.

Religious/Family Programming is supplied by three "religious broadcasters" who offer full-time satellite programming to cable systems. In most cases it is "for free" both ways. In some instances, however, the cable operators are asking a modest fee for time on their systems. The programming consists partly of programs these religious groups are producing for TV station use (*The 700 Club*, *The PTL Club*, etc.) plus other religious and family-oriented programming. The cable operator can use one or more of these services to fill his channels. It provides diversity, it wins him favorable consideration by the community, and it does not count against his distant signal quota.

Distant Signals—of which most cable systems are presently allowed one or two—are being "imported" increasingly by satellite. A common carrier, with specific FCC permission, picks up the signal of an attractively programmed independent TV station at a point within the station's strong signal area and transmits this signal over a leased satellite transponder to cable systems that are clear to carry the station. The cable systems pay the carrier a small fee for transporting the signal. The imported station counts against the system's distant signal quota, and they must pay the standard copyright royalty for carrying it.

Table 9-1: Cable TV Services on the Satellite (April 1, 1980)

Programmer	Service Type	Program Content	Hours Used	Transponder No.
1. Home Box Office (Time Inc.)	Full-service pay TV	Movies & specials	8 hr/day on 2 channels	Tr. 22 & 24
2. Showtime (Viacom/Teleprompter)	"	"	12 hr/day on 2 channels	Tr. 10 & 12
3. The Movie Channel (Warner Amex Cable)	"	"	17 hr/day	Tr. 5
4. Galavision (Spanish Inter. Network)	"	Spanish language programming	10 hr/day	Tr. 18
5. Take 2 (Home Box Office)	Mini pay TV	Selected movies, children's programs	8 hr/day	Tr. 23
6. Front Row (Showtime)	"	Movies & specials	12 hr/day	Tr. 10 & 12
7. Home Theatre Network (New England Cablevision)	"	Family-type movies	2 hr/day	Tr. 21
8. Nickelodeon (Warner Amex Cable)	Paid-for programming	Children's programming	13 hr/day	Tr. 11
9. Calliope (USA Network)	"	Children's movies	1 hr/day	Tr. 9
10. USA Network (UA-Col. & MSG)	"	Madison Sq. Garden and other sports	375 events	Tr. 9
11. Entertainment Sports Programming Network (Getty Oil Corp.)	"	NCAA sports Northeast sports	24 hr/day	Tr. 7
12. Thursday Night Baseball (USA Network)	"	Major League baseball	Thursday nights	Tr. 9
13. UPI Newstime (transmitted by Southern Satellite Sys...)	"	Slo-scan news	24 hr/day	Tr. 6

				Tr. 5
14. C-SPAN (Cable Satellite Public Affairs Network)	"	Proceedings of the U.S. House of Representatives	Variable	
15. ACSN (Appalachian Community Service Network)	"	Educational and cultural community programs	5 hr/day	Tr. 16
16. Black Entertainment Television (BET)	Free programming	Black-oriented programs	2 hr/wk	Tr. 9
17. Satellite Programming Network (Satellite Syndicated Systems)	"	Sponsored programming	22 hr/day	Tr. 21
18. Modern Satellite Network (Modern Talking Pictures)	"	Sponsored films	5 hr/day	Tr. 22
19. Christian Broadcasting Network	Religious/family programs	Religious programs, educational and entertainment programs	24 hr/day	Tr. 8
20. PTL Network	"	"	24 hr/day	Tr. 2
21. Trinity Broadcasting Network	"	"	24 hr/day	Tr. 14
22. WTBS Atlanta (transmitted by Southern Sat. Systems)	Distant signal	Off-air WTBS programs	24 hr/day	Tr. 6
23. WGN Chicago (transmitted by United Video Inc.)	"	Off-air WGN programs	21 hr/day	Tr. 3
24. KTVU San Francisco (transmitted by Satellite Comm. Systems)	"	Off-air KTVU programs	21 hr/day	Tr. 1
25. WOR-TV New York (transmitted by Eastern Microwave Co.)	"	Off-air WOR-TV programs	21 hr/day	Tr. 17

Details of Present Satellite Cable Service

The several *types* of cable services presently offered have been described above. The services in each grouping are similar in how they are offered—and paid for. But there is considerable difference in program content, hours of operation, and pricing. Moreover, because most of the suppliers are in some related business, there are differences in motivation and in manner of operation. Some of these differences are indicated in the Table. Additional details are supplied in the individual descriptions which follow. These are arranged in the same order as in the Table.

It should be kept in mind that most of these services are quite new — and that they are still experimenting with program content, format, and scheduling. Thus the following descriptions, as well as the information in the Table, should be considered very much subject to change. It will be noted that in some instances two or more services share time on the same transponder. In other cases audio, data, or slo-scan services are multiplexed (piggybacked) on the primary video service by the use of "sub-carriers." Such arrangements result in a reduction in transmission costs. In the following list the current "sharing" and "multiplexed" arrangements are briefly noted.

1. Home Box Office (HBO), a Time, Inc. subsidiary, was the first pay TV cable service, and it was HBO that pioneered the development of this new industry. The HBO service was originally launched in 1972 using microwave networks for distribution. In November 1975 it added the satellite distribution. The introduction, development, and present status of the HBO operation (as well as that of the other pay TV program suppliers) is described in detail in Chapter 8 of this book. HBO's present programs are mostly premium movies plus an increasing number of self-produced spectaculars. It programs 8 to 12 hours a day—using an Eastern feed and a Western feed (delayed 3 hours) which go out on separate transponders. HBO also provides an entirely separate mini pay TV service, Take 2, which is described below (No. 10).

2. Showtime is a pay TV service offered by Showtime Entertainment, Inc., which is jointly owned by Viacom International and Teleprompter Corporation. It was started in July 1976 using tape cassettes as a means of distribution. In early 1978 it switched to satellite distribution and has grown rapidly since then. Showtime programming emphasizes movies and specials. It premieres 17 to 20 features a month, of which 3 or 4 are specials produced under Showtime direction. Showtime programs 12 hours a day, using an East-Central feed and a delayed Mountain-Pacific feed (on separate transponders). Showtime, too, has a mini version, Front Row, which is noted below (No. 6).

3. The Movie Channel is a pay TV service offered by the Warner Amex Cable Company, a jointly owned subsidiary of Warner Communications, Inc. and the American Express Company. It was one of the earliest pay TV systems, having been introduced in February 1973. Until recently it was used only in systems owned by Warner Cable. In February 1979, however, the service went on the satellite—and an allout effort to sell it to other systems was launched. A feature of the Movie Channel service is that it runs movies during the day and late at night. In addition to the standard evening showings (7:00 p.m. and 9:30 p.m.), there are Movie Channel showings at 9:30 a.m., 12:00 noon, and 12:00 midnight. Warner Amex also offers a separate fulltime children's programming channel called Nickelodeon (see No. 8 below).

4. Galavision, a Spanish-language premium pay TV service is the pay TV operation of the Spanish International Network (a broadcast service). Started in October 1979, Galavision presently provides approximately 70 hours a week of programming which includes films, sports events, variety specials, and novellas—all in Spanish. None of this programming is "dubbed." Most of it is imported from Spain and the Latin American countries (especially Mexico). At the present time Galavision is transmitted on transponder 18 of Satcom I—which it leases from Reuters.

5. Take 2 (HBO) is a mini pay TV service which HBO began feeding to cable systems by satellite on April 1, 1979, as an alternative or addition to the full HBO service. It is a "family package" which offers fewer movies—and is considerably less expensive than the full HBO service. Most systems charge $4 to $6 a month for Take 2 as compared to $8 to $12 for the full service. Take 2 is programmed independently and is transmitted on its own transponder. Thus cable systems can use it alone or in combination with the full HBO service (or another maxi service) in a so-called two-tier offering to subscribers.

6. Front Row (Showtime) is a mini pay TV version of the regular Showtime service (described in No. 2 above). Subscribers to this less expensive service receive one movie per day, two on weekends. These are extracted from the full Showtime transmissions by a "program separator" which is located at the cable system headend and is automatically controlled by signals on a data subcarrier. This enables the cable system to feed Showtime to one pay channel and Front Row to another pay channel. Subscribers can be offered their choice of maxi or mini service. The Front Row service was started in October 1978.

7. Home Theatre Network (HTN) is a low-cost, family-oriented pay TV service which grew out of the experience of New England Cablevision in designing and originating its own pay TV programming. It is a relatively limited service (8-10:30 p.m., EST, five days a week) which consists of G-rated and selected PG-rated movies and an occasional topical special. Most cable systems bill it to their subscribers at $3.95 per month. There is one new feature film per week, which is premiered on Monday and repeated on Tuesday, Wednesday, and Friday. Thursday is a repeat of a film premiered several weeks before. This simple and relatively inexpensive service appeals to many families, and HTN has enjoyed a high percentage of takers wherever it has been offered. HTN, which went on the satellite late in 1978, shares transponder 21 with the Satellite Programming Network (No. 15 below).

8. Nickelodeon (Warner Amex) is unique in that it is a full 13-hour a day, 7 days a week, service devoted exclusively to children's programming. Nickelodeon is an outgrowth of Warner Amex's experience with its QUBE two-way system in Columbus, Ohio, and is being produced in QUBE's elaborately equipped. studios. The programming, which is advertised as "without violence or commercials," is innovative in nature and includes something for children of all ages. For pre-school children there is the popular *Pinwheel* program developed by Dr. Vivian Horner (of *Electric Company* fame), who is now vice-president/product development of Warner Amex Cable. For teenagers there is the *Bananaz* show. And for all young people there is a show called *Nickel Flicks*, featuring adventure serials a la Tom Mix. Warner Amex has purposely priced Nickelodeon so that it can be offered by cable systems as part of their basic service. The charge to cable systems is 10 cents per subscriber per month (50 cents if it is used as a pay channel). Systems which take Star Channel (see No. 3 above) receive Nickelodeon free as a bonus.

9. Calliope (USA Network) is also exclusively a children's channel. The one-hour a day programs consist of children's movies supplied by Learning Corporation of America. They presently air from 6:30-7:30 p.m., EST, Monday-Friday. The service is marketed by USA Network using transponder 9—the same transponder as used for Madison Square Garden Sports, Thursday Night Baseball, and C-SPAN (see No.'s 10, 12, and 14 below). The charge to cable systems is 15 cents per subscriber per 26-week season for up to 25,000 subscribers ranging downward to 8 cents per subscriber for systems with over 75,000 subscribers.

10. USA Network (formerly Madison Square Garden Sports), which was one of the earliest services on the satellite (1977), expects during the 1980 season to feed 375 live sports events, plus possible play-offs, to a microwave and satellite network which presently consists of over 3000 cable systems with some 2.7 million subscribers. The charge to cable systems is 6 cents per event per subscriber in the New York area, 2 cents per event per subscriber in nearby areas. In other areas it is 50 cents per subscriber per year in the Eastern time zone and 35 cents per subscriber in other time zones. USA Network is carrying some advertising, and expects to attract more. This service is carried on the transponder 9—which is shared with the Calliope serivce (No. 9 above), the Thursday Night Baseball service (No. 12 below), and the C-SPAN service (No. 14 below).

11. Entertainment & Sports Programming Network (ESPN) started full-time, all-sports programming—highlighting National Collegiate Athletic Association (NCAA) events—in September 1979. They have made an arrangement with NCAA which will provide a year-round series of NCAA championships and regular season events in 18 sports. This includes the entire spectrum of NCAA sports "with the exception of specific events and sports programming already committed to another network." ESPN is being financed through an arrangement which provides for Getty Oil Company to acquire up to 85 percent interest in ESP Network, Inc. Cable systems taking the service are asked to sign a five-year agreement which provides for payment of 10 cents per month per subscriber during the first two years, after which there is no charge at all for the following three years.

12. Thursday Night Baseball is the result of a national cable television arrangement between USA Network (No. 10 above) and the office of the Baseball Commissioner. Under this agreement USA Network televises one or two selected major league baseball games every Thursday night during the regular season and distributes these by satellite to cable systems nationwide. The participating systems pay USA Network one cent per subscriber per game. In return they receive proprietary baseball telecasts in which local advertising can be sold. National advertising is sold by USA Network. Baseball selects the games to be telecast. The arrangement is similar to that in which the Monday night games are seen on broadcast television.

13. UPI Newstime is a new kind of 24-hour a day audio-video news service which consists of still news pictures (shown three or four a minute) with voice-over commentary. The hour-long programs, which are recycled continuously, are updated four to six times a day. UPI started this service in July 1978 and is feeding it to a rapidly-growing number of cable systems. Newstime is transmitted by Southern Satellite Systems from its Douglasville, Georgia, uplink station. It is multiplexed (piggybacked) on the WTBS signal (see No. 22 below) and transmitted by the same uplink transmitter and over the same transponder. This saves scarce frequency space as well as cost. UPI charges cable system operators five cents per month per subscriber for the service (eight cents if it is used for pay TV).

14. C-SPAN (for Cable Satellite Public Affairs Network) is another unique service. It offers cable systems (and others) the "live" televised gavel-to-gavel proceedings of the U.S. House of Representatives. The signals are transmitted, morning and afternoon, on the transponder which is used evenings by USA Network services. This enables the cable operator to use the same satellite receiver and (if he wishes) the same cable channel for both—an economical and convenient arrangement. For this service the cable system pays C-SPAN a fee of one cent per month per subscriber. The Cable Satellite Public Affairs Network is a nonprofit organization generally supported by the cable industry. (For more details on C-SPAN programming, see Chapter 10 of this book.)

15. Appalachian Community Service Network is an outgrowth of the Appalachian Educational Satellite Program. ACSN (also referred to as CSN) provides five hours a day of public service programming intended to be non-competitive with PBS and commercial television. This programming is designed to assist communities with a variety of educational, informational, and instructional programs. It is made available to cable systems at a maximum charge of one cent per subscriber per month (with quantity discounts to large systems and MSOs). It is transmitted on transponder 16 of Satcom I.

16. Black Entertainment Television (BET) is a relatively new cable TV service which premiered in January 1980. BET, which is an advertiser-supported service, offers "programming that features Black performers in dominant or leading roles or programming that addresses itself, in fact or fiction, to Black cultural experiences and life styles." President of BET is Robert L. Johnson, formerly vice-president for government relations of the National Cable Television Association. Tele-Communications, Inc., the big MSO, has a minority (20 percent) interest in the operation. At the present time BET programs are transmitted Friday nights from 11 p.m. to 1 a.m. (EST) on transponder 9, Satcom I.

17. Satellite Programming Network (SPN) is another unique programming service available to cable systems. It is described as "non-broadcast programming"—and is offered on something akin to the barter arrangement common in broadcast TV. The programs include celebrity shows, short entertainment and informational features, talk shows, classic movie specials, and the like. These programs come with built-in commercials and are offered free to cable systems agreeing to use them on a regular basis. There are also slots for insertion of local advertising or promos. Most of this programming is supplied by organizations which buy time on the SPN system to air their programs. The selection of programming for SPN is aided by an advisory committee from the cable industry and strict rules have been laid down as to what kinds of programming can be accepted. SPN was started in December 1978 as a 3-hour fill-in on transponder 1. The acceptance, however, was so enthusiastic that it was changed in March 1979 to 13 hours, and in August 1979 to 21 hours a day on transponder 21. The other 3 hours a day on this transponder is used by the Home Theatre Network (described in No. 7 above).

18. Modern Satellite Network is still another non-broadcast service available free to cable systems. It consists of film programs arranged by Modern Talking Pictures, which is the nation's largest distributor of free-loan sponsored films. Modern packages selected films from its library into 60-minute programs complete with a personality host. They have been furnishing these (on film or tape) to cable systems for the past 5 years. In January 1979 they started putting 5 hours a day on the satellite. This is transmitted daytimes on one of the transponders used evenings by Home Box Office (see No. 1 above).

19. Christian Broadcasting Network (CBN) transmits by satellite (it has its own transmit earth station) 24 hours a day of "family" programs—including religious programs (e.g., *The 700 Club*), women's programs, teaching shows, musical variety programs, and youth-oriented shows. Much of this is produced in CBN's own well-equipped production studios. The programming is free to cable systems, and a large number of the systems that have their own earth stations are picking it up and putting it on one of their cable channels.

20. PTL Television Network (PTL) operates very much like CBN. PTL, too, has its own production studio and its own transmit/receive earth station, both located at headquarters in Charlotte, North Carolina. PTL has a six-year $5.7 million agreement with RCA for use of a full-time transponder and began putting programs on this in April 1978. It programs 24 hours a day of "Christian theme" programming, including *The PTL Club*, a two-hour talk variety show, which is aired several times during the day.

21. Trinity Broadcasting Network is the third religious broadcaster that is putting its programming on the satellite. Like the others, it has its own production studios and its own transmit/receive earth station, both located in the Los Angeles area. For satellite cable programming, Trinity Broadcasting expands on the wide variety of programs it produces for its own stations (KTBN-TV, Los Angeles, and KPAZ-TV, Phoenix). These programs are picked up and used by the two television stations and they are also available free to any cable system wishing to use them.

22. WTBS-TV (Channel 17, Atlanta) is transmitted 24 hours per day by Southern Satellite Systems (via its own uplink at Douglasville, Georgia) to cable systems throughout the country. Cable operators who have receive earth stations use the WTBS signal in one of three ways: (1) as one of their allowed "distant signals," (2) as a late-night signal after local station signoffs, or (3) as a "wildcard" fill-in for blacked out programs. Charges by Southern Satellite for carriage of the three services are, respectively, 10 cents, 2 cents, and one cent per month per subscriber. There are discounts for prepayment and a monthly maximum regardless of system size. As of April 1980 about 2000 cable systems with approximately 6 million subscribers were taking the WTBS feed, making this the largest satellite network in existence. The WTBS signals are carried on transponder 6. Multiplexed (piggybacked) on the WTBS carrier are several sub-carriers. One of these carries the UPI Newstime service mentioned above (No. 13). Others will be used for audio and data channels. In addition, a Cabletext service is transmitted in the vertical interval of the WTBS signal. (See Chapter 13 for a discussion of Cabletext.)

23. WGN-TV (Channel 9, Chicago) is a second "distant signal" which is available to cable systems via satellite (Satcom I, transponder 3). The carrier in this case is United Video, Inc., a company that has been in the microwave common carrier business for some years and has been carrying WGN and other stations to a large Midwest cable network. The basic charges for WGN carriage are approximately the same as for WTBS.

24. KTVU-TV (Channel 2, San Francisco) is a "distant signal" which Satellite Communications Systems (now a wholly-owned subsidiary of Warner Amex Cable) started feeding to cable systems in December 1978. Because of its West Coast oriented programming and Pacific time operation, KTVU is attractive to West Coast cable system operators. After KTVU signoff, the late-night programming of KPIX-TV, San Francisco, is carried on the same transponder (Satcom I, transponder 1). The basic charges for the KTVU channel are the same as those for WTBS.

25. WOR-TV (Channel 9, New York) is a "distant signal" which became available by satellite in the spring of 1979 (on Satcom I, transponder 17). After WOR signoff, WCBS is carried on this transponder. The carrier for WOR is Eastern Microwave, one of the earliest and largest microwave carriers with a CATV network that blankets the Northeast. Eastern has been feeding WOR (and other New York stations) by microwave to several hundred cable systems with approximately two million subscribers for some years. For its satellite feed Eastern charges approximately the same as the other carriers.

Resources

Program Suppliers

1. Home Box Office, Time & Life Building, Rockefeller Center, New York, NY 10020.
2. Showtime Entertainment Inc., 1211 Avenue of the Americas, New York, NY 10036.

3. The Movie Channel, Warner Amex Cable Co., 75 Rockefeller Plaza, New York, NY 10019.
4. Galavision, 250 Park Avenue, New York, NY 10017.
5. Take 2 (contact HBO)
6. Front Row (contact Showtime)
7. Home Theatre Network Inc., 465 Congress St., Portland, ME 04101.
8. Nickelodeon (contact Warner Amex Cable)
9. Calliope (contact USA Network)
10. USA Network, 208 Harristown Rd., Glen Rock, NJ 07542.
11. Entertainment Sports Programming Network, 319 Cooke St., Plainville, CT 06062.
12. Thursday Night Baseball (contact USA Network)
13. UPI Newstime, United Press International, 220 East 42nd St., New York, NY 10017.
14. C-SPAN (Cable Satellite Public Affairs Network), 1745 Jefferson Davis Highway, Suite 308, Arlington, VA 22202.
15. ACSN (Appalachian Community Service Network), 1666 Connecticut Ave., N.W., Washington, D.C. 20235.
16. Black Entertainment Television, Suite 300, Prospect Place, 3222 N St., N.W., Washington, D.C. 20007.
17. Satellite Programming Network, P.O. Box 45684, Tulsa, OK 74145.
18. Modern Satellite Network, Modern Talking Picture Service, 45 Rockefeller Center, New York, NY 10020.
19. Christian Broadcasting Network, Pembroke Four, Virginia Beach, VA 23463.
20. PTL Television Network, Charlotte, NC 28279.
21. Trinity Broadcasting Network, Box A, Santa Ana, CA 90053.
22. WTBS-TV, Cable Relations, 1018 West Peachtree St., Atlanta, GA 30309.
23. WGN-TV, WGN Continental Broadcasting Co., 2501 Bradley Place, Chicago, IL 60618.
24. KTVU, One Jack London Square, Oakland, CA 94607.
25. WOR-TV, RKO General Inc., 1481 Broadway, New York, NY 10036.

Carriers

1. RCA American Communications, Inc., 201 Centennial, Piscataway, NJ 08854.
2. Western Union Telegraph Co., One Lake St., Upper Saddle River, NJ 07458.
3. Eastern Microwave, Inc., 3 Northern Concourse, P.O. Box 4972, Syracuse, NY 13221.
4. Satellite Communications Systems, Warner Amex Cable Co., 75 Rockefeller Plaza, New York, NY 10017.
5. Southern Satellite Systems, P.O. Box 45684, Tulsa, OK 74145.
6. United Video, Inc., 5200 S. Harvard, Suite 215, Tulsa, OK 74135.

Publications

1. *Cablecast*, Paul Kagan Associates, Inc., 26356 Carmel Rancho Blvd., Carmel, CA 93923.
2. *Television Digest*, 1836 Jefferson Place, N.W., Washington, D.C. 20036.
3. *Television/Radio Age*, 1270 Avenue of the Americas, New York, NY 10020.
4. *Cablevision*, Titsch Publishing, Inc., 1139 Delaware Plaza, P.O. Box 4305, Denver, CO 80204.

Elizabeth L. Young

10. Public Services by Cable/ Satellite: Experiences and Challenges

The next time you are in your kitchen, take a look at the largest pot or pan cover you have. It will probably be 15 or more inches in diameter, convex on one side and concave on the other, light-weight, and sturdy. Now imagine that a similar piece of metal, only slightly larger, is mounted on your roof (with some modest electronic attachments) and brings the voices, the messages, the sights and sounds from literally anywhere in the world into your TV set and thus into your livingroom.

Impossible? Improbable? A vision for the distant future? Not at all. For we are speaking of communications satellite technology that will make possible direct home reception, and experiments are already going on in Canada and Japan (see Chapter 4 for a comprehensive discussion of the United States position on direct broadcast satellites). Meanwhile, we have increasing access to satellites already through the medium of cable TV. With more than 4,000 cable systems operating in the United States today, some 2,300 were estimated to have satellite receiving earth stations by April 1980.

Elizabeth L. Young is the President of the Public Service Satellite Consortium (PSSC) in Washington, D.C. Formerly she has served as Director of the Telecommunications Center of the Ohio State University, and has held other positions in public broadcasting. She also has held adjunct teaching appointments at The American University and The Ohio State University.

Let's catch our breath for a moment and see where we are. Even though a "direct broadcast" satellite for the United States is only a proposal of Comsat at present, "fixed" satellites (those transmitting signals between several fixed points) are available and are beaming programs to cable systems, public broadcasting stations, and, increasingly, to commercial TV stations. Communications satellites have been operating internationally and experimentally since the early 1960s, but the first commercially owned U.S. domestic satellites began operating in 1975. Since that time, their number and capacity have increased steadily so that capacity have increased steadily so that by 1980 there would be more than 100 transponders available on the communications satellites operated by Western Union, RCA, and AT&T/GTE.

John Taylor, in Chapter 9, describes how the cable industry has benefitted from the advent of communications satellites which have made possible successful networks for cable programming. Some of the programs he describes are of a public service nature. The focus of this chapter will be to examine more closely how satellites and cable are being linked to provide educational and informational services, to explore the challenges involved in aggregating the public service "market" so that it can use technology efficiently, and to hazard a guess or two about the future.

Historical Perspective

It is important to recognize that we have had a relatively brief time to experiment with communications satellites as delivery mechanisms for social services and education. The National Aeronautics and Space Administration (NASA) launched a series of Applications Technology Satellites (ATS) beginning in 1966. Three of the ATS series were used successfully for experiments. The most powerful and versatile, ATS-6, was launched in 1974 and shut down in 1979, exceeding its originally anticipated "life" by three years. It delivered educational and health-medical communications not only in the U.S. but also in India where the satellite was "on loan" for a year.

In 1971, the U.S. and Canada signed an agreement to build and launch a Communications Technology Satellite (CTS), which was launched in 1976 and concluded its service in 1979. As with ATS-6, CTS demonstrated that networks of educational institutions and service organizations can be created using the satellite in the sky as the pivotal transmission mechanism.

Among the experimenters on ATS-6 and CTS were the Veterans Administration (linking VA hospitals together for conferencing and diagnosis), WAMI (a medical teaching project involving the states of Washington, Alaska, Montana, and Idaho), junior high schools throughout the Rocky Mountain area, schools in Appalachia (through a project coordinated by the Appalachian Regional Commission and focusing on teacher education), the public broadcasting organizations, and SALINET (a library information and training project).

What the experiments proved was that under the right circumstances, the satellite is an efficient, cost-effective means of providing information simultaneously to numbers of people who may be widely dispersed. The reasons that the satellites "worked" were apparent. The satellite is "distance insensitive"—meaning that it costs no more in time or money or energy to transmit across long distances than it does to transmit across short distances. For all the exotic technology required to build a satellite and get it into orbit, from the standpoint of the user the system is simply an earth station here, an earth station there, and a satellite in the middle relaying signals. This simplicity leads to flexibility: networks can be configured by rearranging earth stations as the situation demands. In the ATS and CTS experiments, transportable earth stations were used as well as "permanent" terminals that were low-cost and easy to install.

During the experimental phase, transmissions included one- and two-way video, one- and two-way audio, slow-scan pictures, and data. In most of the experiments, provisions were also made for interaction. For example, in the WAMI project, a doctor in Seattle could converse with a medical student in Alaska, or a child in a rural school could ask a question of the "master teacher" in the state capital, with the child able to hear and see the teacher's response.

Given the possibilities demonstrated by communications satellites during the early experiments, NASA determined that it would move out of the research and development business and would let commercial owners provide the needed spacecraft for further operational applications. Accordingly, since 1978, commercial U.S. domestic satellites have been increasingly used for delivery of educational and public services. We will turn now to a brief review of how the satellite services are delivered on the ground, and we will then examine some current uses. As we do so, we may bear in mind one seminal difference between public service and commercial applications of communications satellites and cable. In the commercial world, there has been an explosion of interest and corresponding satellite programming. Why? Because the market exists. The home viewing audience is large and definable. It has a demonstrated capacity for absorbing more entertainment. The market for public services delivered by satellites (or by any media) is there, too, but it is less clear who will pay for delivery, and there are often institutional barriers that preclude quick decisions and effective delivery of programs. These problems will be discussed further on in this chapter.

Terrestial Links

In the satellite business, there is always the problem of the "final mile." Or, how does one get the signal from the satellite receiving station to its ultimate destination, whether that is an institution, a single viewer, or a mass audience?

It is necessary to have in place on the ground complementary delivery systems. One of these is obviously a broadcast station. Currently, all of the TV stations that are part of the Public Broadcasting Service (268) have satellite terminals. By the end of 1980, all National Public Radio stations (more than 200) will have receivers also. ITFS (Instructional Television Fixed Service) and MDS (multi-point distribution service) channels are also delivery systems in use at the present time. Cable TV is currently the more pervasive terrestrial delivery system for communications satellites operating in the U.S.

In communities without cable, an institution or organization (whether public or private) may wish to erect its own earth station, since the Federal Communications Commission (FCC), in October of 1979, deregulated ownership procedures and said, in effect, that licensing of receive-only satellite facilities was no longer required, nor would there continue to be regulations about the size of the antennas.

Some entrepreneural companies such as the Satellite Communications Network (a for-profit company with common carrier status) have been formed expressly for the purpose of building and leasing transmit-and-receive satellite facilities. And as observed at the outset of this chapter, we are not yet at the point where direct broadcast satellites are available for in-home use. Therefore, while a number of terrestrial delivery systems exist or are being built, in many communities cable is and will continue to be the most practical means of getting the satellite signals to the end user.

Current Applications

The PSSC

As noted earlier, during the early 1970s there was a period of experimentation using communications satellites that were designed by NASA. In 1975, a new nonprofit membership organization was formed to conduct certain of these experiments and to bring together the public service community for permanent uses of satellites. It was named the Public Service Satellite Consortium (PSSC) and is currently headquartered in Washington, D.C., with technical facilities and staff in Denver.

In 1978, the PSSC established the National Satellite Network (NSN), which is its service division that coordinates transmissions for its members and others. NSN generally arranges two types of services: long-term or operational services and short-term or "occasional event" services.

Long-term transmissions involve services that are intended to continue over an extended period of time. The best example of such a service offered by the PSSC has been the NSN Hospital Interconnect, which was started by May 1979. To establish the HI, PSSC initially purchased two hours of time from the Satellite Program Network (using transponder 21 on RCA's SATCOM 1 satellite), and programs were transmitted between 1 p.m. and 3 p.m. Eastern time, Sunday through Saturday. Since an increasing number of cable systems have installed earth stations that are pointed toward SATCOM 1, PSSC obtained agreements from 30 cable systems with earth stations that they would receive the programs and would retransmit them to hospitals.

Program content consisted of health care information appropriate for those recovering from illnesses or needing other medical attention. Initial programs included such topics as coronary care, diabetes, and nutrition. Programs were obtained from the Greater Cleveland Hospital Association and were rotated every few days. Participating hospitals began in July 1979, to pay one cent per patient per program hour for the service.

After this service had become operational, the American Hosptial Association (a PSSC member) began examining the feasibility of offering an expanded service that would include continuing professional education for hospital personnel. The initial Hospital Interconnect series concluded at the end of October 1979, and it was anticipated that AHA would contract with PSSC to mount the expanded service, following a period of research and test marketing, before the end of 1980. This initial offering proved the feasibility of using satellites and cable to deliver daily services to an interested user population.

Short-term transmissions or "occasional events" may take place over a period of hours or days and may involve two or more participating sites. Table 10-1 summarizes a number of the occasional events PSSC has coordinated since late 1978. PSSC's task usually consists of the following steps: assisting the member organization in assessing its specific communication goals; advising the member in the production of program content (PSSC itself does not produce or select programs or content); purchasing the required time on one or more of the available communications satellites; providing uplinking of the program from the most convenient site; arranging for reception at the appropriate earth stations; and arranging for the "hand over" of the program from each receiving earth station to an appropriate local facility, e.g., a campus closed-circuit television system, a cable system, a viewing room in an adjacent facility. Since PSSC operates a satellite uplink in Denver and has a teleconferencing facilities, it can provide a complete service using its

Denver facilities. PSSC also has access to teleconferencing production facilities in Washington, D.C., New York City, Chicago, and other locations where it can lease the facilities as required. By mid-1980 the Consortium had a transportable earth station (for both transmitting and receiving) housed in Denver and available on a lease basis for use in conjunction with all of the domestic satellites.

Table 10-1: PSSC National Satellite Network Transmissions Aug. 1978-Nov. 1979

Date	Satellite	Transmission
Aug. 15, 1978	CTS & WESTAR 1	Greater Cleveland Hospital Association/ REACH
Sept. 6, 1978	WESTAR 1	American Dietetic Association
Sept. 12-14, 1978	CTS & WESTAR 1	American Hospital Association
Sept. 12, 1978	CTS & WESTAR 1	Greater Cleveland Hospital Association/ REACH
Dec. 13, 1978	CTS & WESTAR 1	Greater Cleveland Hospital Association/ REACH
Jan. 18-19, 1979	WESTAR 1	Women Writers Satellite Teleconference
March 27-29, 1979	CTS & WESTAR 1	American College of Physicians
April 7, 1979	Telephone conference	American Law Institute/American Bar Association (ALI/ABA)
April 16, 23, & 30, & May 7, 1979	CTS	American Journal of Nursing Company and American Nursing Association
May 2, 9, 16, 23, & 30, 1979	WESTAR 1	Medical University of South Carolina
May 18, 1979	CTS & WESTAR 1	Indiana Higher Education Telecommunications System
June 13, 1979	SATCOM 1 & WESTAR 1	Radio and Television Commission of the Southern Baptist Convention
Aug. 27, 28, 29, & 30, 1979	SATCOM 1	American Hospital Association
Sept. 4, 11, 18, & 25, & Oct. 2, 9, 16, 23, &30, 1979	SATCOM 1	McGeorge School of Law
Oct. 25-26, 1979	WESTAR 1	Teachers Corps Youth Advocacy Loop/ Alan Brown
Nov. 13, 1979	WESTAR 1	American Dietetic Association

The occasional events generally involve one-way video plus audio and return audio. The entire transmission can take place via satellite, or the originating video plus audio may be fed on a satellite transponder with the return audio ordered via an AT&T WATS line. For example, in May 1979, the Medical University of South Carolina (a PSSC member) produced a series of continuing educational programs for physicians and nurses on epilepsy. The objectives were to explain adult and childhood epilepsy and the medical therapy and surgical treatment needed; to demonstrate the use of diagnostic tests and therapeutic monitoring; to identify referral resources, such as comprehensive epilepsy centers and the National Institutes of Health; and to provide new information and modify attitudes as well as behavior. Programs originated from Charleston, South Carolina, and were fed via the WESTAR 1 satellite to 51 public television stations in 37 states. Seventeen medical schools, 13 campus facilities, 23 public television viewing rooms, and 218 hospitals throughout the U.S. received the program. Viewers could ask questions by means of conventional phone lines.

On two occasions, the American Dietetic Association has used the National Satellite Network to offer seminars to particpating dieticians who have viewed and listened to the program, phoned in questions, and been able to acquire continuing education credits for taking these "short courses." The video portions of such transmissions are usually originated from a teleconferencing facility which can best be described as a modest TV studio. There are cameras and lights and (usually) facilities to show slides, tape, or film during the program. Teleconferencing which is by no means new with the satellite has become a service that satellites can offer with cost effectiveness. In a study done by Western Union under contract to NASA, it has been estimated that teleconferencing will comprise some 35 percent of all communications satellite traffic by 1990. Cable may not be the only terrestrial delivery system to be used in satellite teleconferencing but it should continue as a principal system.

ACSN, AETV, Others in Education

An educational project which has used satellites successfully and is now expanding into its operational phase is that of the Appalachian Regional Commission. The Appalachian Education Satellite Project (AESP) in the summer of 1974 used ATS-6 to reach 15 classroom sites from New York to Alabama with teacher education programs. Operations continued to April 1975, when the satellite was lent to India, and AESP resumed service (when the satellite returned) between 1977 and 1979. The classrooms were equipped to receive live and taped feeds. Five of the 15 sites were also equipped to receive and transmit two-way audio via ATS-3. Eventually, 46 earth stations were in operation for the project. Evaluation of the project indicated that learning gains did take place.

Because of the success of the initial AESP project, ARC appropriated funds for an Appalachian Community Service Network to be created. (ACSN will also use funding from NIE.) ACSN, which became operational in October 1979, is delivering adult education and other public service programming via transponder 16 on SATCOM 1. Cable distribution provides for most of the reception, but some community-based receive-only satellite earth stations can also beam the programs directly into schools and community centers. Initially, programming is offered between 7 a.m. and 11:30 a.m. Eastern time. ACSN has its own uplink in Lexington, Kentucky, and intends to both produce and acquire appropriate courses for distribution. The intent is to also offer teleconferencing services. In the early stages, ACSN programs have included "Coping with Kids," "Personal Finance," "Energy Forum," "Home Winterization," and "Freehand Sketching."

ACSN charges cable systems one cent per subscriber per month. There is no advertising. Additional ACSN revenues are anticipated from formal courses (via paid enrollments), teleconferencing, and off-hour distribution of materials. The headquarters of ACSN remains in Washington, D.C., with the Appalachian Regional Commission. ACSN is exploring the feasibility of establishing production facilities and an uplink in the Washington area.

Late in 1979, the creation of the American Educational TV Network (AETV) was announced. It is to be an adult educational service, using transponders 10 and 12 on SATCOM 1, beginning in 1980. Its goal is to offer post-professional training for those required to take continuing education courses to retain professional licenses—including doctors, dentists, nurses, and others. Those using the service will pay to enroll in the courses. There will be no charge to the participating cable systems. The project is located at the California State University in Long Beach.

The University of Mid-America in Lincoln, Nebraska, has had a successful history of multi-media course distribution since its incorporation in 1974. Presently, its Board is examining whether some distribution should move to satellite. Most UMA courses include a mix of print, audio, and visual materials. Public television stations already broadcasting UMA courses could receive more timely distribution if WESTAR 1 were utilized. In addition, if UMA were to lease transponder time on SATCOM 1, the course offerings would also be available to cable systems.

In Maryland, plans are underway to study the feasibility of implementing a national telecommunications-assisted learning system much akin to Great Britain's Open University. Indeed, initial plans call for adaptations of the Open University materials. This project, tentatively titled "The National University Consortium for Telecommunication in Teaching" is a joint effort of the University of Maryland and the Maryland Public Broadcasting Center. Television components of the courses would be fed via both terrestrial facilities and satellites to public broadcasting stations beginning in the fall of 1980.

Given the growing number of satellite receiving earth stations and the growing interest in distributing courses or elements of courses by satellite, we may expect to see more new organizations forming for the purposes of acquiring and distributing adult materials. The most critical factor in the success of such endeavors will be economics—are there enough people willing to pay money to meet costs—and the availability of transponder time. All of the educational and public service satellite projects described thus far in this chapter rely on sharing arrangements with other users who own one or more full transponders. With the demise of the ill-fated RCA SATCOM III, transponders will be exceedingly scarce at least until mid-1981.

C-SPAN, QUBE

Another type of informational service now available through satellite and cable is C-SPAN, the Cable Satellite Public Affairs Network. C-SPAN, which has its own satellite uplink outside of Washington, D.C., relays televised sessions of the House of Representatives via SATCOM 1, transponder 9. C-SPAN is carried by more than 550 cable systems with a potential audience in excess of 5 million homes. The project is run by a nonprofit organization, the National Cable Satellite Corporation.

C-SPAN originally offered its service to commercial and public broadcasters who declined to carry the feeds regularly, but the cable industry was interested and underwrote the initial costs. While Brian Lamb, who heads C-SPAN, acknowledges that there is no way to have an accurate head-count of who is watching, more and more cable systems are signing on. The production of the House coverage is controlled by the House itself, and fixed cameras are used. Thus far, they have not been obtrusive during sessions. It is interesting to note these days that the service has an enthusiastic audience in the offices of Representatives who, with their staff members, can now easily monitor the "action" on the floor.

C-SPAN also offers weekly transmissions especially designed for high schoolers but viewable by all cable subscribers. Each Wednesday morning, high school students are invited to the Capitol to interview and talk with a prominent government leader or newsmaker. The sessions, which are run in cooperation with the CLOSE-UP Foundation, are then televised and beamed via the satellite as part of C-SPAN's service. In 1980, C-SPAN began transmitting luncheon speakers from the National Press Club. Thus, C-SPAN is a "first" in enabling people to watch their government at work, unedited and uninterrupted. Such a service has obvious value in classrooms as well as for the at-home viewer.

Probably the most ambitious cable experiment which is also making use of satellite transmissions is the Warner Amex QUBE system in Columbus, Ohio. QUBE offers 30 channels of service and permits interaction by means of digital responses. Viewers have a channel selector much like the touch-tone dial of a telephone, and it is used to select channels as well as to respond numerically. A computer at the "headend" controls the system, tabulates responses, and records who is watching which channels. (For a detailed presentation on two-way interactive cable TV, see Chapter 12 of this book.)

Two channels on the Columbus system are devoted to credit and non-credit general enrichment courses which are offered both by QUBE itself (through acquisitions of programs from educational producers) and by local institutions such as Franklin University and The Ohio State University. The colleges and universities have formed their own consortium, the Higher Education Cable Council, to coordinate course offerings. Certain of the courses offered (one in personal finance, one in introductory accounting, and one in small business management) have been taught "live" and have made use of the interactive capability of the QUBE system. Students respond to questions about the content or answer test questions by touching the appropriately designated buttons on their QUBE consoles. It is conceivable in the future that QUBE might offer, for example, courses beamed directly from the University of Mid-America or the Maryland Center for Public Broadcasting via satellite. It is even possible, although considerably more complex and expensive, that interactive responses from students could be relayed back by satellite to the program's point of origin.

In Columbus, Warner Amex has begun another service on QUBE called "The Home Book Club," in which the Public Library of Columbus and Franklin County and OCLC (formerly the Ohio College Library Center) are participating. The service enables viewers to watch and participate in a discussion of a current best-seller. Questions are asked by the moderator, e.g., "Do you think this is Updike's best novel?" and the home QUBE viewer "touches the QUBE" to respond—the No. 1 button registers a "yes" vote, the No. 5 button means "no." This type of interactive video could also be shared among a number of QUBE communities using the satellite.

Warner Amex is planning to add its QUBE to new markets it will serve and to convert its present systems at least in those markets (probably those with over 100,000 viewers) where QUBE would be economically viable. Greater Cincinnati will have QUBE by the end of 1980, and Houston is also a target market. Warner Amex is bidding on franchises in Minneapolis, Atlanta, and Pittsburgh, where, if they are the successful bidder, QUBE would also be installed. Thus, several major QUBE cities could be linked by satellite for one-way and two-way transmissions with full interaction.

Another spin-off of QUBE (as noted by Taylor in Chapter 9) is the creation of a children's service, "Nickelodeon." Through its vice-president for education, Dr. Vivian Horner, Warner Amex is clearly committed to producing, acquiring, and distributing quality educational programs. But once it has developed the programs for its own systems, it has a market among other cable owners. By the end of 1979, Warner Amex was programming three transponders—No.'s 12, 18, and 19—on SATCOM 1. When additional satellite time becomes available, Warner Amex will be a likely candidate to expand its services via satellite.

Problems and Challenges

Losing a satellite is not a pleasant thing to have happen and involves economic loss, but this happens infrequently and can be compensated for with redundancy. When we review the short history of satellite-cable networking for public service and education, we realize that the easiest problems to solve are those involving the technology. For example, while cable penetration in the U.S. was only about 20 percent by mid-1979, it is growing and in some cities is much higher.

The relative scarcity of satellite earth stations is also temporary. The FCC's deregulation of ownership rules has already produced an expanded market of users and lower prices for the receive-only dish antennas. By the end of 1979, it was possible to purchase and install a 3-meter dish for around $10,000, and by mid-1980, manufacturers were offering dishes at a price under $3,000. Whether many homes will have their own receive-only satellite facilities remains debatable, but institutions and businesses undoubtedly will.

Another temporary problem—little available time on the current domestic communications satellites (especially after the December 1979 loss of SATCOM III shortly after launch)—will ease as the new generation of satellites is launched in the 1980s. RCA plans to launch two satellites in 1981s, with Western Union's "Advanced WESTAR" scheduled to go up on NASA's space shuttle (launch date uncertain due to delays in completion of the shuttle).

Given the improving technology, availability of terrestrial facilities, and history of successful experiments, will the public service market become a big customer of satellites and satellite-cable networks?

The evidence warrants a cautious "yes" but it may be too soon to know. PSSC estimates that from first point of contact with a member-client, a period of 18 months to 2 years may be required before that client actually signs up for an occasional event transmission or long-range operational service. The long lead-time seems to be necessary because for the member organization using satellites (and sometimes using cable) this is a new experience. Everyone from the director of communications for the company all the way to the president or even the board of directors must be convinced that such a new venture is worthwhile. This involves educating the individuals involved about the technologies and giving evidence of past successes. When we look at the history of public television's involvement in education we note that this reluctance to adopt new technologies is not unique to the satellite era. Despite its beginnings in education, public TV has never become a major force in formal education in the U.S. Partly this is due to institutionalized patterns and habits. Partly, too, it is a question of funding or lack thereof.

Who will decide what the service is to be? Who will pay? Who will benefit? All three questions must be answered for a public service to be viable. All too often, three different groups with different agendas fill each of the roles. The great virtue of the entertainment market for broadcasters and cablecasters is that the public decides (perhaps not on which programs get on the air but on which to watch), the public benefits, and the public pays (either directly as in pay TV or by product advertising). Such questions are not so easily answered in the public service arena.

For example, if we all agree that it is valuable for older adults without a high school diploma to be able to take courses by television (or cable), who is going to be able to aggregate the funds to produce the necessary materials and who is going to pay to watch? Sometimes the target audience has a real need but limited resources. In this case, the paying party may need to be government or some social service group. And then, how does the funder measure benefits? And who makes the programming decisions?

Even well-funded public service and educational institutions (which may spend anywhere from two to ten percent of their budgets on communications) may not be highly motivated to decrease costs and move to more efficient methods of distribution (satellites, cable) or may not know how to make the transfer. Decentralization of funding and decision making may hinder regional and national aggregation and cooperation.

The University of Mid-America has found, for example, that adoption of its courses is often hindered by professorial resistance at the departmental level of participating institutions. It is not enough for UMA to find a broadcast outlet; it must gain support from a recognized educational institution willing to grant credit to UMA students. (UMA itself offers no degrees.) This becomes difficult on occasion with our highly decentralized universities and colleges.

In the second year of its existence, PSSC undertook a study of major service organizations and their communications activities to understand more fully which groups would be the most likely to take advantage of new communications technologies. From that study and subsequent experience, it has become evident to PSSC that health-medical groups, followed by religious organizations, local and state government agencies, libraries, and educational institutions, would be most desirous of service from a combination of satellites and related technologies. This list is in approximate descending order of likelihood of use. Decentralized decision making and lack of significant "venture capital" is at the heart of the difficulty for most of these potential users with the exceptions of the health-medical organizations and the major religious communicators. Indeed it is interesting to note (see Chapter 9) that religion has already become a major user of satellites and cable.

National, state, and local governments often have well-defined needs but bureaucratic procedures make movement to innovate difficult. However, there are bright spots. For example, in Columbus, Ohio, the City passed cable regulations that included reserving a portion of the franchise fee for the City to administer a cable bureau which, among other things, is looking at construction of a City studio from which programs about local and state government could be originated. Some of the local governments providing programming on cable are Tulsa, Oklahoma; Madison, Wisconsin; and New York City in Manhattan. And the state of New York produces programming carried by cable systems in many municipalities as well. In another example, the city library in Abilene, Kansas, has equipped a very modest studio in its basement to originate programming on one cable channel. Not only can groups meeting there have their sessions televised, but there are reading programs originating from the library. (For more examples and discussions of government, library, and other public sector or "community" access programming, see Chapters 6 and 7.)

Apart from questions of funding and decentralization, one must recognize that adopting new media and technologies is a question of innovation. A body of research exists that tells us innovation is a process, one that takes time and often encounters quite predictable resistance. Successful innovations usually involve a "change agent"—a person or organization that shows what is possible and leads the way. Home Box Office was a pioneer and thus a change agent in establishing cable-satellite networks. Warner Amex may be such a change agent in opening up interactive video services. ACSN, C-SPAN, PSSC, and others are now acting as innovators in bringing together users and new technologies for the successful provision of educational and social services. Such early leaders illuminate the pathway and break down the barriers.

The Future for Cable, Satellites, and Education

We seem to be in one of those eras when the media of delivery are outstripping our ability to form the messages. We may also be on the threshold of such great changes in communications that we will look back on our expectations of the 1970s and call them naive. We do not yet know, for example, the role video discs will play, nor that of fiber optics. (The reader unfamiliar with these two technologies can find a helpful starting place with Chapters 13 and 12, respectively, in *The Cable/ Broadband Communications Book (Vol. 1) 1977-1978.*)

We do know that the market for education is growing for those past the traditional college years and that we are moving into a service economy. What is less certain is whether the somewhat fragmented public service community can be aggregated or brought together to present itself as a real market to potential programmers and distributors. Many of the existing programs and distribution systems that supply education and public service programming are heavily backed by federal and state funds. This may have to continue. On the other hand, in the fields of health, medicine, and religion, there are indications that people will pay for services and the funding if not totally sufficient is enough to guarantee viability of communications.

We also have learned that new technology seldom completely replaces or destroys an older one. This observation would lead us to believe that satellites bridging vast distances in the sky and cable weaving its extensive network on the ground have a natural role to play individually and together in serving the end user. The question is not whether service can be provided. The question is how much, and how soon?

Resources Mentioned

1. Miller, Jonathan, Managing Editor, *Satellite Week.*
2. Bramble, William J., Ausness, Claudine, and Marion, Roger, *Education on the Beam: A Progress Report on the Appalachian Satellite Project,* AESP, Evaluation Component, 301 Frazee Hall, University of Kentucky, Lexington, Kentucky 40506 (1976).
3. Lamb, Brian, President, C-SPAN, 3800 North Fairfax Drive, Arlington, Virginia 22203.
4. Huffman, Lucy, "Home Satellite Terminals—Boom or Bane?" *Satellite Communications,* December 1979, pp. 24-28.
5. Young, Elizabeth L., "President's Report, October 1979," Annual Report to the PSSC Membership. Unpublished paper.
6. Potter, James G., "Public Service Requirements for Private-Line Networks," Unpublished memo to Howard Hupe, Department of Health, Education and Welfare, May 15, 1978, p. 3.
7. McBride, Jack, Executive Consultant, University of Mid-America.
8. PSSC, "Developing Satellite Communications for Public Service: Prospects in Four Service Areas," NASA Contract NAS 5-23865, September 30, 1977.
9. McNeil, Donald R., President, University of Mid-America, Testimony before the Senate Subcommittee on Education, Arts and the Humanities, October 3, 1979.

Other Resources

1. Carlisle, Robert D.B., *Media and the Adult Student: One Man's Journal*, (Lincoln, Nebraska: Great Plains National Instructional Television Library, 1976).
2. Polcyn, Kenneth A., *An Educator's Guide to Communication Satellite Technology*, (Washington, D.C.: Andromeda Books, 1975).
3. Weinstock, Ruth (ed.), *Communications Technologies in Higher Education — 22 Profiles*, (Washington, D.C.: Communications Press, Inc., 1977).

Gary H. Arlen

11. Computers and Cable: An Overview

"Cable" and "television."

The two terms are used together so often that they have become intrinsically wed; even when someone says the word "cable" alone, it is generally assumed that the "TV" part is included. In the process, unfortunately, the emphasis has been strictly on cable as a video medium — which is, of course, a fact of thirty years' standing.

But the cable itself is a broadband transmission device, capable of carrying a variety of electronic signals. In the past few years, communications experts—within and outside the cable TV industry—have begun to exploit that capacity. The recognition of cable's data capabilities is now so great that many leading cable companies are setting up special departments to go after data communications and other business services. In the process, non-video uses of cable TV company facilities is rapidly increasing.

Gary H. Arlen heads his own communications research and consulting firm, Arlen Communications, Inc. He has been editor of several authoritative trade publications including VideoNews, Satellite News, The Pay TV Newsletter, *and most recently* The International Videotex Teletext News. *He contributes extensively to communications industry publications. Mr. Arlen has been on the faculty of the American University Graduate Business School since 1975, now holding the rank of adjunct professor.*

Such companies as Satellite Business Systems are encouraging cable TV companies to offer "local loops," i.e., local distribution, services for distribution to SBS customers in cabled communities. In fact, after more than a year of lobbying to find cable TV systems willing to participate in such a venture, SBS announced in early 1980 that it would set up such a venture, beginning in early 1981. SBS is a joint venture partnership of IBM, Comsat General, and Aetna insurance company. It expects to begin operations in early 1981 after its own satellite is launched and in place. Its primary offerings will include data communications, private line voice, and limited video teleconferencing.

For its initial tests, SBS will beam signals across the country—with Manhattan Cable (a subsidiary of Time, Inc.) and Viacom handling local distribution within their franchise areas of New York City and San Francisco, respectively.

Actually such local loop services—as an alternative to telephone company circuits or other data transmission links—is just one of the two major ways in which computers and business services fit into the cable TV industry. The second major activity is computer-fed information via cable TV as part of the growing world of the so-called "home information utility." This includes variations on teletext, viewdata, and other computerized information retrieval methods (see Chapter 13 and later in this chapter).

(There is also a third area of cable-computer involvement—namely internal accounting, billing, and day-to-day data processing activities of the cable TV company. Such activities are obviously much the same as those of any other retail or service business; they are generally handled internally, by service bureaus or by automatic data processing companies which specialize in cable TV billing. As cable TV services become more complex—with the addition of tiers of programming—such automated accounting becomes even more essential. Obviously, major cable companies are also employing data processing for their planning, engineering, and other activities involved in running the business. Such uses are excluded from this report on Computers and Cable, however, because they don't actually involve transmission of data and information through the cable system to service outside customers.)

Cable TV's ability to handle broadband communications—such as computer services—is so promising that the industry is plunging ahead in several directions to assure itself a stake in these non-video, non-entertainment uses of their facilities.

Business Services

Cable TV industry leaders have already identified and developed markets for their business services, by leasing dedicated circuits to corporate customers for local loop service—sometimes in direct competition with telephone company circuits.

Banks, brokerages, and other companies with several local branches are likely customers for such a service. In addition, companies needing to feed information (or exchange data) with other firms within the community can use such a service. Another possible customer is the national firm with scattered offices around the country; by using a cable TV satellite earth station as a downlink, the company could then use the cable system for local distribution within the communities—in essence replacing the telephone company or any other microwave carrier for intracity or local distribution. Of course, such a plan relies upon satellite transponder capacity being available and upon cable feeds to areas where the customers' plants, offices, or stores are located; it appears likely that some sort of arrangement—including a possible cable TV interface with specialized business communications firms (such as SBS)—will become widespread.

Growing Market for Local Services

The demand for local distribution services is perhaps best underscored by the flurry of activity among data processing firms. Xerox—through its proposed Xerox Telecommunications Network (XTEN) and its Ethernet (intra-building communications) systems—exemplifies the anticipated value of intracity broadband links. Although telephone company circuits, local microwave facilities (such as multipoint distribution service), and other offerings are available, many telecommunications industry leaders have identified cable TV systems as ideal for local distribution. Compared to over-the-air transmission, the coaxial or fiber optics cable offers equal or greater security, less use of spectrum space, and—once cable is nearly universal—almost complete access to the nation's cable/satellite network, i.e., every street in America.

Not surprisingly, one of the most advanced business/data offerings available on a cable TV system today is in the borough of Manhattan, New York City. Manhattan Cable TV, which serves the lower half of the borough—including the central business district, Wall Street, and the corporate headquarters strips—has been providing low speed data services to financial institutions and other customers since 1975. Those facilities and experiences are part of the reasoning behind SBS's decision to work with Manhattan Cable for New York City local loops.

Among Manhattan Cable's early customers were Manufacturers' Hanover Trust, Banker's Trust, American Express, and other financial institutions. The transmissions—with a 75 kilobaud capacity—terminate in the customers' main frame computers.

The revenues for intra-Manhattan data communications transmission are estimated to be in excess of $400 million annually—so there is ample reason to pursue such a market. While most analysts believe that few other metro areas would have such a concentrated demand for business/data services, it is generally acknowledged that most urban areas do have a continuing and growing need for computer communications services.

When its service began, Manhattan Cable dedicated two channels on its regular cable for its data customers. Anticipating considerable growth in the area, the company has now placed a special cable ("dedicated trunk") with 130 circuits and has started a marketing campaign to sell the service. Predictably, AT&T (via its local operating company, New York Telephone) complained to the New York State Public Service Commission that such a service was improper, but the PSC declined to stop Manhattan Cable from offering business services.

Although the company's current business communications ventures are in the data transmission realm (with the apparent blessing of the PSC), the eventual entry into private line voice service would also seem possible. Manhattan Cable's business trunk could even be used for digital transmission. Eventually, Manhattan Cable's features will include facsimile transmission, electronic mail, digitized voice, and a variety of other communications services.

Manhattan Cable is not the only cable TV firm pursuing such non-video ventures. A cousin company under the Time, Inc. banner, American Television and Communications, has also set up a separate division to develop data communications business, as a common carrier when necessary. (A common carrier service is, as defined by the FCC, an organization providing electronic communications "for hire"; that means companies such as the telephone company, satellite operators, or other communications firms will carry your message for a fee along their facilities. Such a set-up is different from broadcast or cable TV transmission in which, presumably, the communications company has a hand in choosing the programs to be sent out over its facilities.)

American TV and Communications, one of the three largest cable TV firms in the country, now operates as a microwave common carrier within the New York metropolitan area, specifically to carry data between a local bank's data processing center on Long Island and the bank's main offices in Manhattan. Such activities are separate from the cable TV business which ATC is pursuing in several of the area's jurisdictions. Presumably, under current laws, the common carrier services would continue to be regulated separately from the cable TV services. Nonetheless, such mixing of activities again underscores the immense interest on the part of cable TV operators in business data activities; it also contributes to the constantly blurring picture of what is cable.

Several other major cable TV operators are also eyeing similar projects, with some of them (like ATC) already dipping a toe into the common carrier waters via such routes as multipoint distribution service applications. MDS is a common carrier service, now widely used for pay TV delivery to apartment buildings, but also capable of one-way business communications to many locations within a metropolitan area. In spring 1980, the FCC began a massive proceeding looking into ways to expand the NDS business—and many cable TV companies, already active in the industry, are likely to be affected by any changes.

Many new cable TV franchise applicants are including business services directly in their proposals. One of the best examples of this situation is in Fairfield County, Connecticut—a posh jurisdiction which includes the city of Stamford. The county is a corporate headquarters haven, with many Fortune 500 firms located there. At least two of the cable franchises being considered in Fairfield as of early 1980 spelled out plans for business services. One of the applicants went so far as to specify plans to use Western Union satellite circuits to distribute business services locally and interconnect them with Western Union's own headquarters a few microwave hops away in New Jersey. Since one of the companies headquartered in Stamford is General Telephone and Electronics, it is easy to imagine several other scenarios in which data, voice, or other traffic could be served via local distribution arrangements marrying the satellite and cable technologies (although GTE presumably won't go to a cable TV circuit if its own facilities could be used).

The Touchy Issue of Rate-Setting

Building a road into business communications services is fraught with difficult questions. Not only are there no answers yet—but some insiders acknowledge that in many cases, the questions haven't even been asked.

One of the touchiest issues is in the realm of rate-setting. So far when a cable company itself has leased a circuit to a business customer for data communications, the offering has been on a contractual basis. Cable companies are reluctant to post a tariff of rates and services because that would make them look suspiciously like a common carrier, which in many cases the companies want to avoid at this time. To a great degree, cable firms have relied on the "flinch method" to establish prices on their leased channels. (That is, salesmen quote a price and if the potential customer flinches because it is too high, a lower fee is cited; if the client is too eager for that sum, the salesmen up the fee by saying hardware isn't included; the process of give and take continues until the flinches and winces end.)

Facilities Are Scattered

America is still a patchwork of franchised and unfranchised territories when it comes to cable TV. Moreover, even within the franchised areas there are substantial pockets of the community where wires have not been strung and where equipment has not been installed. Because of this scattered arrangement, the cable TV industry often cannot provide local loop facilities to national companies seeking service in specific areas.

More to the point, the current trend to create multiple franchises within a big city (witness the Houston example, where four different companies are wiring the city itself), not to mention other companies for the suburbs, creates another problem for major corporate users. The current nature of American businesses is to cluster a number of plants or offices within a single community. Just as chain stores or financial institutions have branches around town, so do major manufacturing or retail companies.

If each of those offices, stores, or plants is in a different cable TV franchise area, there may be problems in linking up all the sites. Obviously technical standards of the different cable TV companies should be compatible. The more serious question, however, is how to connect each system so that a local communications network is established by hopscotching across jurisdictions and cable TV facilities.

This issue is of prime concern to companies like Satellite Business Systems, which is encouraging the idea of cable TV systems as local loops. To some of SBS's customers, the concept is very attractive: bring a satellite signal into one ground station, then distribute it locally via cable. The only missing link in the web could be the absence or inability of local cable TV systems to handle such a service.

Analog versus Digital

Almost every telecommunications expert has declared that the 1980s will be the "Digital Decade," an era when transmission systems convert to the higher-quality signals which digital communications provide. As an indicator of the digital momentum: Intelsat, the international satellite organization, has targeted the full conversion of its worldwide network to digital facilities by 1986.

In simplest terms, digital communications—a companion technology of the binary computer era—involves pulses of discrete or discontinuous signals; in contrast, analog transmission (generally represented by a flowing wave) is a continuously variable signal. To convert signals from one transmission format to the other, some form of "modem" (modulator/demodulator) is used.

The significance of this technological development is underscored by a number of factors. For example, "computer talk" (which is generally in digital languages) is the heftiest part of SBS's business. Hence SBS is establishing a digital system which it would prefer not to clutter with modems. But most cable TV systems, even the newly built ones, use analog technology. Such a situation obviously will pose problems in the short-term.

Common Carrier Regulation

Still another issue which must be confronted is the question of common carrier status. "Common carriers" face rate regulation, tariffs, and other aspects of government oversight at the federal and state levels which are anathema to most cable TV operators. As indicated above, some cable TV companies don't wince at the thought of common carrier status for parts of their operations (such as MDS subsidiaries), but the entire concept is a sensitive political issue—especially as the revised Communications Act proposals have moved through Congress in recent years.

Exactly how raw a nerve the issue touches is exemplified by a minor brouhaha which surfaced in Washington in late 1979. An authoritative trade publication reporting on a speech by National Cable TV Association President Thomas Wheeler noted that Wheeler voiced hesitation about his industry doing anything which could be construed as common carrier activities. But many leading cable TV operators apparently didn't care to hear their industry spokesman seemingly cut them off from additional revenue avenues. Wheeler defended his stance— emphasizing that his underlying objective is to keep the *entire* cable TV business from being regulated as a common carrier. Conceivably that leaves room for cable TV companies that desire it to create their own common carrier ventures. Nonetheless, as cable TV companies move deeper into local distribution of other companies' transmissions, the issue will continue to crop up.

System Capacity

Finally—and perhaps most significantly—is the matter of system capacity. Many of the nation's cable TV systems simply do not have enough channels to carry what they *must* retransmit under current FCC rules, let alone what they would like to carry. The problem has already become a difficult one just in the matter of video signals—the must-carry broadcast stations, the attractive and profitable pay TV, tiered programming, and other new offerings.

The newest urban cable TV systems are being built with 35, 80, or more channels; one franchise proposal in the metropolitan New York area calls for 125 channels. On the other hand, older systems (generally in small towns) often have only 12 or 20 channels. While it can be argued that the small-town systems would face less demand for dedicated leased channels to be used for data communications, many cable industry leaders recognize the need to make such facilities available everywhere. That is because many national corporations have branch offices, plants, or customers with which they want to communicate in all parts of the country. Indeed, in this example lies the reason why AT&T is such a formidable competitor: its system can and does go *anywhere.*

How serious is the problem of capacity to the cable TV industry? According to the experts, about two-thirds of all the cable systems in the country have only 12 channels of capacity. But because most of them are small-town, classic cable systems, they serve fewer than half of the nation's cable TV homes. That ratio will change even further in the early 1980s because high-capacity urban cable systems are being built at a rapid rate. Observers believe that by 1984 almost every cable system in the country will have increased channel capacity—most likely with enough room for the extra services demanded by business/data users.

The Home Computer-Cable Connection

Among the new services many cable TV systems will offer directly to their subscribers is a variety of computer-linked offerings. These broadly fit into the concept of the "home information utility" which can take a variety of forms. The cable TV industry is already experimenting with several of these ideas, as are other major communications/information companies ranging from AT&T, RCA, CBS, GTE, and IBM to a variety of other hardware and programming sources.

The home information utility involves delivery of "alpha-numeric" material (words and numbers) to a TV screen. It comes in a variety of forms, such as "teletext," which is carried encoded within the normal broadcast signal, and "viewdata" (sometimes called "videotex"), which is transmitted via a telephone line and hooked into the TV screen. (See Chapter 13 for a fuller discussion of these.)

By using a device at home, viewers can request information to be displayed on the TV screen. The home device may be as simple as a pad which resembles a hand-held calculator; or it may be a computer-keyboard which permits complicated interactive "conversations" with the system's computer.

The data in the system may be as simple as airline timetables or stock market figures; or it can be as complicated as financial planning, budgeting, and tax-return calculations. Depending on the extent of the data bank, customers can call up weather forecasts for different parts of the world to which they'll travel, educational programs, interactive videogames, and personal business information.

Entertainment, Catalog Shopping Come First

Not surprisingly, cable TV is taking its first steps into this computerized world via a number of routes which are fundamentally oriented toward entertainment—with some informational components.

The first example is the much-discussed QUBE system, the two-way cable TV operation in Columbus, Ohio, established by Warner Cable (and now operated by its successor company, Warner Amex Cable). The system has also been franchised for Cincinnati, parts of Houston, and other Warner Amex systems. In its earliest stages, QUBE's two-way capacity was largely used to poll viewers instantaneously on various topics of public concern.

When American Express bought a half interest in Warner Cable in late 1979, one of the first new projects was to extend that capacity. Warner Amex Cable announced that it would quickly launch a computerized catalog shopping service. QUBE subscribers could look into a special video version American Express gift "brochure" (similar to the ones which come stuffed into credit card monthly statements) and, by pushing buttons, order items and charge them to their account. Soon thereafter Sears, one of the nation's major catalog shopping services, indicated it would step up its long-rumored interest in similar shop-at-home services via cable TV. (A detailed discussion of two-way interactive programming by QUBE in Columbus, the cable system in Reading, Pennsylvania, and others—including opportunities and issues involved—is presented in Chapter 12 of this book.)

In a slightly different realm, a way to marry the services of the home computer into cable TV technology surfaced with the creation of PlayCable—a project of Mattel Electronics (the big toy company's electronic games unit) and General Instruments (via its subsidiary Jerrold Electronics, one of the nation's leading cable TV equipment suppliers). Mattel was developing its entry into the home computer business: Intellivision. Like most other companies, Mattel decided to take a go-slow approach and translated the computer capacity into the marketable format of videogames. Hence the first versions of Intellivision were modular units—which could be bought separately. One component was strictly for videogames; the other was a keyboard which could convert the cartridge game component into a small data processing unit. Such a device, similar to those of many other consumer electronics companies, is a self-standing unit.

Now enter Jerrold and General Instruments: by hooking the Intellivision components into a two-way cable feed, it would be possible to avoid investing in the home cartridges, memory units, or other ancillary devices. The cable customer could merely use the remote terminal (plus accessories to plug into the cable system) and then access a data bank at the cable TV headend. That data bank might include a variety of videogame offerings (hence the term PlayCable) but it would also—eventually—have a far greater array of material such as accounting programs, research information, and other data. As with most other current information utility services, PlayCable is capable of "time sharing." For example, a cable customer can query the computer for information; if the project does not need "real time" response, the data can be transmitted down line when circuits are available and loaded into a microprocessor memory cartridge or cassette at the viewer's terminal. Then the viewer can play back the information at his convenience. The same process can be used for simply playing a videogame—without the expense of going to the store to buy a cartridge.

Mattel and General Instruments began tests of PlayCable on four U.S. systems in April 1980—at about the same time the Intellivision units went on sale around the country. Thus homes without cable could use the stand-alone Intellivision games, while cable families in the test markets could go a step further and use the PlayCable technology.

Other Information Retrieval Systems

While QUBE and PlayCable represent substantial, sophisticated ventures into computer-cable system interaction, a variety of other home information projects are also being examined by the cable TV industry. For example "CableText," a joint venture of Satellite Syndicated Systems and Scientific-Atlanta, will beam a national information bank down the cable/satellite network aboard one feed from a video signal. Since this is strictly a one-way offering, it may have severe restrictions on a national scale; that is, typical teletext information (such as airline schedules or emergency medical advice) would not be adaptable to a national audience. Nonetheless, a substantial amount of information could be incorporated into such a nationwide feed.

On a local level, Dow Jones is experimenting on a Texas cable TV system in business information services, which subscribers can call up. A number of other tests are underway around the country, as information companies and cable TV operators examine ways to apply the broadband transmission capacity of cable TV to the information retrieval ability of today's computer technology.

A Promising Future

It took cable TV nearly 30 years to make its first major plunge into expanding its broadband capabilities for services other than one-way video transmission. The strides of the past few years—plus the indications of what the industry will do during the next few years—appear to hold great promise for cable's leap into the role of a major transmission medium for all forms of computer-related services. In part the current enthusiasm is being motivated by a reawakened sense of competition— a feeling that if cable TV doesn't do it, someone else will. To a great degree, the new leaders of the cable TV industry have recognized the tremendous capacity of their facilities, pushed along by demands from other industries which want to take advantage of this capacity.

There is no reliable gauge to predict today what share of the transmission market the cable TV industry will capture during the

1980s. That is because its development will be taking place concurrently with a number of other changes in transmission facilities. The rapid proliferation of technology coupled with the notoriously slow regulatory consideration (even in this age of "deregulation") means that all these offerings can and will face unforeseen struggles. Moreover, the tender economy of the 1980s may necessitate unexpected turns from plans envisioned when the ventures were originally promulgated.

Whatever the final scenario, it appears certain that cable TV will have a substantial role in the expanding world of data communications and computer-related services. The exact nature of that role will be hammered out by the technology and marketplace developments ahead.

Resources

Because the development of the cable-computer is so new, very little authoritative information has surfaced other than the private reports and promotional material of organizations involved in the industry. Material in this report is based on the author's research in the development of material for *Satellite News, VideoNews,* and *The International Videotex Teletext News.*

Organizations involved with this emerging industry—whose executives have been particularly helpful in supplying information—include Manhattan Cable TV, Satellite Business Systems, American TransCommunications, National Cable Television Association, American TV & Communications, and the Federal Communications Commission.

John Wicklein

12. Two-Way Cable: Much Promise, Some Concern

Two-way cable has been heralded as the opening to communication of tomorrow. The service it can provide could obviously be of great benefit to us all; its potential for intruding in our lives makes us wonder if these benefits will cause us losses of individual liberty. But two-way, blessings and threat, is here: it cannot be ignored.

To talk of two-way cable development today is to talk primarily of three innovative experiments, one commercial and two in the area of public services:

1. The QUBE system installed by Warner Cable Corporation (now Warner Amex) in Columbus, Ohio;

2. The N.Y.U.-Reading project involving community-access programming for the elderly;

3. Japan's investigation of two-way as a means of community development.

John Wicklein, in charge of news and public affairs programming for the Corporation for Public Broadcasting, is writing a book on the social consequences of the new technologies of communicatiion, which will be published by Viking Press in winter 1981. He is the co-author, with Monroe Price, of Cable Television: A Guide for Citizen Action, *Pilgrim Press, New York, 1972.*

These systems are fully-realized interactive uses of the two-way technology. Canada's Department of Communications has some experiments in the works that may prove equally interesting. But most other two-way cable operations (of which there are few) have been installed to let subscribers select sports, entertainment, and film programming on pay cable channels. Because they give a broad picture of two-way systems to come, this report will focus on the operations in Columbus, Reading, and Japan.

Columbus Discovers Two-Way

In doing research for a book, I spent several days in Columbus talking to executives and producers who were developing QUBE:

"Go in," said my host. I stepped through the door into what appeared to be a carpeted inner office lighted from above by fluorescent panels. "Take three steps." I did as he told me. From across the hall, I heard the clatter of a teleprinter springing into operation.

"The room has sensed your presence — it sent the alarm to our computer," my host informed me. "The computer activated our printer across the hall—but it could have activated one at police headquarters, as well."

My host was Miklos Korodi, general manager of QUBE, the two-way, interactive cable system Warner Amex has installed in Columbus, Ohio.

The motion-sensing burglar alarm is one of several home-security services QUBE plans to offer its subscribers. "Here, watch this." Korodi held a piece of burning rope up to a smoke detector in the ceiling. A raucous buzzer alarm sounded in the room, and the computer printer kicked in again. In a live installation, information on the location of the house, flammables inside, and the position of the nearest fire hydrant would be printed out at the firehouse while the alarm is rousing sleepers in the burning home.

QUBE has announced it will also offer a "duress" button to call police in a situation threatening the subscriber's safety and a medical emergency button to call for an ambulance. A personal security medallion will be an optional extra: an elderly woman could wear the medallion around her neck, to press should she slip and fall on the ice while putting out the garbage. The alarm, relayed by radio through the "black box" inside the house, tells the ambulance crew her medical history—what medication she is taking, any medicines she must avoid.

QUBE's engineers designed the black box, a microprocessor that controls the home protection system. The Data General computer at QUBE's "headend" queries the box continually, asking, in effect, "Is everything all right there?" If it isn't, the microprocessor, a compact computer in its own right, spells out the problem so the city's emergency forces can respond.

(Security services are beginning to be offered by some other systems, but none as yet has been reported to be a commercial success in urban systems. In some cities in Japan, Australia, and France, utility meters are now "read" by the system, rather than by an employee of the utility.)

Inventing the New Wheel

Korodi, an outgoing, enthusiastic man in his early forties, seems delighted by the things the new two-way cable system can do. So do members of his staff; the ones I talked to obviously believe they are inventing the wheel for the new communications. Both Korodi and the Warner Amex management in New York think that the sale of multiple services will make this cable system, technologically the most advanced in the country, a commercial success. QUBE (a trade name that stands for nothing in particular) is never referred to by its developers as "cable television." They speak of "two-way cable": one line carrying signals from the headend out to the customer, one line relaying his responses back to the headend. Or, better yet, "two-way, *interactive* cable."

There are reasons for that. After all, a burglar *is* interacting with the system when he takes three steps in your home and sets off an alarm. Most of the television services of QUBE's multi-service offering are built around its two-way, interactive capability. This permits subscribers at home to make decisions about what the system is offering them and then, through the adapter on their standard TV sets, tell the computer what those decisions are. On the interactive channels, it allows them to "talk back" to their televisions.

"They like to play the system," says one Warner Amex executive, and, indeed, they are being programmed to do that by QUBE's promotional campaign. "Touch the button," says the large, four-color, slick paper brochure, "and enter the era of two-way participation in the infinite, unfolding, never-ending worlds of QUBE."

30 Channels to Play With

These worlds include 30 channels controlled by touch buttons on a keypad console about the size of a plug-in electronic calculator. Ten channels provide the commercial and public television stations, a public access channel, and a program guide channel. A second 10 supply "Premium" selections—primarily movies that have not yet played on commercial television. Premium channel 10 supplies something else you don't see on commercial television. For $3.50 a touch, you get soft porno (to use the QUBE staff's reference, "hard-R") films with predictable titles such as *Dr. Feelgood* and *Hot Times*. The soft core channel is fed into the home only if a subscriber specifically orders it. In addition, it and all other Premium channels can be locked by removing a key that, presumably, can be kept out of the hands of the children. Premiums also include entertainment specials produced or purchased by QUBE, self-help courses (such as *Shorthand* and *How to Prepare for College Entrance Examinations*), and local college sports. Unlike Home Box Office, which charges subscribers a fixed fee for each month of pay-TV programs, QUBE's computer bills viewers for each selection, at prices that range from 75 cents for *Shorthand* to $9 (in football-maniacal Columbus) for a live telecast of an Ohio State football game. This is in addition to the $10.95 QUBE customers pay every month for the basic service.

You are not a passive viewer when you push a Premium channel button, because it is going to cost you. The computer is solicitous about your having to make such a decision, and allows you a two-minute grace period before it enters your selection into its memory.

Even greater participation is demanded by the system in the third group of 10—the Community channels, where viewers are solicited to "interact" with their sets. Most of the interaction centers on the "Columbus Alive" channel, which offers programs every weekday, produced out of QUBE's studio building on the Olentangy River Road. This is the "headend," rebuilt from a large-appliance warehouse. It has three television studios equipped with color minicams that double as cameras in mobile units on assignments around Columbus. And here is housed the computer that is the heart of the interactive system. This is a "polling" computer, which gathers billing and response data from subscribers. The computer sweeps all subscribers' homes at six-second intervals, asking: Is the set turned on? What channel has been punched up? What was the last Response Button touched?

The home console has five Response Buttons in addition to the channel-selection buttons. The first two can be used as "Yes-No" buttons; all five can be used to answer multiple-choice questions or punch up number codes to indicate, as one possibility, selection of products displayed on the screen.

One evening I went to the Olentangy studio to watch the staff produce *Columbus Alive*, a variation of the original *Today* show on NBC. The two co-hosts and their guests would be in two-way communication with 30,000 subscribers in QUBE's franchise area, which encompasses 104,000 homes. The night I saw the show, an attractive, articulate woman was interviewing a priest and a former nun on "What is it like to be a homosexual in Columbus?" She told her audience that it had been estimated there were 80,000 homosexuals in the Columbus "metro" area, which has more than a million people. "Let's find out how many of you know homosexuals," she said. A statement, superimposed on the livingroom furniture in the set, appeared on the screen:

I have a friend, relative or acquaintance who I know is homosexual.

"If you do know a homosexual," said the host, "push Button Number 1 for Yes; if you do not, press Button Number 2 for No. Touch in now."

Within seconds, the computer supplied a result to the studio's character generator, which printed it out on the screen:

Yes   65%

No   35%

The host continued the interview, with interruptions to throw similar questions to the audience and get their responses. When the show got slow, I used the keypad to do some channel-switching. I punched up the porn channel to find out if it was really there. It really was. On another channel, I found a young, bearded instructor from a local college presenting a three-credit course on basic English composition. He took attendance by asking individual members of the class (who had paid tuition directly to the college to "Touch in." He salted his lecture with Q and A. segments asking students to use the response buttons to answer true or false, or pick the correct answer from five multiple choices flashed on their screens. (In some "QUBE Campus" classes, if an enrolled student gets the answer correct, the red Message Light on his keypad lights up: Instant reward.)

The Commercial Process

Back at *Columbus Alive* I found the male co-host seated beside a man in a dark gray suit who looked like a bookstore clerk. He was indeed introduced as a representative of Readmor Bookstores in Columbus who had come to talk to us about hardcover versus paperback books. After a short exchange with his guest on the merits of each, the host asked the audience a series of interactive questions about their reading habits. The computer reported back the not-surprising information that more people bought paperbacks than hardcovers, and the surprising information that 41 percent said they bought more than 10 paperbacks a month. This may reflect the fact that QUBE's franchise area is in the affluent western side of the city and suburbs, and encompasses the Ohio State University campus. (Three other cable companies cover the rest of the city.)

As the segment is ending, the titles of four books mentioned on the program are posted on the screen, numbered one through four. "If you would like to order one of these books," said the host, "touch the corresponding buttons. The computer will gather your name and address, and Readmor will send you the book."

Now the interesting thing about this "book interview" is that it was actually a commercial, paid for by Readmor Bookstores. At no time was it identified as such to the audience. When I asked one of the show's producers why it was not, she said it was because they wanted the show "to flow into informal commercials so it won't interrupt the rest of the content." QUBE sells this eight-minute segment as an "Informercial," charging the advertiser about $75 in the *Columbus Alive* slot. A two-minute version called a "Qubit," sells for half that rate.

Informercials and Qubits have also been used for test marketing. Advertisers and market research firms have long used Columbus, with its 600,000 middle Americans, as Test City USA. *Us* magazine asked QUBE viewers to "Touch in" their judgments on five proposed magazine covers, and then published the two that rated tops: John Wayne and The Incredible Hulk. From the willingness of their responses, subscribers apparently enjoyed becoming part of the commercial process. Korodi sees advertisers asking viewers to choose between pilot commercials or rate their "interest level," at 10-second intervals, as they watch situation comedy (sitcom) pilots.

Computerized two-way systems, if they catch on, can make Nielsen and Arbitron ratings obsolete. No "sampling" guesswork—the QUBE computer knows, down to the last household, how many sets are tuned to one of its channels. Korodi: "We can give the advertiser demographics he never had before—how many people in the $20,000 to $30,000 bracket are watching this commercial, that sort of thing," The computer, he went on, can cross-reference answers to opinion questions with income groups, to tell which economic class wants what.

The computer is capable of charging an order for a book or other merchandise to the subscriber's credit card or to a charge account at a department store, if the subscriber provides the number to be fed into its memory. This is only a step from another service— called Electronic Funds Transfer or EFT—which QUBE expects to test in a year or so. In this, subscribers could, for example, select products and pay for them immediately by transferring funds from their bank accounts to the accounts of businesses that advertise goods and services. To do this, each subscriber would have a confidential Personal Identification Number that he could punch into the system to tell the computer that it is really he, and not an electronic embezzler, who is ordering the money to be transferred.

"This is all possible today," Korodi told me, "but on each service we have to ask: Is it a business? We are addressing ourselves to people's needs, then looking at it to see if it is economically justifiable, then we will market it."

Potential for Major Economic Success

After two years of experience with QUBE (the system went into operation December 1, 1977). Warner Amex is convinced that some form of two-way is economically viable. The company has put at least $20 million into QUBE to find that out. To recoup this, and, it hopes, begin realizing a profit on such operations, the company wants to expand two-way service to others of its 138 cable systems around the country. It has been granted two-way franchises in Houston and Cincinnati, has applied for another in Pittsburgh, and plans for a third in Boston. Other cable companies have experimented with this form of service in a limited way, but so far only Warner Amex has staked a lot of money on the idea that two-way may be the wave of the future.

Cable industry leaders say they are watching QUBE closely, on the possibility that interactive cable may provide the new element that will make the industry achieve the "critical mass" of 30 percent saturation of American homes—agreed by many to be the magic figure that will make it a major economic success—by the early 1980s. Cable now reaches into 19 percent, or about 14 million homes.

Financial analysts are again looking at cable as a growth industry. In the backs of their minds is the forecast by Arthur D. Little Co., the research firm in Cambridge, Massachusetts, that movies you pay for in the home will put movie theatres out of business by 1985. Promoting the use of two-way to charge subscribers only for the specific films and shows they watch may make this form of home entertainment become big business. It is two-way's capability of selective payment for entertainment and consumer services that intrigues cable executives responsible for profit and loss. As one Teleprompter official put it. "We feel definitely that two-way will be here ultimately; it just has to be ecomically viable."

Supplying only those services that can produce a profit makes sound business sense, but it leaves something to be desired from the standpoint of giving people the services they need. Some needed services that a two-way system can provide will never turn a profit. A channel whereby a city clinic could conduct a medical diagnosis with responses from a person who is housebound is a sure money-loser. So are channels that could be used for two-way communication between city security forces and the people in their homes during a local disaster. Two-way system operators may find that they have to provide some nonprofit services to the community in return for being franchised to make a profit off of the community. (Chapter 5 presents a discussion of community needs assessment and some of the services that might be offered; Chapters 6, 7, and 10 describe many specific public service applications of cable television, some of them two-way, some of them including the use of satellite in the delivery of services.)

QUBE has already acknowledged this obligation by offering channel facilities for participatory "town meetings " and government hearings, at no cost to the community. One such meeting was held in Upper Arlington, a prosperous suburb in QUBE's franchise area. Using multiple-choice questions, the Upper Arlington Planning Commission asked QUBE subscribers to comment on a draft plan for renewing an older part of the city. The computer was programmed to "narrowcast" the hearing only to those subscribers who lived within the suburb. Two previous public meetings on the issue drew a total of about 125 citizens each. The meeting held by two-way, the computer reported, attracted a total of 2,000 residents during its two and one-half hours. "The point of doing this was to involve the people of the community in their own future," said Patricia Ritter, an Upper Arlington administrator who co-produced the event for the city. In that, she said, the televised hearing was a success.

Among the questions the Commission asked was, "Should a building maintenance code by adopted?" The computer, knowing where each response was coming from, reported that sentiment in favor of such a code ran about 12 percent higher in the older section, which contains a number of apartment houses, than in the newer, single-family areas of town. Residents who "touched in" their responses to the questions knew immediately if they were in the majority or the minority—results were displayed within seconds after they pressed the buttons. To make subscribers feel free to express their views, the QUBE hosts assured them that the computer was set in a mode that would not identify any answer as coming from an individual home. If the computer had been set differently, it could have pinpointed the answers supplied by each household and produced a profile of each subscriber's participation for the evening. If any of the participants had qualms about feeding their opinions into the system, they did not express them. Most, apparently, thought the experiment was an advance in participatory democracy. Asked if they wanted to do it again, 96 percent pressed the Yes button, and within 10 seconds the computer, having worked out that percentage, relayed it to the home screens.

Can Privacy Be Safeguarded?

As in other parts of the system, the people of Upper Arlington took part enthusiastically in the interactive programming. They had previously been hooked on two-way by being asked to give preferences on products, opinions on political issues, and suggestions for social issues to be discussed on *Columbus Alive*. Some had been hooked on the audience-participation game shows presented by QUBE. In one program, similar to the national *Gong Show*, viewers can direct the show by pressing the Yes-No buttons to tell whether an amateur act should continue. When a majority of those watching press No, the talent is dumped in mid-performance. Now that kind of power gives you a certain satisfaction. It is fun. Two-way cable is *fun*. Playing the system, subscribers are only vaguely aware that the preferences they state, the products they select, the personal opinions they express can all be stored in the computer's memory and tallied, analyzed, and cross-referenced with demographic and financial information that is known about them. Several subscribers I interviewed said they were not concerned by this. One young working woman told me, "I don't feel that I have any reason to be afraid—I may be naive, but I don't care if my opinions are recorded." Their attitude seemed to be, Who would *want* that stuff, anyway? Who could profit by it?

Someone might.

Since the QUBE system was installed and its capabilities became known, reporters, city officials, and others in the community have considered the possibility that two-way might prove to be a method of invading subscribers' privacy. When I discussed this with QUBE executives, they replied, in effect, "Yes, it *could* happen, but it won't happen here."

Dr. Vivian Horner, Warner Amex vice-president in charge of program development, expressed it to me this way: "People don't think of the telephone as an invasion of privacy. Yet each call you make is recorded. When people get as used to two-way cable as to the telephone, they will take it much as a matter of fact. If people feel threatened by it, they will drop it—the economic base will keep it honest." A QUBE sales executive echoed this idea: "We have a time bomb here. We have to be extremely careful and set up very strict rules. If we abuse them, we're fools."

The Warner Amex management, aware that the issue of privacy would inevitably be raised, drew tight security around the system's polling computer. Access to the computer's records, the company says, is restricted to three top-level executives; entrance to the master control room, which houses the computer, is restricted to those who work there.

At a meeting of the Communication Commission of the National Council of Churches in New York in the fall of 1978, Dr. Gerry Jordan, QUBE's director of educational development, said that on-air talent and moderators of public affairs programs always caution viewers whenever the computer is set to record names and addresses of those who push response buttons. They don't warn them, he said, when questions relate to purchases—if a name has to be recorded in order to send, or bill for, a product or service. When Commission members pressed Jordan on what safeguards had been built in to protect the individual's right of privacy, he said: "I think we at QUBE are more concerned than the subscribers are. We expected it to be much more of an issue with the public than it has turned out to be." Early on, *The New York Times* put the question to Gustave M. Hauser, president and chairman of Warner Amex. "People who buy the service will simply have to accept that they give up a bit of their privacy for it " he replied. "Beyond that, we'll try to protect their privacy all we can."

When I interviewed Hauser at the company's headquarters in New York, he said he felt the issue of privacy was "a serious one for the whole society." The amount of personal information QUBE collects is trivial compared to the total amount that the computers of government and businesses are amassing, he added. "For us, it is a question of responsibility and using the system properly."

Will people drop out of a two-way system if they find out that their "interactions" are being monitored? First of all, they do not have to be told they are being monitored: No law requires the cable operator to tell them. But beyond that, people will probably get used to it. Once the services provided by two-way cable TV become almost indispensable, people won't worry about them. They won't, that is, unless objections are raised by consumer protection groups and by legislators concerned with two-way cable's implications for civil liberties. Federal, state, and local legislation is nonexistent in this area. Most systems are franchised by local municipalities, using guidelines set by the Federal Communications Commission. The guidelines say nothing about restrictions on two-way cable.

Bob Kindred, who publishes *Cable TV Programs*, a guide to what can be found on local cable television systems in the Midwest, would like to see two-way thrive. But he is afraid that sometime in the future people will rebel against two-way cable, unless restraints are placed on how it uses the information that its computer collects. "A number of questions they ask, I don't answer," he said. (A vice-president of a Columbus bank had the same thought: "I won't put anything in there I don't want people to know.") People are going to want protection built in by law, Kindred added, "and this will probably help cable."

Reading's Service for the Elderly

About the time the QUBE system was establishing its commercial credentials, another pilot project was demonstrating the usefulness of two-way cable in providing public services. This was an experiment involving elderly citizens in Reading, Pennsylvania, a residential city of 88,000 about 60 miles northeast of Philadelphia. The project was developed by the Alternate Media Center of New York University under a grant from the National Science Foundation (NSF).

Privacy was not a particular problem in the Reading system, because the technology was deliberately planned to be very simple, without the benefits (and drawbacks) of the computer, so that elderly citizens could run it themselves.

In 1974, NSF asked for proposals for experiments in the delivery of social services via two-way cable. The Center, which had spent three years helping to develop one-way cable systems across the country that would promote citizen access, came up with an idea that won the Foundation's support. It proposed linking three neighborhood community centers—one a multipurpose center and two housing projects for the elderly—in Reading, to permit older citizens to exchange ideas about mutual problems. The set-up also allowed them to contact government and social welfare officials at remote origination sites such as City Hall, the County Courthouse, the Social Security office, schools, and other community facilities.

"Technology by itself is an idiot," Red Burns, executive director of the NYU center, told me. "What we wanted to do was set up a system of users who would use the technology in ways that would meet their needs."

Professor Burns, whose hair confirms the name she uses, said the designers deliberately set out to use the system as a socializing force. To do this, and stay within the economic restrictions of the grant, the system was designed primarily to bring elderly people together at the three centers, rather than have them interact, as in the QUBE system, only through their sets at home. However, to test the possibility of interactive participation by people who were housebound, the Center paid the local cable system to adapt the television sets of 117 elderly persons so they could view the cabled activities and take part by phone. (ATC-Berks County TV Cable Co. provided the cable lines free, but was reimbursed for installing return lines to the centers and for maintenance of the system.) As the experiment progressed, the response from these people was so positive that the cable system decided to carry the service for all of its local subscribers, so that they, too, could phone in their comments.

What Needs Can It Serve?

As the final report to NSF pointed out, most technological innovations are designed to assist the producer, rather than the consumer, of public services:

"Rather than asking how public agencies can use cable television to provide public services, we asked: How can citizens use cable television to obtain public services and provide services for themselves?"

At first, the elderly citizens of Reading showed a desire to "make television"—copy the programs they had seen on commercial TV. But then they caught on to the real benefits—to them—of two-way: exchanging ideas and experiences, talking back and forth, and producing simple, interactive segments that gave them the information they needed.

The Alternate Media Center asked them to organize their own local Community Policy Board to decide what kind of programming should be attempted. In the opening stage, it hired a group of older people with no professional television experience to operate the system. Basically, this consisted of one black-and-white camera and a TV monitor at each location, and portable videotape camera for use at remote points and for interviews in the field There was a small control room with switching equipment that could cut back and forth, allowing speakers and listeners at each location to be seen and heard by those at the other locations.

Almost all the programming was live, with some tape inserts, used mainly as discussion leaders. The system transmitted two hours a day, five days a week.

The content the participants chose included weekly sessions in which they talked about their problems with the mayor, city council members, county commissioners, and representatives of social service agencies. As they got into it, citizens and the mayor began calling each other by their first names. Evening sessions were scheduled to allow them to take part in city budget hearings and in hearings on the allocation of federal community development funds. Other programs included discussions of local history, cooking lessons, group singing, and poetry reading. More than 70 public and nonprofit agencies were invited to use the system to communicate with older citizens. Members of the community held discussions on the cable to decide what kinds of programs would be most useful and what should be dropped.

Since many expected to end their lives in nursing homes, the group asked for a series on such homes in the Reading area. The producer used videotape for this one, because the audience wanted to see what the insides of these homes were like. On several occasions, the operator of a home was brought in to a center and questioned by elderly citizens in the studio after a tape had been shown on that particular home.

At the request of a citizen who was housebound, a retired volunteer fireman produced "The Changing Face of Reading," on what was happening to the city. One outdoor sequence at night required extensive lighting, and the producer prevailed on his friends in the Fire Department to provide ladders and lights.

To get people to use the system, the community board realized they could not make every program a serious discussion of welfare concerns. So lighter entertainment was presented, usually involving the participants themselves: sing-alongs, reminiscences, quiz shows, and the like. On several occasions, the community used peer-group counseling on insomnia, sex, and when to stop driving a car.

People coming to the televised sessions often recognized friends at other centers whom they had not seen for years. Waving and calling out became so prevalent during "serious" discussions with public officials that the system operators decided to include a 10-minute "Party Line" segment at the end of each day's programming, so that people could socialize with their neighbors at other centers. Gathering together in the familiar community rooms that were used as studios helped people feel comfortable with the system, and lose their early inhibitions concerning the technology, Professor Burns reported.

End of a One-Way Medium

Programming got under way in January 1976, after eight months of preparation. A year later, the Alternate Media Center withdrew, turning the project over to the Community Policy Board. The project, now operated entirely by elderly citizens, was continued under the name Berks County Community Television. The Center had done what it set out to do: establish a two-way interactive system to meet the needs of users, as *they* perceived them, to the point where it had viability to continue on its own.

The costs of equipment, installation, and local personnel to operate the system during the initial period came to $160,000, and were paid for under the NSF grant. The city saw the system's value: local government and local merchants raised enough to cover operating costs of $2,000 a week on a continuing basis. In terms of television production, programming was mounted extremely cheaply—an average of $326 an hour. Of course, this did not provide "professional" quality television, with highly polished production. Rather, the idea was to produce a *service* using television as a community medium.

In developing such a system, older people in Reading liberated themselves from the concept of television as a one-way medium aimed *at* them. They took control and made it two-way communication. In it they found an avenue to influence decision makers whose decisions affected their lives. It gave them freedom to transcend the boundaries to which many of them felt confined—senior citizens' housing projects. And it provided them a chance to socialize with people they no longer had a chance to see in person.

The Reading operation tilted against the image that is emerging of two-way as a dehumanizing force, with each person sitting alone in front of his home communication set (HCS), in communication with a computer.

A questionnaire evaluating the experiment at the end of the Center's involvement indicated that the citizens' participation in the system led to participation in other social and political activities as well. It led older persons to renew former friendships, and to take an active part in Senior Citizen Clubs and other community-action meetings held apart from the cable. It helped retired persons use skills they had developed over a lifetime and develop new skills as well. The weekly citizen-government teleconferences, for example, were moderated by a 77-year-old woman who had once been active in local politics.

Participants responded that the programming had reduced isolation and served as a source of human contact. About 25 percent of those who attended the televised sessions and 80 percent of those who took part from their homes identified the interactive cable television system as the major improvement in their lives over the previous year.

Interactive Cable in Japan

In the late seventies, two rival Japanese government agencies conducted experiments that combined two-way elements of QUBE and the
NYU-Reading project. The first, at Tama New Town on the outskirts of
Tokyo, was by the Ministry of Posts and Telecommunications; the second, at Higashi-Ikoma in the Nara Prefecture, by the Ministry of Trade
and Industry. Both experiments reflected the high interest in electronics
of the Japanese government, industry, and public. But they were
mounted when they were mainly because of each agency's desire to
stake out the turf in the new communications area. Officially, they were
done to test concepts, not as projects that would progress immediately
from the pilot stage to operational systems such as QUBE or Berks
County Community Television.

Plans for the new town were announced in 1971. The Toyko Metropolitan Government and housing agencies were to construct a large
bedroom community of 90,000 homes for 330,000 people. Posts and
Telecommunications realized Tama would be ideal for a two-way experiment, since it is much easier to lay coaxial cable in a city as it is being
built than it is to cable an existing city. It coined the term CCIS, for coaxial cable information system, to describe the project, and set up two CCIS
research panels. One was to determine the flow of communication
among the people and propose ways to enhance this flow. The other
studied how to put a local information system into practical use. The
panels included representatives of NHK (the public Japan Broadcasting
Corporation), commercial broadcasting organizations, newspaper
publishing companies, the Nippon Telegraph and Telephone Public Corporation, and the electronics industry. (The Ministry of Trade and Industry had set up a research panel in the same area a few months before.)

500 Experimenters in Tama New Town

From this planning arose a scatter-shot experiment meant to test a
number of electronic communications options. To do that, 500 households were cabled into a computerized system. As usual in cable systems
in Japan and elsewhere, the cable system retransmitted regular television programs of the public and private networks. It offered a number of
unusual services, as well.

The most popular was a memo-copy service. A user at home wrote
her message on a piece of paper the size of a postcard, and inserted it into
the HCS transmitter. Automatically, the message was printed by the facsimile terminal of the neighbor to whom it was addressed. (This, of
course, amounted to a form of electronic mail service.)

Eighty of the households tested a Broadcast and Response service
using a keypad response system similar to the one at QUBE. In the Tama

New Town tryout, it was used primarily for educational purposes. A large number of families with school-age children lived there, and parents were interested in having the system test home-teaching techniques. Students were taught English and arithmetic, and parents could take a course in how to help their children study these subjects. Pupils at home saw the teacher in the studio. They could use the five-button keypad to respond to her questions and the telephone to ask questions of their own.

The idea of using two-way for education of children in the home has been around for a long time. Some who promoted it saw the possibility of reducing the costs of school construction, since children could sit in their livingrooms, rather than take up space in classrooms. Others felt a more useful application would be to use the system for students who were housebound, either temporarily because of illness or permanently because of physical disability. This idea was tried out as early as 1971 in Overland Park, Kansas. A 17-year-old student confined to his home after a series of brain tumor operations was connected by two-way coaxial cable to a classroom four miles away. A camera and microphone attached to his television set let him respond directly to questions; he could also punch in responses via a digital keyboard. Over a six-week period, the student took a course in American history, for which he received credit. Designers of the experiment pointed out that the teacher could conduct a class for several home-bound students at once, conserving the time she would otherwise have to spend visiting each individually. Although the technology worked well, the classroom-in-the-home did not take off at that time, largely because few systems had installed the equipment necessary for two-way interchange.

In Tama, the Broadcast and Response mode was used outside of classroom hours for origination of local television programs. A sampling of the titles indicates the community's interests: *Tama TV News, History and Culture of the Tama Area, Shopping Information, Medical Hour, Japanese Cakemaking for Sixty Years.*

Regular "access" programs were presented by people in the community. One of them was *Report from Housewives,* another, an on-the-spot telecast of the meeting of the PTA at Kita-nagayama Elementary School. About 30 percent of the families monitoring the experiment took part in the community programming. Later evaluation showed this service to be second to the memo-copy function in the community's assessment of usefulness.

Another popular feature was a Flash Information Service, which "flashed" news and emergency information by characters superimposed across the bottom of the regular television picture. The information transmitted alerted residents to local emergencies and breaking news while they were watching other programming.

The Ministry found that 50 percent of those who took part in the experiment said that their interest in local matters had been increased because of it. This was considered to be a good percentage because of the truism that commuters often look on their suburban towns as only a place to sleep. "I have become conscious of the solidity of this local community," one man told a researcher. And another said, "I've come to exchange greetings with people I've seen through Tama TV."

Testing the Hi-OVIS System

The test system set up in 1978 by the Ministry of Trade and Industry at Higashi-Ikoma was more complex than that at Tama. That fact is reflected in its title: Hi-OVIS, for Highly Interactive Optical Visual Information System. Optical fibers, rather than coaxial cable, were used to tie the system together, and greater use was made of computers. One hundred fifty-eight homes in an extended neighborhood were "wired" by pairs of glass fibers. The system was programmed from a nearby center with studios and computers. Local origination included services similar to those in Tama New Town, but added mobile TV units to report on developments in the area.

Hi-OVIS tested what was considered the "next step" in interactive television systems: An audio and visual return capability provided by a camera and mike built into the HCS. This made it possible for people at home to be seen and heard throughout the system when they participated in a discussion of community affairs. They could also indicate their reactions via "conventional" keypads.

Participants got a foretaste of another still-developing service: they could request the computer to play for them, individually, movies, reruns of broadcast programs, and locally-produced video programs that had been stored on cassettes. The center's computer reserved a time for playback, since each cassette could be accessed by only one home at a time. Later generations of this kind of equipment are designed to store the programming, not on cassettes, but digitally in the computer, so that any number of households can receive a specific program in the same or overlapping time periods.

Residents could also access information, such as words in a dictionary, from a microfiche file; the computer found the requested fiche and transmitted to the home screen. Useful information that had to be up-to-the-minute—weather and road conditions, for example—was stored digitally in the computer, for transmission on request in Japanese characters on the screen. Audio information was stored digitally and transmitted via the speaker.

The Hi-OVIS experiment had the same social goals as the Tama experiment; testing the usefulness of a local information system in increasing communication, understanding, and cooperation among people in the community. Its evaluations showed that the users felt the system had achieved this result, and that community consciousness had been raised.

A Glimpse of Things to Come

Dr. Masahiro Kawahata, managing director of the Visual Information Development Association in Tokyo, reported that Hi-OVIS showed sufficient usefulness to the public to warrant development as an operational medium. "In this," he said, "we can catch a glimpse of what the transition to a new service-oriented society will be like."

The most significant discovery from the experiments I have described is that, rather than isolate users in their homes, as conventional TV tends to do, two-way cable television can put people in greater touch with their neighbors and their communities. It can lead to more, not less, personal interchange with the people who live around them.

If the community, through legislation and social policy, can solve the problems presented by two-way's potential for invasion of privacy, it would appear that the benefits to society of interactive cable will in the long run far outweigh its drawbacks.

Resources Mentioned

1. Information Services, Department of Communications, Government of Canada, 300 Slater St., Ottawa, Canada K1A OC8. 613/995-8185.
2. Warner QUBE, 930 Kinnear Rd., Columbus, Ohio 43212. 614/297-2000.
3. Burns, Red, Executive Director, Alternate Media Center of NYU, 144 Bleecker St., New York, NY 10012. 212/598-3338.
4. Moss, Mitchell L. (ed.), *Two-Way Cable Television: An Evaluation of Community Uses in Reading, Pa.*, The NYU-Reading Consortium, Alternate Media Center, New York, April 1978.
5. Tadokoro, Izumi, "New Towns and an Advanced Cable TV System," *Studies of Broadcasting*, Nippon Hoso Kyokai, Tokyo, March 1978.
6. *Report on Tama CCIS Experimental Project in Japan*, Ministry of Posts and Telecommunications, Tokyo, 1978.
7. Kawaheta, Dr. Masahiro , Managing Director and Chief Engineer, Visual Information System Development Association, Sanko Building 4-10-5, Ginza, Chuo-ku, Tokyo, Japan.

Other Resources

The following persons are knowledgeable about interactive systems in the United States:

1. Elton, Dr. Martin C. J., Director, Master's Program in Interactive Telecommunications, School of the Arts, New York University, 144 Bleecker St., New York, NY 10012. 212/260-3990.
2. Jennings, Dr. Ralph, Executive Director, Telecommunications Consumer Coalition, 105 Madison Ave., New York, NY 10010. 212/683-5656.

3. Lawrence, Steven, Director of Programming and Development, Center for Non-Broadcast Television, Inc., 49 East 68th St., New York, NY 10021. 212/628-1010.
4. Lewis, Harry, Citizens for Privacy in Cable TV, Suite 1108, J. C. Bradford Building, Nashville, TN 37219.
5. Nyhan, Michael, Institute for the Future, 2740 Sand Hill Rd., Menlo Park, CA 94025. 415/854-6322.
6. Rice, Michael, Program Director, Aspen Institute Program on Communications and Society, 2010 Massachusetts Ave., Washington, D.C. 20036. 202/466-6120.

The following persons are knowledgeable about interactive systems in Europe:

1. Giraud, Alain, Engineer in charge of research in communications, CNET (Centre National D'Etudes des Telecommunications), 38-40, rue du General Leclerc 92131 Issy les Moulineaux, France. 1/638-47-34.
2. Pye, Roger, Communication Studies and Planning Ltd., Circus House, Great Titchfield St., London LW1P 7FD, England. 637-9757.
3. Ploman, Edward W., Executive Director, International Institute of Communications, Tavistock House East, Tavistock Square, London WC1H 9LG, England. 388-0671.
4. Thorngren, Dr. Bertil, Long-Range Planning Office, National Swedish Telecommunications Administration (Televerket) S-123 86 Farsta, Stockholm, Sweden. 713-1000.

Kathleen M. Kriner

13. Videotex: Implications For Cable TV

Videotex,* which is used here as a generic term, has been defined as a system(s) for the delivery of text information into the home usually using the television set as the display device. Videotex systems have undergone substantial development since their inception in the early 1970s. Major field trials have been initiated or are being planned in Canada, Japan, Britain, France, and in many other European countries. As these systems are being implemented, however, questions have arisen concerning the terminology, classification, and even their purpose.

Neither the technology nor the services are entirely new. Television or computer terminals have been used as display devices for information retrieval systems for some time. Similarly, information services for specialized or business users such as the New York Times Information Bank

---

*There is considerable disagreement and confusion over terminology. I have used videotex as a generic term, viewdata for telephone-based systems, and teletext for broadcast systems. It should be noted that videotex has been adopted by the CCITT (a European Communications technology standards organization) as a generic term for telephone-based systems, although the British prefer to use the term viewdata to refer to telephone-based systems.

At the time she prepared this chapter, Kathleen M. Kriner was a Program Manager, Home Information Systems, National Telecommunications and Information Administration. Currently she is Director of Telecommunications, American Newspaper Publishers Association.

or Reuters News Services are well established. In fact, there is some confusion over whether videotex is best viewed as a service or as a technology.

The situation is exacerbated by the rapid development of the technology and the diversity of applications. Early videotex systems consisted of either a broadcast-based or telephone-based version; as described in the following section, there are now five classifications of systems including a rather inauspicious category entitled "hybrids." Similarly, initial systems were directed at the consumer market; now videotex systems are being implemented as business services. Videotex is also being viewed as a delivery system for specialized applications like banking, mail, and shopping. More fundamentally, concerns exist regarding who should provide these services. The cable TV, telephone, computer, broadcast, and print industries are increasingly in competition for the ownership and control of these systems. In short, no one is quite sure what videotex is—or will become. A consensus is emerging, however, that videotex, in one form or another, will be implemented over the next decade.

For the cable TV industry, videotex systems could represent an opportunity to develop a major new market. Certainly, cable TV operators are in an excellent position to offer these services. In contrast to the common carriers, there does not appear to be any regulatory barrier to the provision of videotex services over cable. Moreover, there is a wide range of technological and service options, which will be discussed later, for a cabletext service. This chapter is intended as a general introduction to videotex systems and offers some thoughts on the implications as well as opportunities for the cable TV industry. (Also see Chapter 11 and Chapter 12.)

Technology

For the present, videotex systems can be classified into five categories based on transmission medium.

1. Narrowband interactive systems, known as viewdata, use the telephone system to distribute information to users at relatively slow speeds, i.e., 2,400 bits per second. Telephone videotex systems are two-way; hence, users may directly interact with a virtually unlimited number of data bases. Information is displayed on either a television set or a computer terminal

2. Broadcast teletext refers to systems in which digital information is inserted into the vertical blanking interval (VBI), that is, the unused portion, of the television signal. Broadcast teletext systems are inherently one-way. At present only 400 pages of information can be broadcast at one time. (Theoretically, more information could be transmitted at one time, but since services are broadcast in a continuous cycle, the addition of more "pages" would cause an unacceptable delay in access time.)

3. Wideband broadcast or cabletext systems operate on the same principles as a broadcast teletext system but utilize a full video channel for information transmission. A wideband system could be configured to offer up to 50,000 pages of information or a smaller number of raster-scanned frames of information such as stock-exchange prices. Wideband systems can be implemented either over a cable TV channel or over an unused VHF, or more likely a UHF, over-the-air TV channel.

4. Wideband two-way teletext is a fourth category of systems which could be implemented over two-way cable TV systems. A two-way cable TV system could combine the advantages of broadcast transmission with the selectivity of an interactive system. Experiments such as TICCIT in Reston, Virginia, and the Warner Amex QUBE system have demonstrated the feasibility of this approach. For a videotext service, users could respond to inquiries, or conduct a search of a data base, or access a transaction service, e.g., banking, using a return cable link from the home to the cable headend. However, such systems are extremely expensive and it may be some time before two-way wideband systems are economically feasible.

5. Hybrids. A number of innovative approaches are being developed which combine diverse technologies to deliver videotex services. Telephone/cable TV, or telephone/broadcast television hybrids have some promising advantages. The telephone could be used for an upstream link to enable users to interact directly with a data base. The cable TV or broadcast channel could then be used for transmission of selected information back into the home. This hybrid system would be less expensive than a two-way wideband system and would have the performance advantages of an interactive system.

In addition to the systems described here, other transmission technologies could be used for delivery of videotex services on a national scale. For example, satellites, using either a full channel, or the VBI, could be used for national distribution of videotex services to cable TV systems, broadcast stations, or translators. Similarly, a direct broadcast satellite system (DBS) could distribute videotex services directly to the home as part of its offering. In fact, from a technical perspective, DBS might be a desirable approach for the distribution of electronic newspaper services. Videotex services have also been identified as applications for fiber optics experiments in Canada.

System Capabilities

The transmission options are only one facet of a videotex system. Equally important components include system capacity, information retrieval structure, user terminal, and services or applications.

Capacity

Narrowband teletext services are fairly constrained—only about 400 pages of information can be broadcast over the VBI. But if memory and increased intelligence are added to the terminal, then larger quantities of information could be transmitted and stored in the home terminal. Use of intelligent terminals will greatly increase the information storage and handling capabilities of a teletext system. For example, a journal or newspaper could be broadcast over-the-air, stored in the terminal, and viewed at the user's leisure. A wideband system on a cable TV or over-the-air TV channel could offer substantially larger quantities of information. For example, up to 1,000 pages could be transmitted with a waiting time of 10 seconds. The information-handling capacity of a narrowband telephone or two-way cable TV system is essentially limited only by the size of the supporting computer and sophistication of its software.

Information Retrieval

Information retrieval techniques currently are virtually the same on all videotex systems. Information is organized in a tree structure, or hierarchical system. Using a simple 12-number keypad device which looks like a calculator, viewers key in the page number (if it is known), of the service, and the information is displayed on the screen. For example, to obtain information on local restaurants a user would go through the following steps: (1) By examining the index the viewer would note that an entertainment and dining guide was located on page 50. (2) By keying in the page number the viewer would then see the listing of topics contained in the guide. From the index the viewer could determine that restaurants are organized by location on page 50, by nationality on page 60, or cuisine on page 70. (3) By keying in 70, the viewer would then see a listing of restaurants by cuisine. (4) For further information, another page or location number could be listed for a review of that restautant. Printed indexes usually are prepared for each service. Alternatively, a user could first examine an on-line index or to obtain the appropriate page number. Usually both alphabetical and subject indexes are available on-line. In viewdata systems, separate indexes for each service provide a guide to specialized topics or services.

This method of information retrieval is awkward and cumbersome, especially when compared to the sophisticated systems developed for similar business information services. Despite its limitations, the tree structure approach has the distinct advantage of being easy to use, especially by people unfamiliar with information retrieval systems. Many of the other existing retrieval systems would require special training; hence they would not be easily adapted to a consumer service. It is likely that in the future, as videotex systems become established, there will be a shift towards improved retrieval systems.

Terminal

Current videotex terminals utilize a relatively simple numeric keypad device with 12 or 16 keys. This is another area of videotex technology which is likely to change in the not-too-distant future. As the cost of electrical components drops, additional memory and intelligence will be added to videotex terminals. (In fact, the Canadian Telidon system has been developed with the premise that storage capability should be an optional feature for both broadcast- as well as telephone-based systems.) By adding storage capacity to a videotex terminal, large amounts of data could be transmitted using either broadcast, cable TV, telephone, or satellite technologies into the home and stored in the set. Thus, the entire contents of a newspaper, journal, or even an educational course could be transmitted and stored, permitting viewers to view the contents at their leisure.

Similarly, alpha-numeric keyboards could easily be used with videotex systems. This type of terminal with a viewdata (telephone) or two-way cable TV system, while more costly, would permit users to exchange messages and utilize transaction or data processing services. Similarly, an alpha-numeric keyboard with substantial storage capacity might also be used with a broadcast teletext system to simulate an interactive system, particularly for educational applications.

Videotex terminals of the future may also be equipped to handle a variety of different peripheral devices, e.g., videocassettes. Similarly, printers may be desirable for hard copy. Devices such as tele-typewriters and braille printers would also provide the means for delivery of services to the handicapped. Consideration is already being given by equipment manufacturers to the development of a range of terminals with different capabilities and price levels. This approach may well be the most desirable from the manufacturers' and the consumers' perspective.

Services

Despite the technological development of videotex, little is known about what services businesses or consumers want. Most of the systems implemented to date have adopted the approach of presenting a smorgasbord of services; however, attempts are being made to target services to respond to identified needs or users.

As seen from the listing of current applications in Table 13-1, most videotex services have been adapted from existing print or broadcast